# THE MOTLEY FOOL INVESTMENT GUIDE FOR TEENS

EIGHT STEPS TO HAVING
MORE MONEY THAN YOUR
PARENTS EVER DREAMED OF

BY DAVID AND TOM GARDNER

WITH SELENA MARANJIAN

A FIRESIDE BOOK
PUBLISHED BY SIMON & SCHUSTER

New York • London • Toronto • Sydney

FIRESIDE
Rockefeller Center
1230 Avenue of the Americas
New York, NY 10020

Manufactured in the United States of America

10   9

Library of Congress Cataloging-in-Publication Data
Gardner, David, date
    The Motley Fool investment guide for teens : eight steps to having more money than your
parents ever dreamed of / by David and Tom Gardner with Selena Maranjian.
        p.   cm.
    Summary: A guide to becoming financially independent with tips on saving and investing.
        1. Investments—Juvenile literature.    2. Teenagers—Finance, Personal—Juvenile literature.
    3. Saving and investment—Juvenile literature.    [1. Investments.    2. Finance, Personal.
    3. Saving and investment.]    I. Gardner, Tom, 1968–    II. Maranjian, Selena.    III. Title.

HG4521.G1926 2002
332.6'0835—dc21                                                                    2002066905

ISBN 0-7432-2996-7

For information regarding special discounts for bulk purchases, please contact Simon & Schuster
Special Sales at 1-800-456-6798 or business@simonandschuster.com

To the teens who helped us on the book, to the many teens who
participate in The Motley Fool Online, and to you, our reader

# Acknowledgments

• • • • • • • • •

We are glad you're taking the time to read our acknowledgments section because we sincerely want to thank our coauthor, Selena Maranjian. From her early days at The Motley Fool, Selena has been a dedicated advocate for providing more personal finance and investing material to young people. Selena tirelessly assembled the working draft whence this all comes. The book you hold in your hands, among our favorites ever written, would not have been possible without her dedication to the journey.

We'd also like to thank our team here at The Motley Fool for dotting *i*'s, crossing *t*'s, and making sure we met all of our deadlines. They are Jonathan Mudd (former teenage rock star), Alissa Territo (master juggler of deadlines, edits, and brothers), Brian Bauer (holding the final Fool stamp of approval), and Rex Moore for getting our on-line community involved.

Up in New York City, our publisher, Simon & Schuster, was extremely committed to this project. Thank you, Mark Gompertz, for demanding that we sit down and write this book. Kudos also to Doris Cooper, our editor, who matched a drive for accuracy with a belief that having fun is critical. Finally, and dearly, thanks to our longtime loyal agent, Suzanne Gluck.

We want to thank our community members at The Motley Fool Online. Their passion for learning together about money and life is ever a source of inspiration. For years, they've been pleading for a fun, thoughtful, useful book for young people. We hope they think we've got it right.

David and Tom Gardner

# Contents

# Introduction

◆　◆　◆　◆

For God's sake, give me the young who have brains enough
to make Fools of themselves.
—*Robert Louis Stevenson*

You have a brain, and it's extraordinary. While you're off playing soccer or your banjo or cards with your grandparents or U2's great new CD, your brain won't stop. It's calculating. It's remembering. It's planning. It's making decisions and adjustments, millions of them. It's dreaming. Then reasoning. Then reconsidering.

Your mind is a wonder.

We believe that, at your age, the diligent use of your mind is the single best way to be financially independent. What does *financial independence* mean? It means being able to live where you want to, work when and where you want to, and provide generously for yourself and those you love. It means being able to give money to a charity you believe in without having to worry about going into debt.

More specifically, financial independence means being able to fly off to wander the coves and beaches of the Bay of Islands in New Zealand. It means being able to buy a great mountain bike, buy and care for your first car, rent an apartment that you like. It means being able to afford to go to cooking school or to pay down the cost of medical school or to get an advanced degree in physics or philosophy. Financial independence means being able to take a year off to paint murals or to study the migratory path of the short-toed treecreeper (a delightful, rare bird) or to start your own band.

It means not being anxiously nervous about your money, ever.

The mission of *The Motley Fool Investment Guide for Teens* is simple. We want you to be financially independent. We want you to be able to direct your life without financial care. At first, it would seem an impossible task, what with millions of American adults up to their ears in credit card debt. The last five years have seen more personal bankruptcy filings than any period in American history. Virtually none of the nation's high schools or universities offer even basic tutorials on saving, investing, and planning for your future. And today's college graduates have more credit card debt than ever before.

My oh my. Do we really think we can help you toward financial independence?

Yes.

Here's why.

1. You already have more than you think going for you. You probably know a lot more about making good financial decisions than you'd think. And you have a gigantic financial advantage over adults—*Father Time*. We will soon prove that very small investments of $5 and $10 today can create enormous rewards for you in the years ahead.

2. Most adults were never taught that they'd make far more from their investments throughout life than from their working salary. If you learn this now, and apply the lessons, you can have more than enough capital to enjoy your life (and likely become a millionaire before your teeth fall out).

3. You will soon realize that every dollar you spend is an *investment*—whether you invest in a case of Coca-Cola or in a share of ownership of Coca-Cola stock. You can buy two pairs of cargo pants from Abercrombie & Fitch, or you can buy just one pair and spend the rest on a share of stock in Abercrombie & Fitch. Every dollar you pay out—in fact, every hour you spend in life—is an investment. Our aim is to help you find the best way to invest.

4. Contrary to popular opinion, you don't have to be rich to succeed at investing. Twenty-five years from now your financial life will be defined more by how well you figured out the world around you than by how much money you started with. Investing is open to everyone. A dollar bill and a share of stock don't know if their owners are male or female, black or white, thin or wide, short or tall, rich or poor.

5. Perhaps best of all, growing a pile of money can actually be darned *fun*. You don't have to swear off ice cream or snowboard-

ing or buying your favorite books, or all three, in a desperate attempt to save every last nickel. Of course, you can expect that we'll advise you *not* to blow all your savings on the Power ZX-5000 Sports Coupe or that thousandth pair of new shoes, but let's not go overboard here. The aim of our brief time together is to help you enjoy life and grow rich—*simultaneously.*

All we need is for you to put your mind to use, creatively and diligently. It won't take all that much, and we may even have a bit of Foolish fun along the way. Make no mistake about it, though, our aim is to give you the means to freely pursue your interests in life.

## Teen Financial Concerns

Your parents and their friends may think back fondly to their youthful days, often remembering the good times and ignoring the rest. But you know now, as a teenager, that your life is busy, complex, filled with joys but also anxiety. Are you succeeding in school? What does he think of you? What does she think of you? How will you pay for college? What will you do after that?

Life's fun. But life's complicated. Every single one of the teenagers we talked to, in preparing for this book, had some sort of financial question or concern. As Dustin, a seventeen-year-old, told us, "Everyone worries about not having enough money. I worry about my parents not having enough. I want to help them out as much as I can." Fifteen-year-old Emma adds, "I really am worrying about how I'll pay off my massive college debts. It's terrifying."

Other teens' financial thoughts are less far away. Most can relate to fourteen-year-old Deb's financial goals: a car. Eighteen-year-old Jason says, "I'd like to get a really nice cell phone." Sixteen-year-old Rae dreams of a new computer and a fish tank. Daniel, also sixteen, would "like to try flying remote-control airplanes, but it costs $350 or more to get entry-level equipment."

All of us, at every age, have financial needs and wishes (and one of the keys is recognizing the difference). Your parents may want a second home in the country. Your grandparents may need a bit more money to improve their medical care. Your aunt and uncle may be budgeting to take a two-week trip to Milan this year. And no doubt you have your own list—clothes, music, travel, adventure?

Now if you come to this book with very little understanding of high finance, you have plenty of common ground with just about everyone on the planet. Few people ever receive any kind of formal education

## Keep in Mind

### "Fool" = Good

If The Motley Fool is new to you, understand that our references to capital F "Fools" and "Foolishness" are positive. We wear the title of Fool proudly. The Motley Fool is a company founded in 1993 to help people make better financial decisions—saving more effectively, spending more intelligently, and investing more profitably.

Our name comes from act II, scene vii, of William Shakespeare's play *As You Like It*. Often in Elizabethan drama, the Fool was the only one able to speak the truth to the king—without getting his head cut off. We aim to be that very kind of Fool, telling the truth about financial matters and entertaining you along the way. To us, *you're* the king or queen.

about money. Most adults are playing it by ear, hoping they didn't overpay for that car or house, hoping they have enough saved to retire someday. Sure, adults have bank accounts and mortgages and even some stock and mutual funds. But believe it or not, many of them are very insecure about their money. They make regrettable financial decisions here or there. And quietly, if not openly, many people feel ill equipped to face the challenge of managing money throughout their lives.

They had no education, and they did not start early enough.

Fortunately, you have a chance to get a head start. And contrary to the abounding evidence in America, it actually isn't hard to be smart with your money. All you'll need to do is make a series of smart choices today, and you'll be well on your way to mastery. Saving and investing will seem more like a game, more like a series of opportunities than a sequence of nightmares.

## Take It from Me

### You Know More Than You Think

My first experience with investing came vicariously through my parents. When I was thirteen, my mom and dad thought they'd discovered a great stock. LA Gear was a new clothing and shoe line for kids and teens that had met with recent success. One night when I slipped into the kitchen for a late night snack, my parents were discussing their portfolio and contemplating buying shares of LA Gear. My dad turned to me. "Jess," he asked, "what do you think of LA Gear shoes?" I told him that I wouldn't be caught dead in a pair of LA Gear sneakers. I walked out of the room in my sparkling Nikes, aghast that Dad could even think LA Gear might be cool.

My father didn't heed my advice, and my parents lost just about every dime they invested in LA Gear. Nike's shares, meanwhile, are up 300 percent over the last ten years. Always remember, you know more about investing than you think you do—if you're truly familiar with the product or service. Your intuition and experience can help you tune out the white noise surrounding investing and tune in to some potentially great opportunities.—Jessica J. Powley, 24

### How This Book Is Organized

This book aims to explain how money can help you pursue your interests in life. It does so in nine key steps:

1. Set goals (and reach them).
2. Make and save money.
3. Be smart about your money.
4. Avoid financial blunders.
5. Know what to expect.
6. Your new friend: the mutual fund.
7. Actually invest!
8. Learn together.
9. Win $1,000 being a Fool.

## Keep in Mind

### You're Worth a Lot Already

If you dig through your pockets and look at your bank account, you might turn up that you're worth just $175, or so . . . but you'd be wrong. Billionaire investor Warren Buffett, one of the world's richest people and brightest minds, speaks often to classes of high school and college students. At the 2001 annual meeting of his company, Berkshire Hathaway, he explained, "I tell students what a valuable asset they have in themselves. I'd pay a good student plenty of money in exchange for 10 percent of what they produce for the rest of their life."

Warren Buffett's onto something. Think about all the promising people around you in school. Imagine all the amazing things they'll do. Some will travel the world. Others will start companies. Some will perform as musicians or actors. Others will be exhaustive and diligent scholars. Others will design and build homes. Any of them who learn the basics of personal finance and investing now are virtual shoo-ins for financial comfort in their adult lives. They'd make for a great investment.

Those steps make up the main course, nutritious and balanced and designed to give you a substantial head start on your money and your life. This digested, you can legitimately start dreaming about that ski chalet or that whiz-bang computer or that extended trip in space (hey, that'll happen in your lifetime). For those with greater ambition, budding enthusiasts for our subject, this Foolish book offers a substantial dessert tray, in the form of six more steps. It is our "Bonus Section":

10. Finding great companies.
11. Tracking your companies.
12. Launching an investment club.
13. Understanding the business.
14. Crunching the numbers.
15. Managing your portfolio.

As you read, you'll discover that it really is all up to you. You can take small amounts of money in the years ahead and turn them into a lifetime of riches. Or you can spend your life trying just to eke by, spending more than you have, and asking your parents for handouts.

We'll make as strong a case for the former as we can, but it's your decision.

Onward.

## Keep in Mind

### Teen Consultants

This book was written with the help of a team of several dozen teen consultants who responded to our on-line call for help. They're a diverse group. Some have invested for a few years, have read books about business, and have many answers. Others aren't sure if they even want to invest. Some have literally never thought about money as a tool in their lives.

Here are examples of who we're talking about.

Adam Kaufman admires great scientists and wants to be a geneticist or oncologist. Shashank lives in England and has already started a small Internet company of his own. Deb Sperling is always reading: "If I'm not reading a book, I'll be reading a magazine, newspaper, or whatever is put down in front of me . . . pamphlets, billboards, you name it."

These and other teens weigh in on many topics throughout the book, sharing their experiences and suggestions. Some of the book was tested on them, too, to make sure we were ready for prime time. And we'd also like to thank a handful of adults as well, people who offered advice based on things they did right and wrong in their youth. The adults are mostly employees, friends, or members of the The Motley Fool community (www.Fool.com). Throughout the book, expect to see references to these people and to their contributions.

# PART I

# EIGHT STEPS
# TO WEALTH

# ·STEP 1·

# Set Goals (and Reach Them)
· · · · ·

Success to me is having ten honeydew melons, and eating
only the top half of each one.
—*Barbra Streisand*

What does success mean to you? If you're like many teens, success might be excelling at school or in athletics, getting into and thriving at the college of your choice, preparing for a career you'll love, finding the perfect boyfriend or girlfriend, or just not making a complete idiot of yourself in public!

Since this is a financial book, think for a moment about what success means to you financially. Hey, we know that up till now, you might not have given it a moment's thought. So humor us. You might start by thinking, Success is . . . well . . . hey, I just want to be rich! So let's start there. How would you define "rich"? Today, 40 percent of the world's population, more than two billion people, struggle to live on *less than $2 per day*. Viewed from that perspective, you're already stinking rich. In that context, virtually all Americans are.

We asked a bunch of teens to define "rich," and the answers varied widely. Some thought that if you made $250,000 per year, you were rich. Others thought having $2 million or $5 million stashed in an account would do it. One explained that if you had enough money in the bank to live comfortably just off the interest (payments a bank makes to you for keeping your savings with them), without working, then you were rich. The common thread running through most of the responses was that you're rich if you're able to buy what you want, within reason.

What's "reasonable"? It's probably not reasonable to anticipate owning mansions in three different countries, driving a Porsche with a Bentley in the garage, and having a large staff (masseuse, fan waver, grape feeder, foot rubber, and palm reader) tending to your every wish. You may not even want any of that stuff. It *is* reasonable, though, to aspire to someday own a house you love, one or two cars for your family, and enough of the things that give you pleasure that you call yourself content with life. Stuff like musical instruments, pets, maybe a boat, a home entertainment center, a fast computer, a decent wardrobe (um, less than fifty pairs of shoes, please), workout equipment, shelves full of books . . . and an android (gotta have an android).

Take a few minutes now to list some of your goals and dreams, both long- and short-term. You might think this a silly exercise. But ain't it peculiar how few people spend time thinking out and writing down their dreams? Dream a little. What do you want to be, to do, to call your own? Then estimate how much you think each one would cost (some will be easier to guess at than others—and some will have no associated financial cost).

## My Goals and Dreams

I want to be:                                    Estimated Cost:

_____ $_____

_____ $_____

_____ $_____

_____ $_____

_____ $_____

_____ $_____

I want to do:

_____ $_____

_____ $_____

_____ $_____

_____ $_____

_____ $_____

_____ $_____

I want to own:

_____ $_____

_____ $_____

_____ $_____

_____ $_____

_____ $_____

_____ $_____

We've got some good news for you. And then some even better news. Chances are you can meet a bunch of your goals even if you don't read our book. Just be ambitious for them—whether it's hiking the Himalayas or starting your own bookstore or writing for *The Simpsons.*

All of that said, if you do learn the basics of your money with us, you'll likely reach more of them—perhaps even all of them. Without robbing any banks, without saving and overpolishing every penny you ever get your hands on, without sacrificing joy, you can finance the dreams that need financing. If you get started now.

Time for a relevant tale.

### Anne Scheiber: From Simple to Substantial

In 1932, Anne Scheiber was a thirty-eight-year-old auditor for the Internal Revenue Service. Attracted by the promise of the stock market, she forked over most of her life savings to her brother, a young stockbroker on Wall Street. Disastrously, his entire brokerage firm went bankrupt, and Anne lost all her investments. (Moral of the story—and you'll find us nodding our heads at this one: Keep a *darn* close eye on your brother.)

Determined to try again and do it on her own, she then saved $5,000 and plunked it back into stocks in 1944. By the time she died in 1995 (at the age of 101)—get this—her money had grown to *$22 million*— far more than any of us need in this life.

How'd she do it?

Well, to start, she was a long-term, involved investor. She wasn't trying to strike it rich overnight. She didn't buy stock today and then sell it tomorrow (something that too many people try, with little success). She attended shareholder meetings and followed her companies closely. She bought big, name-brand companies like Pepsi, Chrysler, and Coca-Cola. She reinvested the money that companies sent her as "dividends," buying more shares of stock with it. And she placed her faith— and her money—in these growing companies and patiently watched their earnings expand over decades.

Some years, Anne's companies struggled. Other years, the stock market got hammered. In 1973 and 1974, the market lost nearly half its value. It was a very discouraging time. President Nixon left the White House in disgrace. United States Armed Forces left Vietnam in defeat. The nation's over-reliance on oil from the Middle East sent our economy into a tailspin. And everyone thought the new bell-bottom pants were really cool. We had just about hit rock bottom. But Anne Scheiber held on to her investments. She was rewarded for doing so. When she died, she donated her $20 million plus to Yeshiva University in New York.

How the heck did she do it?

Anne invested relatively little money in the middle of her life, then watched it grow to an enormous sum. You may be thinking, Yeah, but that was decades ago; things are different now. Not so fast! Although a lot has changed since 1944, the stock market is still around, still making people like you wealthy. We'll explain how in subsequent chapters.

Or you might think, Geez, I don't want to wait *fifty* years to become a millionaire! And that's a fair point. Note, though, that she ended up with more than $20 million. If you're happy with just $5 million, you won't need fifty years. Also, she started with just $5,000 and added very little after that. You can put more than that away in the years ahead, if you're motivated. Start saving and ask your extended family to match every dollar you save. We'll show you how. You'll be there in no time.

If you get started, we think you can have whatever money you'll need to finance your dreams. If you get started now, you'll win, just as Anne Scheiber did. Errr . . . well, mostly. Because you might not want to do it *just* the way she did. Why not? According to those who knew her, Anne kept to herself, lived alone in a small New York City apartment, wore the same coat day after day, year after year, and often skipped meals rather than use her money.

So that part's actually quite sad—sad because it obviously wasn't necessary.

Check this out again: She was worth millions of dollars, but she skipped meals, wore old clothes, and basically had no friends. We're going out on a limb here and speculating that she didn't ever pick up her Motley Fool teen guide and fill out what you just did—your list of dreams in life. What's clear is that she settled for the sole pursuit of money, rather than the pursuit of money *to enhance her life and the world around her.* There's a big difference between the two—a difference that makes all the difference.

Fortunately, you don't need to pinch every penny to succeed in saving and investing. And you *have* filled out your list of dreams above (if not, go back and complete the task!). We Fools generally love investing and creating wealth *alongside* the many other pleasures that life has to offer. Stuff like reading books, whipping a Frisbee around an open field, tossing a dart at a world map and traveling there this summer with our two best friends, sleeping late on Sunday, going to movie festivals, swimming the English Channel, or just sitting around making jokes about Dad wearing black socks and tennis shoes. Ya know, the regular stuff.

Anne Scheiber's investment legacy provides a powerful example of what you can achieve if you're methodical and patient with money. She also reminds us, though, to stop, plant, water, tend to, and smell the roses now and then. Both matter.

### Great News for You: The Millionaire-Making Magic of Compounding

If you're not the type who enjoys math class, that's okay. If you don't delight in figuring out how long it'll take that plane to get from Phoenix to Denver, no problem. If you don't put on big sloppy grins at quadratic equations, breathe easy. We're going to do a little math together that *all* of us can enjoy.

It's time to talk about the magic of compounding growth. This mathematical force applied to your money depends on three key factors:

1. How much money you invest.
2. How long you set aside your money.
3. How much your invested money grows each year.

Let's look at some examples. We'll start with a simple one.

We'll start with $100. Your $100. The hundred bucks you set aside after mowing half a dozen lawns or changing a bunch of diapers or just cracking open the birthday check from your grandparents (you lucky dawg). Let's take that $100, invest it in the stock market, and see what happens. It'll earn the market's average yearly gain of 10 percent. Look there, you're already making money. After the first year, your $100 grows to $110. You made ten bucks. After the second year, the $110 grows to $121. Look at that. You made $11. Then after year three, your money grows to $133. Even though it climbed the same 10 percent, you made $12.

Interesting. But kinda boring, right?

Well, now let's watch it over longer periods of time.

## Growing $100 over Time

Start with $100. Grow it by 10 percent per year. And here's what happens:

| Year | Total | Add 10% |
| --- | --- | --- |
| 1 | $100 | $10 |
| 2 | $110 | $11 |
| 3 | $121 | $12 |
| 4 | $133 | $13 |
| 5 | $146 | $15 |
| 10 | $236 | $24 |
| 50 | $10,672 | $1,067 |
| 100 | $1.25 million | $125,278 |
| 300 | $238 trillion | $23.8 trillion |

Do you see what's happening? It's like watching water trickle, then roll, then storm over a dam. The more water pressure and the more time, the greater the flood. Your initial bundle of $100 is growing, and the dollar amount by which it's growing is also growing. That's compounding. It's a flood. It's the flood responsible for creating the majority of wealth in America today.

Another way to think about this is that the $10 you added kept growing by 10 percent per year, and so did the $11 you added next, and the $12, and so on. It all kept piling up and growing. In just eight years, you double your money. Which isn't that inspiring with just $100. But after fifty years, your measly hundred bucks is worth more than $10,000. And after three centuries of steady growth, your small investment is worth $240 trillion—enough for your ancestors to own a few planets (and put them all in your name) in the year 2400. And if these numbers don't inspire you, imagine what happens when you save and invest $100 *each year,* or *$1,000* each year, or more. This is how enduring wealth is created.

## Growing $100 at a Time

In our example above, we had you set aside just $100 and grow that 10 percent every year thereafter. Now let's look at *noncompounding,* or linear, growth. In this example, as in the first example, you're setting aside $100 today. But in this one you just add another $100 in savings to your initial sum every year thereafter, *but with no annual growth of those savings.* No investment, just savings.

As you can see below, you're pretty psyched as you enter year two, when your money doubles to $200 (because you added $100 of savings to it). Remember, you had to wait eight full years for your $100 invest-ment above to double. Congratulations, your savings just doubled your hundred bucks in a single year. Upon the conclusion of year two, you then jumped to $300. *Blowout,* right? But look what happens after that, and compare to the table from the first example:

| Year | Total |
|------|-------|
| 1 | $100 |
| 2 | $200 |
| 3 | $300 |
| 4 | $400 |
| 5 | $500 |
| 10 | $1,000 |
| 50 | $5,000 |
| 100 | $10,000 |
| 300 | $30,000 |

Wow, what a difference. In our compounding example—where the growth was in percentage, not total, terms—you have more than $1 million after you tortoised your way through a hundred years. In our linear example, even though your hare got a great start out of the gates, you have just $10,000 to show for your efforts a hundred years later. Truly hare-y. (That will be the only bad pun in this book . . . we promise.) (Except for the others.)

Compare them against each other.

| Year | Linear Savings Growth | Geometric Investment Growth |
|------|----------------------|----------------------------|
| 1 | $100 | $100 |
| 2 | $200 | $110 |
| 3 | $300 | $121 |
| 4 | $400 | $133 |
| 5 | $500 | $146 |
| 10 | $1,000 | $236 |
| 50 | $5,000 | $10,672 |
| 100 | $10,000 | $1.25 million |
| 300 | $30,000 | $238 trillion |

To create wealth and live without financial worry, you absolutely must participate in the compounding growth of the bond and stock market. And the sooner the better. Which is why we keep shouting, "Great news for you!" throughout this book. The more years you have, the better the news gets. When you put the linear growth of savings into the geometric growth of investment, you have both columns above working in your favor. In this book, we'll show you how to achieve both.

## The Growth Rate

Now that you're getting the hang of things, let's dig just a little bit deeper together. The growth rate—how fast your money grows, on average, from year to year—is very important. Let's start over, using $100 again. This time we'll compound its growth at three other yearly rates: 5 percent, 11 percent, and 13 percent. Five percent is what you might earn in interest in a money-market account (a long-term savings account at a bank). Eleven percent is the historical average growth rate of the stock market for most of the last cen-

> ### Famous Words
>
> *Everyone has the brain-power to follow the stock market. If you made it through fifth-grade math, you can do it.*
> —Peter Lynch

tury. Thirteen percent is how fast your money might grow if you wound up being an interested, self-motivated, and successful stock picker. The first two rates, 5 and 11 percent, you can earn with virtually no effort. We'll show you how in the chapters ahead. Thirteen percent, though, will demand extra work on your part. More on that later.

### Compounding at Different Rates of Growth

If you start with $100 and it grows at 5 percent, 11 percent, and 13 percent, here's how much you'll have after the following periods of time.

| Year | 5% | 11% | 13% |
|------|------|--------|---------|
| 10 | $163 | $284 | $405 |
| 20 | $265 | $806 | $1,152 |
| 30 | $432 | $2,289 | $3,912 |
| 40 | $704 | $6,500 | $13,278 |
| 50 | $1,147 | $18,456 | $45,074 |

And that's just a lousy $100 set aside today. That doesn't include any additional savings you might have in the years to come—savings that will very significantly improve your results.

Consider three lessons from the numbers above.

1. Wow, look what happens to money over time. The measly $100 getting 11 percent yearly growth turns into more than $18,000 in fifty years.

2. The different growth rates really affect the results. Getting the stock market's average return of 11 percent makes a huge difference over that 5 percent return (comparable to putting your money in a bank account).

3. Yes, we know we've presented very long time horizons. But you're a teenager. You have years and decades ahead of you. Can you really not stick $100 aside for fifty years and just see what happens? How about $1,000? What if you could put away $10,000 for fifty years and get the stock market's average return? The answer is, you'd have more than $1.8 million. Let's meet up on the beaches of New Zealand a few decades from now, eh?

### Interest vs. Stock Market Returns

Keep in mind that not all growth rates are the same. If your bank is paying you 3 percent interest on your savings, that's pretty much guaranteed. If a savings bond is paying you 5 percent interest, that's also darn close to a sure thing.

The stock market, however, particularly over short-term periods, is anything but a sure thing. Same goes for bonds (we'll explain bonds in the chapters ahead—they represent loans that you make and draw interest from). The "returns" (what you make) of these investment classes can fluctuate dramatically from one year to the next. There are good years, great years, so-so years, and years we'd much rather forget (like 2000 and 2001). Over long periods of time, though, the stock market has averaged an annual 11 percent return.

Similarly, many individual companies remain strong for a decade or more, some even for a century. Others fail—sometimes quite quickly. In fact, the great majority

> **Famous Words**
>
> *I don't know what the seven wonders of the world are, but I do know the eighth— compound interest.*
> —Baron Rothschild

of new start-up businesses fail within the first five years. If you focus on investing in truly solid, growing companies, on average you'll be much more likely to earn something like that annual 13 percent we mentioned above. If you select one or more companies that turn out to be remarkable growers, such as Microsoft, the average growth rate for your investments might be higher than 13 percent. We'll spend the latter pages of this book helping you find some of these wonderful companies.

### The Amount of Money You Invest

You should now have a sense of how money can grow over time and how much growth rates matter. Now let's turbocharge our results. Let's increase your up-front savings. Instead of starting with an initial investment of just $100, let's see what happens with $1,000. A thousand bucks shouldn't seem like an unthinkable sum of money. That's just savings of $20 a week for an entire year. And saving $20 per week isn't as tough as you might think. In fact, in the next chapter, we'll help you do just that. For now, let's see what happens to your $1,000 in savings.

### Growing $1,000 over Time

If you start with $1,000 and it grows at 5 percent, 11 percent, and 13 percent, here's how much you'll have after various periods of time.

| Year | 5% | 11% | 13% |
| --- | --- | --- | --- |
| 10 | $1,629 | $2,839 | $3,395 |
| 20 | $2,653 | $8,062 | $11,523 |
| 30 | $4,322 | $22,892 | $39,116 |
| 40 | $7,040 | $65,001 | $132,782 |
| 50 | $11,467 | $184,565 | $450,736 |

Notice that the numbers in the table for $1,000 are simply ten times greater than those in the $100 table. When it comes to your money, the most important math is pretty easy. But it's crucially important. The teenagers around you who'll be surfing off Oahu, taking a year off from work, or retiring early when they're forty-seven are in so many cases the teenagers who learn to save and invest today.

---

### Take It from Me

*Compounding can be your best friend. It's more powerful than gravity!*
—Matt Burnham, 16

---

### How Compounding Can Work in *Your* Lifetime

Let's add a little twist here. Opposite are two tables you've already looked at, with spaces for you to insert your age. This will help you see how this compounding scenario might apply to *your* life.

## How $100 Can Grow in Your Lifetime

Enter your current age in Year 0. Then calculate and enter your age after ten, twenty, thirty, forty, and fifty years.

| Year | Your age | 5% | 11% | 13% |
|------|----------|-----|-----|-----|
| 0 | | | | |
| 10 | _____ | $163 | $284 | $405 |
| 20 | _____ | $265 | $806 | $1,152 |
| 30 | _____ | $432 | $2,289 | $3,912 |
| 40 | _____ | $704 | $6,500 | $13,278 |
| 50 | _____ | $1,147 | $18,456 | $45,074 |

---

## Keep in Mind

### The Rule of 72

If you want to know how long it'll take to double your money, here's a neat trick.

First, pick an average annual growth rate. Then divide 72 by *that number.* For example, to see how long it'll take money growing at your bank's 4 percent rate to double, just divide 72 by 4. Your answer? Yep, 18. It'll take eighteen years to double your money in a bank account earning 4 percent. Now what about at the stock market's average return of 11 percent per year? Divide 72 by 11, and you get 6.5 years. It takes nearly three times longer to double your money in a typical savings account than in the stock market. Let's not forget that.

---

## How $1,000 Can Grow in Your Lifetime

Let's try this again with $1,000 up front.

| Year | Your age | 5% | 11% | 15% |
|------|----------|-----|-----|-----|
| 0 | | | | |
| 10 | _____ | $1,629 | $2,839 | $3,395 |
| 20 | _____ | $2,653 | $8,062 | $11,523 |
| 30 | _____ | $4,322 | $22,892 | $39,116 |
| 40 | _____ | $7,040 | $65,001 | $132,782 |
| 50 | _____ | $11,467 | $184,565 | $450,736 |

Pretty remarkable what happens if you put some money away, invest it, and patiently let it grow over time. You can secure your retirement. Invest $1,000 a year, get the stock market's returns for fifty years, then cash out with a fortune. What's the challenge? Getting started early.

### Is Your Head Hurting?

Is all this math stressing you out? We're almost done. This is extremely important stuff—stuff that could dramatically improve the life you live. So don't think of it as math—think about what the tables represent! They show you how small sums of your money can grow into large sums. You start with enough money to buy a CD player and end with enough to buy a car or house. All the while, you're not actually doing any intense labor to make it grow.

### Investing Money Regularly

Let's tweak these tables one last way, to make them more realistic. After all, how likely is it that you'd invest just $100 or $1,000 in one shot when you're a teen and then add nothing else? Here's what happens when you invest money regularly.

### Investing $100 Each Year

If you start with an initial investment of $100 and add $100 every year, and your little bundle of wealth grows at 11 percent per year, here's how much you'll have in the years ahead.

| Year | Total |
|------|-------|
| 10 | $1,700 |
| 20 | $6,500 |
| 30 | $20,129 |
| 40 | $58,827 |
| 50 | $168,706 |

Again, that's just $100 per year. C'mon. That's chicken feed!

Compare this table with the one showing you how a single $100 grows over time at 11 percent, and you'll see some interesting things. A number that pops out at us is $6,500. That's how much you'll have after forty years, if you just invest one $100 bill. But as you've just seen, if you're plunking down $100 *each year,* you'll reach $6,500 in just twenty years—half as long. That's the power of both saving and investing.

---

### Famous Words

*Don't wait until the time or the market is just right to start investing—start now. The best time to plant an oak tree was twenty years ago—the second best time is now.*

—James Stowers Jr.

---

Now, we know twenty years probably sounds like a *reaaaaaal* long time. But what we're trying to teach here is the extraordinary benefit of setting aside a little of your money now for long periods of time. Your money will double, then double again, then double that doubled double. And if you're patient with those small sums, you'll find yourself with enough money to enjoy the opportunities of life. If that sounds silly, keep reading, young Fool. Mayhaps what sound like just notes will turn into song in the pages ahead.

### The Incredible Power of Time

You're probably a fan of the power of compounding already, but we'll give it one more shot. Imagine two people of the same age. Let's call them Marge and Homer.

Marge begins investing at age fifteen. Via bake sales and newspaper routes and household chores for her parents, she manages to save and invest $1,000 in the stock market each year. She stops doing so at age thirty, having invested a total of $15,000. After this, she never invests again. Never. Not for the rest of her life. On the money she's already invested, she gets the market's historical average return of 11 percent.

Homer, meanwhile, is a late bloomer. He doesn't get his financial wake-up call until he's thirty-five. Unfortunately, that's not unusual. Beginning at age thirty-five, Homer then scrapes together not $1,000, but *$5,000 each year* and invests it. Let's hear it for Homer. He keeps at this, putting away $5,000 each year, until retiring at age sixty-five. That amounts to a total of thirty years, and $150,000 invested. And Homer also gets the average rate of return of the stock market, 11 percent growth per year.

Homer has invested ten times more than Marge. But he started twenty years later.

Who ends up winning this race?

Here are the numbers:

|  | Marge | Homer |
|---|---|---|
| **Begins investing at age:** | **15** | **35** |
| Stops adding money at age: | 30 | 65 |
| Invests each year: | $1,000 | $5,000 |
| Invests a total of: | $15,000 | $150,000 |
| Total grows each year by: | 11% | 11% |
| **Total worth at age 65:** | **$1,473,172** | **$1,104,566** |

Hard to believe, ain't it?

The big lesson here is *time.* It's the critical advantage that you, as a teenager, have over every adult—including the authors of this book. In fact, since we, the authors of this book, are in our thirties, we are like Homer to your Marge. Even if we invest $10 to match every $1 you invest, we won't be able to catch you in retirement. And were we your parents' age, somewhere from forty-five to fifty-five years old, we'd literally have to invest $20–$40 for your every $1 just to stay even with you in retirement. For every $1,000 you put in, your parents would have to put $20,000–$40,000 just to have as much for their retirement.

Amazing, really.

The lesson, brothers and sisters, is obvious, is it not? Start now, with a dollar or two here and there, week by week. One less coffee, one less pair of shoes, one less trip to the snack bar, one less CD. The little commitments of today will lead to enormous rewards throughout your life. A thousand dollars a year saved and invested in stocks from ages fifteen to thirty should, based on historical record, generate just shy of $1.5 million in your retirement account.

### The Keys to Compounding

To summarize, remember that the power of compounding depends on

- how much you invest (and how regularly).
- what your growth rate is.
- how long you let your money grow.

You need not follow neatly any of the examples we've shown. You might start sooner or later. You might invest $300 each year in your first two years, $3,000 in later years, then more as you're able to. You might earn an average yearly return of 10 percent over many decades. Or perhaps your annual return will be 7 percent or 13 percent or more. You can't control every variable, but to a great degree, you can control how much you invest, how you invest, and how long you let your money grow.

Remember also that you can still enjoy your life while you're saving and investing. We're not talking about trading all your old clothes for money on eBay—though come to think of it, that's not a bad idea. And we're not talking about never buying that brand-new car even though it'll lose the value you paid so incredibly quickly—though, actually, that's not a bad idea, either. We're not talking about avoiding lottery tickets like the plague—though why would you or anyone want to throw your money away like that? And we're not talking about renting movies rather than hitting the theaters (and paying six bucks for greasy popcorn)—though like everything else in this paragraph . . . maybe that's not a bad idea.

---

## Keep in Mind

### You Can Do It!

Our aim with this book is to help you make simple, smart decisions *now* that will give you all the time in the world in your forties, fifties, and sixties. And really, this stuff can be routine. All you need to succeed at saving and investing is

- a brain.
- time.
- patience.
- discipline.
- curiosity.
- a Foolish heart.

That you are presently holding this book proves to us you have at least five of the six listed attributes. As for *discipline,* you'll prove that as you turn the final page. Anyway, applying a bit of each of these is fundamental to creating financial independence . . . as well as to enjoying the world around you.

All we're talking about is saving a few hundred or few thousand dollars each year and investing it throughout your lifetime. You can amass great wealth by regularly investing just a portion of your savings—not all of it. That wealth will probably be the best shot you have at choosing the job you *really* want in life (many people work out of necessity rather than love), or moving to your favorite island (or perhaps owning it), or helping out the less fortunate in your state (perhaps the greatest reward). Savings and investment wealth will create opportunities for you throughout life. You need only get at this early.

### So . . . Why Do You Want to Save and Invest?

We hope you're convinced that through planning and investing, you *can* earn your financial freedom and make a good deal of excess cash. It's important to remember *why* you want to do so, though. You wouldn't want to pursue money for the sake of having money. Don't make your life little. Don't get petty. Don't be a miser. Instead, dream. Think of how you'll use the money to make both your life better *and* the world a little bit better place to be.

At the beginning of this chapter, you listed some of your goals and dreams. By now you should understand that you'll be able to realize many more of them by investing. So let's dig a little deeper into your thoughts and discover more reasons. Think about what a substantial amount of money will mean to you in your life. Here are some possibilities. Put a check mark next to the ones that ring true for you, then add in others below.

_____ Money will *help* me do what I want to do in life.
_____ Money will *help* me enjoy life more.
_____ Money will *help* me be less stressed out.
_____ Money will *help* me pursue amazing adventures
and opportunities.
_____ Money will *help* me help others in the world.
_____ Money will *help* me make my mark on the world.
_____ _____
_____ _____
_____ _____
_____ _____

Obviously, money itself—the green and the gold of it—won't make your life better. It won't pursue adventures for you. It won't leave your

# Keep in Mind

### More Anne Scheibers

Anne Scheiber isn't alone in having started with very little and then building up great wealth over many years. Here are a few more inspiring examples:

- Monsignor James McSweeney earned a sub-poverty-level income for decades as a Catholic priest. But he focused on his investments in his free time and left assets of nearly $1 million when he died.
- Gilmore and Golda Reynolds seemed like ordinary next-door neighbors in Osgood, Indiana. But when they passed away, they surprised their hometown by leaving it $22 million that they had accumulated by investing in stocks over many years.
- Thomas Drey Jr., a retired teacher, spent a lot of time researching companies at the Boston Public Library. Upon his death, he shocked the library by leaving it $6.8 million.
- Jay Jensen, also a retired teacher, lived frugally, investing steadily in blue-chip stocks for some forty years. He never earned more than $46,000 per year, but he turned that into several million dollars. Today, he's in the process of giving most of it away.
- Florence Ballenger is another teacher who lived frugally but well (often traveling around the world). Through investing, she and her husband accumulated more than $6 million.
- Oseola McCarty was a washerwoman in Mississippi who never owned a car and never earned more than $15,000 a year. But she amassed several hundred thousand dollars by saving and investing.
- _____ (Insert your name here) began saving and investing when still a teenager and fifteen years later had a nest egg of $55,000. Ten years later, that had grown to $210,000. This young, investing Fool now enjoys a nice car and a spacious home, is on track to pay for her or his children's college educations, is looking forward to retiring early, and likely will have millions of dollars when that time comes.

mark on the world. If it could, you wouldn't have very wealthy people falling into dark depression or even sometimes doing cruel things. Even with money, you'll have to work to be a productive, helpful, happy person. But certainly money can *help* in the pursuit of your dreams and visions.

Next up, we'll discuss how to make and save money for your future. But before that, pause and recognize that you already know more than most adults about the power of investing! It's true. Tap some of your parents' friends on the shoulder and ask them about the power of compounding applied to money. Ask 'em—*Stumper time!*—to provide a quick explanation of the rule of 72. We suspect you'll be teaching them a lesson or two before your discussion ends. Try not to be too smug about it, eh?

# ·STEP 2·

## Make and Save Money

. . . . .

*When your heart is in your dream,*
*no request is too extreme.*
—*Jiminy Cricket*

I f we teach you nothing else in this book, we hope to help you garner the financial means to pursue your dreams *and* have the courage to follow through on them. The third planet from the sun (um, that's Earth) is covered all the way round with heavy adult hearts and weary adult eyes. Too many either don't have the resources to go dream hunting or, when they do, chicken out and choose the safe road instead. Don't let it be you.

To get you started, let's begin to build up some financial savings to fund your future.

### Making Money

The fast-growing newspaper *Investor's Business Daily* just flat-out calls a whole section of its paper by these two simple words alone:"Making Money." And certainly, making money is a perfectly worthy aim in life. *An* aim, not *the* aim. Money is a means to an end, not an end in itself. What a shame when it consumes us. Likewise, though, what a shame when we disregard our need to, yes, make money to fund our lives and dreams. (On a side note to budding investors, at Fool.com those eighteen years old and up can claim a few weeks free of *Investor's Business Daily.*)

Naturally, there are lots of ways to make money and unfortunately many more ways to lose it. Let's concentrate on the former.

## An Allowance

Not every teenager gets one, of course. But we can provide you with some information to help you out, here. According to the 1997 National Longitudinal Survey of Youth, the average allowance for teens in America is $50 per week. That's $200 a month. That's $2,400 a year. And really, that's an awful lot of money. Actually, the statistic shocks us.

For starters, okay, if you're getting less than $50 per week, it's time to sit down with Mom and Dad and talk about equal opportunity! And if you're already getting more than $50, you might want to tuck this book out of their sight.

## A Reward

All sorts of circumstances might arise that make it difficult for your parents to offer you a regular allowance. So how about pursuing rewards within your extended family? That's right. Let your parents, grandparents, aunts, uncles, great-aunts, great-uncles, cousins, and anyone who looks like a relative know that you've outlined some goals. Would they be willing to pay you a cash stipend for achieving them?

Some examples, in no particular order, are 1) a straight-A average in school; 2) acceptance to the college of your choice; 3) performance on the athletic field; 4) excellence in the creative and performing arts; 5) completion of your own writing projects; 6) reading a certain number of books per year; 7) agreement not to smoke cigarettes; 8) ability to keep your bedroom neat every day; 9) ability to save certain amounts of money each year; 10) successful completion of multiple Nintendo game cartridges (good luck with that one!); and so on.

We're willing to bet that your parents, your adult relatives, and their friends will welcome the opportunity to put some carrots out in front of you to encourage excellence (go ahead and show them this page of the book!). Jiminy cricket, that makes sense.

## Selling Stuff

If your closet or basement is full of belongings that you no longer need or want, consider selling them. Studies show that the average teenager gets bored with more than 128 pounds of material belongings each year. Okay, we made up that statistic. But it can't be far from true.

If you're a *stuff* hound, think about selling as much of it as you can. Toys, games, comics, clothes—even that weird ceramic pig your great-aunt Henrietta gave you last Columbus Day (wow, someone needs to talk to your great-aunt about gift giving!). And frankly, with services like eBay, it's never been so easy to unload your unused stuff for cash as it is now. (If you're under eighteen years old, you may need to ask an older sibling or parent to help you use eBay's service.)

## A Job

Yeah, we listed it fourth because we know you're not hankerin' to stand behind a counter wearing that gold-and-green Yuckie Yogurt uniform and mixing smoothies all summer. But it doesn't have to be that way. If you sit down and make a list of the three things you love to do, you'll almost certainly find part-time jobs available in your fields of interest. Why not get started on your professional life in small ways today? Be enterprising, young Jedi.

If you're interested in playing the piano, give a paid concert for your friends and family. If you love to read, get part-time work at the public library. If you love playing tennis, offer yourself as a tennis coach to the parents of young kids in your area. Set your mind to it, and you'll find professional opportunities right in the middle of your favorite hobbies.

## Start a Business

This is an ambitious undertaking for anyone, teen or adult. It can lead to loads of responsibility and mountains of stress. But you'll never learn so much about human nature and how the world works as when you start and run your own organization—even if it only ever has one employee. And remember, as unrealistic as it might seem that a teenager can start a business, some of our greatest companies were started by

---

## Keep in Mind

### You're Worth More Than You Know

Odds are, you have some skills. You may be musically gifted, or a good writer, or able to speak French. Perhaps you can swim well, or you can explain to your parents' friends how to customize their computer operating software. Believe it or not, people will both pay you for your expertise and pay to train you for future work. If you're creative and resourceful, you may be able to make much more money than you could have imagined . . . for work that is valuable.

teens. Bill Gates left Harvard to start Microsoft. Michael Dell launched Dell Computer from his dorm room at the University of Texas.

### How Are *You* Going to Earn Some Money?

Take a few minutes to brainstorm. Think about the moneymaking ideas mentioned above. Think about your own life and interests. Dream a bit. Then jot down some ways that you can increase your income.

My moneymaking ideas:

_____

_____

_____

_____

_____

You've just generated a bunch of ways to earn some cash (you did complete the exercise, right?). Those are important ideas you've written out. Why? Because there are many more ways to *lose* and *spend* money. As you go through life, you'll face an endless string of decisions about how to use your money. At times, your cash will grow; other times, it'll shrink. The game, of course, is to have enough savings to follow your dreams and help others around you do so as well, all the way along, right on up until you're 117 years old, wrapped in mohair blankets, surrounded by generations of your family, sighing your last breath.

### A Plug for Education

*Education costs money, but then so does ignorance.*
—*Sir Moser Claus*

Moser Claus was a wonderful statistician in Great Britain. And some of the best numbers he ever ran are expressed in his quotation above.

Since you're currently reading this book to learn about investing, you clearly value education (or, er, whoever gave you this book does). But you might not yet realize how financially valuable education can be. We know, some of your teachers are boring. Maybe calculus is getting you down. You're struggling with European history. Or all those biology terms are confusing you. But the net results, if you stick with your education, can be astounding. Check out the average salaries associated with different levels of education.

## The Earning Power of Education

| Education Level Achieved | Yearly Salary | Weekly Salary |
| --- | --- | --- |
| Not a high school graduate | $22,074 | $425 |
| High school graduate only | $27,975 | $538 |
| Some college but no degree | $33,948 | $653 |
| Bachelor's degree | $51,644 | $993 |
| Master's degree | $61,296 | $1,179 |
| Ph.D. | $80,225 | $1,543 |
| Professional degree (medical doctor, lawyer, etc.) | $95,175 | $1,830 |

Source: U.S. Bureau of the Census, 2000

You don't need to attend a fancy (and expensive) private college in order to be successful in life. In fact, lots of private colleges are badly overpriced. And lots of private college students waste their time on campus. State universities can be a bargain. Even private colleges can be affordable, with scholarships, financial aid, and loans. Here's a sampling of some people you may have heard of and where they went to school:

## Public Schools

| | |
| --- | --- |
| Warren Buffett (investor extraordinaire) | University of Nebraska |
| Katie Couric (TV personality) | University of Virginia |
| David Gardner (Fool co-founder) | University of North Carolina |
| Stephen King (writer) | University of Maine |
| David Letterman (TV personality) | Ball State University |
| Colin Powell (secretary of state) | City College of New York |
| Oprah Winfrey (media personality) | Tennessee State University |

## Private Schools

| | |
| --- | --- |
| Madeleine Albright (former secretary of state) | Wellesley College |
| Ruth Bader Ginsberg (Supreme Court justice) | Cornell University |
| Tom Gardner (Fool co-founder) | Brown University |
| Selena Maranjian (Fool coauthor) | Brown University |
| Steve Jobs (Apple co-founder) | Reed College |
| Denzel Washington (actor) | Fordham University |
| Meg Whitman (eBay CEO) | Princeton University |
| Tiger Woods (golfer) | Stanford University |

---

### Take It from Me

*When you reach my age and you find yourself eating light bulbs for a living, you know you've made some bad career moves along the way.*
— forty-six-year-old circus performer Matt Hely
(in *Newsweek,* 1/8/01)

---

### Jobs for Teens

Lisa, if you don't like your job, you don't strike:
you just go in every day and do it really half-assed.
That's the American way.
—*Homer Simpson*

With your commitment to keep learning throughout life, let's look at the sorts of jobs you might want to take on today. We'll start by thanking the Homer Simpsons of the world. They'll make your working life a lot easier. If you're one of those who take their jobs seriously and do top-notch work, you'll most likely stand out and be treasured by your employer. You'll also probably find it easier to move from job to better job.

But let's back up a bit. Maybe you don't have a job right now, and you'd like one. There are countless standard jobs for teenagers. Like that one wiping counters at Yuckie Yogurt. But if that doesn't float your smoothie, how about these part-time and summer jobs for teens?

- *Baby-sitting,* the classic teen job, for good reason. Babies are being born right now in your neighborhood. Young children need supervision. Many parents find it difficult to find dependable baby-sitters. Even beyond that, parents may find other chores they need help with. Charge!
- *House-sitting.* When someone in your neighborhood goes on vacation, there's often a pet that needs looking after. Lights need to be turned on and off. Plants need watering. And you might even get some free HBO watching out of the deal.
- *Parks departments.* If you enjoy being outside, here's a great option to explore. You may end up giving tours, watering greenery, or cleaning the grounds (hey, someone has to do it!).

- *Working for your parents.* If your mom or dad has a business, they might be able to use your help. Even if they work for a company, they may be able to hook you up with a part-time job there. Just make sure to negotiate a good salary!
- *Tutoring.* Some teens reported that they earn anywhere from $5 to $20 per hour for tutoring. If you're good at a subject, you may be able to earn money by helping others to understand it.
- *Lifeguard.* Some parts of the country have been hit with a lifeguard shortage. In certain areas, you can earn $10 per hour or more to hang out in red with the likes of David Hasselhoff and Pamela Anderson. If you have the skills, consider it.
- *Gardening.* If you enjoy and are skilled at garden work, offer your services to others in your neighborhood. Many people don't have the time to rake all the leaves, mow the lawns, clip the hedges, and chase Old Man Hank's vicious ferrets out of the yard. Some people might even pay you to build and tend a vegetable garden for them.
- *Camps.* If you look into it early enough, you can line up a job at a summer camp—you might work with kids, tend the grounds, prepare food, run the archery range (be careful of that one—it's pretty darned boring!).
- *Day care helper.* If you enjoy working with young children, see if any day care centers near you could use some help.
- *Mowing lawns, raking yards, shoveling snow.* These can all be part of the same job. Once your customers know you and the good work you do, they may use your services doing other jobs in other seasons. This might seem boring, but it can be very lucrative. If you make $20 mowing each lawn and can do five in one day, then you just netted $100 in a day. If your parents put in fifty cents for every dollar you earn, that's $150. Keep this up and before long you can begin scouting out oceanfront property in the Caribbean.
- *Factories.* Factory work tends to be boring, repetitive, and sometimes dreary, but it can pay well—sometimes very well.
- *Movie theaters, amusement parks, and other entertainment venues.* These places hire teenagers almost exclusively. Get with a few friends and run that local movie theater (and eat free Dots).
- *Department stores.* A big perk with these jobs is that you often get to enjoy employee discounts (which can be substantial). At certain stores, you can also make commissions on items you sell. Plus, experience will teach you how the retailing business works. Chances are, you'll be the fashion royalty at school.
- *Create Web sites.* If you know enough about computers to create well-designed Web sites, you can make some good money. Many

small companies and organizations pay thousands of dollars to have Web sites built for them. You might charge very little at first, but once you have a few impressive Web sites to show potential customers, you can hike your rates. It's very possible that companies would also pay you to help maintain their sites, adding content and troubleshooting.

- *Be crafty.* If you enjoy arts and crafts, you might make jewelry or other items and sell them—perhaps on eBay, where you'll have instant access to a large customer base. Some painters and photographers are making money selling their work on-line, too.

- *Serve the elderly.* Not only might you find work in an old age home or retirement community, but you might also serve older people in your neighborhood. Many older people find that they can't get around as much. They may welcome your services delivering groceries, running errands, or doing odd jobs around their home. And you can pick their brains on what matters in life.

- *Be a computer guru.* In recent years, more and more Americans have bought personal computers and gone on-line. They frequently run into problems, though. They struggle to install software or a printer or scanner. They wonder why certain programs keep crashing. They can't figure out how to send a photo out via e-mail. In many cases, they could use just one hour of instruction from a young guru. If you have even an intermediate familiarity with computers, you might offer your services as a local computer consultant. You can set things up, solve problems, answer questions, teach programs, and show people how to complete tasks, such as on-line searches. If you're really organized, you might even develop short courses that you offer to people for $20–$100 an hour.

- *Caddie at a golf course.* This can help you learn more about a sport you might enjoy for the rest of your life. It can also introduce you to lots of adults who might have useful advice or a great contact for you in your field of interest.

- *Use your skills.* Think about things you're good at that you could teach others—adults or children. You might offer piano lessons, for example, or horseback riding lessons, or juggling lessons. If you play an instrument, you could play at weddings. If you write, you might start your own newsletter. That's how we started The Motley Fool.

### Brainstorm Some Job Ideas

Okay, let's really focus on some job opportunities for you. We just provided you with a ton of ideas. These may have sparked a few of your

## Take It from Me

### Be the Bearer of News

I highly recommend that a teenager looking for some nice pocket cash take up a newspaper route. My best friend delivers for *USA Today.* He makes $250 per week (delivering to businesses and hotels, among other places). He has to get up at 3:50 A.M. and finishes about 7:00 A.M. This is a job for a very responsible teenager, because if you're not disciplined enough to go to bed on time, you won't last too long. But at $250 a week, that's $12,000 a year. Not bad.
—Catherine May, 18

own. So what do you love to do? What comes naturally? What will others pay you for? Each of us has marketable interests and talents. We just have to think carefully about what they are.

In the space below, jot down any job ideas that seem like promising possibilities for you. Refer back to this list whenever it's time to look for some gainful employment.

1. _____
2. _____
3. _____
4. _____
5. _____
6. _____
7. _____
8. _____
9. _____
10. _____

### Consider Internships

Another kind of job to consider is an internship. Most internships offer a pittance, if anything. But they can pay off down the road. Obviously, you don't just want to take a random internship. You want to pursue

## Take It from Me

### Take the Initiative

At the end of my freshman year in high school, I wanted a membership to this athletic club that was two blocks from my house. I needed a place to lift weights to prepare for football. I sent a letter to the club. Several days later, I received a phone call asking me to come in. I was told that I would receive a membership in exchange for working about four hours a week in the maintenance department. After six months of doing so, I asked if I could start getting paid. The club owner said he was impressed with how well I got along with people. He agreed to pay me $6.50 an hour and let me keep the free membership. Six months later, I received a fifty-cent-per-hour raise.

I'm now getting paid $7.50 an hour. I get to choose my own hours. I work with minimal supervision. I receive a free membership. And I've met a lot of influential people. Why? Just because I decided to be enterprising. I wrote the club a letter, something no one else had thought to do. I must have had at least twenty to thirty people ask me in the past if they could get a job there, but unfortunately for them, they didn't take the initiative.—Bryan Sims, 18

something in your field of interest. If you'd like to be a computer programmer, for example, see if you can snag an internship at a software firm or a larger business that needs technology help.

Another benefit to the internship is that it can show you if a certain kind of job or industry is actually far less interesting than you'd thought. For example, one of us (David, for the record) spent an entire summer working on Wall Street—enough to teach him that despite his love of stocks and investing, he would *never* want to work in an investment bank as an adult. That internship alone probably saved him three years of unhappiness—what an eye-opener!

Truly, there are millions of adults in America working at jobs they don't enjoy. Why? Because as younger men and women, they didn't take the time to pursue their dreams and interests. They didn't go relentlessly after jobs and experiences that fulfilled them. Obviously, part of that pursuit is learning that some of your early interests don't hold your enthusiasm for long.

In case you haven't given enough thought to internships, think of some industries or careers that you're interested in. (Examples: law, health care, animals, journalism, politics, aviation, computers, architecture, ministry, and teaching.) Jot them down.

_____

_____

_____

_____

_____

Next, think about all the adults you know: your parents' friends, your neighbors, your coach, people from church, people you run into at the golf course or gym, and so on. Think about what they do for a living and what companies, if any, they work for. List below all those adults in whose careers or companies you're a little or very interested. If you find that you don't know what they do or where they work, ask.

| Name | Job | Company |
|------|-----|---------|
| _____ | _____ | _____ |
| _____ | _____ | _____ |
| _____ | _____ | _____ |
| _____ | _____ | _____ |
| _____ | _____ | _____ |
| _____ | _____ | _____ |
| _____ | _____ | _____ |

Now, referring to the last list, write down some local companies or organizations where you might be able to pursue part-time jobs in the fields you've listed above. To find more companies, ask around.

_____

_____

_____

_____

_____

_____

_____

_____

If you're interested in working at a company, be sure to start to contact their human resources or employment group and ask about opportunities as early as possible. The following general job-landing tips will also come in handy. In fact, starting with them in your teenage years will give you great practice for the rest of your life.

### How to Land a Good Job (or Any Job)

First off, at the very least, make sure that you're shooting for a job that will pay you more than you plan to spend. If your plans are to do a lot of shopping and to save and invest as well, eight hours a week at minimum wage may not serve your purposes very well.

### Take It from Me

#### Be Assertive

When you're looking for a job, don't shuffle in quietly, looking sideways. Introduce yourself, smile, call them by name, and give more than yes or no answers. Look semipresentable, but be yourself. *Show your interest in their work* (after all, if you're not interested in what they do, why are you applying?). And if you do get a form to fill out, get it back to them posthaste! Don't wait a week—get it back to them the next day. I've learned this by watching and by experience.—Clayton Smalley, 16

Here are some tips on how to maximize your chances of landing—
and keeping—a job you want:

- *Start early.* This can make a big difference. You might apply in May,
  for example, to work at an amusement park for the summer. The
  hiring manager there may really be impressed with you, but if he's
  already hired all the help he needs, you're out of luck. There's no
  harm in starting to line up a summer job in the winter. Prospective
  employers will be impressed by your organization and initiative.
- *Use connections.* Hey, use them. Talk to your parents, teachers, and
  friends about ways to get in touch with people at the organizations
  where you want to work. This so-called networking is not just a
  great business practice, it can also be good fun in life. Make some
  friends. Get up off the couch. Come on! For all we know, this is
  your one life on this planet.
- *Follow your interests.* Why try to get a job at McDonald's when
  you're a vegetarian who'd like to be a chef one day? You're better
  off seeking work in a more upscale restaurant. Think about the
  kinds of work environments and fields that appeal to you and seek
  work there. Even if you have to start out low on the totem pole, it
  pays to stick with what you really are interested in.
- *Have or develop skills and look for jobs that use them.* If you find
  and take a first-aid course and study how to deal with emergencies,
  you may be able to ask for and receive a higher baby-sitting wage.
  Many parents will be willing to pay more for a more qualified sitter
  who puts their worried minds at ease. The Red Cross offers many
  safety training courses (check out www.redcross.org/services/
  youth). In recent years, when there's been heavy demand for computer programmers, some teens found that they could work for
  local companies and earn more than $1,000 per month. This rule
  works in the adult world, too. Jobs that require more skills pay the
  highest salaries (think lawyers, accountants, engineers, and so on).
  Orderlies in a hospital make much less than nurses, who make
  much less than doctors. What does the world *really* need out
  there? (One suggestion: not more lawyers!)
- *Do every job well.* Even if you don't like a job, do it well. The better you do your work, the greater your chances of advancement.
  Having your boss be your fan can be extremely important when
  you need references later. Obviously, a glowing recommendation
  makes a great impression. In the business world, people often notice who's dependable and efficient and top-notch. These people

## Take It from Me

### Use Your Friends, and Look Smart

Ask for help from friends who have a job you want. Get them to hook you up with the person in charge where they work. That's how many teens get jobs. Friends are important. Also, *dress up*. When I go to an interview in a dress shirt and tie, I get a lot more respect and make a much more positive impression. You show that you are serious and intelligent. Look good, dress up, look smart—it's key.—Robert Morgan III, 17

are sometimes lured from job to job. They don't even have to seek out new opportunities—the opportunities come to them.

- *Be professional.* Hey, get started early in earning praise from your boss. Professional employees show up on time. They're dependable. They're courteous and friendly. They don't toss out cynical comments from the peanut gallery. If they're not happy with work or their boss, they confront the problem calmly and directly. Mind you, you don't have to abandon your personality and your sense of humor to be professional. But tackling work with passion, dedication, and professionalism is of benefit to all.

- *Do the job to get the job.* This is an idea promoted by Nick Corcodilos, author of the idea-generating book *Ask the Headhunter.* He suggests that when you're being interviewed for a job, instead of just explaining why you want the job, you can stand out by showing what you can do to specifically help the company. If you're interviewing to be a day care helper, for example, offer to spend an hour with a group of kids, just to show how good you are with them. Help your prospective employer imagine you in the job. This will make you stand out among other candidates.

## Take It from Me

### Be Resourceful

Find a service or organization that you use frequently and befriend some of the employees. When it comes time to find a job or internship, just ask. Ask friends what their parents do. If they work in a field that interests you, see if they have any positions available. Draft a résumé. Prospective employers will be impressed and have a better idea of your skills and interests. Dress nicely for the interview.— Alexis Neuhaus, 18

## Now That You've Made Some Money, Save Some!

*You cannot bring about prosperity by discouraging thrift.*
—*Abraham Lincoln*

We hope you're getting the sense, a few chapters into our book, that all of your money does *not,* should *not,* can*not,* and will *not* come exclusively from your work. If you save and invest some of the money you make, it'll start working for you, creating more money. Given your age, it can create untold sums of wealth throughout your life. Thousands of dollars. Tens of thousands of dollars. Even millions.

We think it's great to get up and go to work most of the days of your life, especially when it's work that you love. That's the way we feel about our work. But note this critical bit of good news: If you're an investor, then all your invested dollars will be getting up and going to work, too! Furthermore, as they grow, so will your opportunity to direct your life. You'll work not out of desperate necessity, but out of choice.

Close your eyes for a second and try to visualize the beauty of it: hundreds (or thousands) of little dollar bills, all of them going to offices of their own, working hard from morning to night (and often through the night). Imagine the little fellers huffing and puffing and wiping the sweat from their brows. Imagine them drawing paychecks of their own, then turning and passing all that money back to you.

This is why we save. This is why you should save. Really, this is why you *must* save if you're going to live a fulfilling life. The greatest life you can live is to have the means, the curiosity, and the perseverance to follow your heart and your mind down every path of adventure and every route to goodness.

So before we can talk investing, we need to master the practice of saving.

## How Much Should You Save?

This is about as tough a financial question as exists. The answer depends on so many factors. But for working adults, a general guideline is to save around 10 percent of your salary each year. That means not blowing every earned dollar at the mall. But it also means having the resources to enjoy your life from day to day.

Now, because many teenagers don't have to pay rent, buy food, pay the cable bill, cover the dog's vet and the car insurance and a dozen other expenses, you might actually be able to save substantial percentages of your money today. While your parents care for you, in theory you could save almost 100 percent of your money. But does that mean you *should* save all your money? Certainly not. It's good practice to get started spending, and knowing how to spend well, right now, too . . . to say nothing of the enjoyment you'll get. The best way to develop good habits is to make saving and spending regular, complementary aspects of your life.

But good saving is so much less explored as a topic, and as a universal human experience, that we're going to devote most of our effort to just that.

## Ways to Save and Keep Saving

Here are a few techniques that help some people save.

- *Save before spending.* Whenever a wad of money hits your hands, from a job or an allowance or your generous uncle Arthur, take some savings out immediately. And make a practice of that. Out of all the money you get, always immediately put away 10–25 percent of it, at least. That $50 birthday check? How about putting away $10 of it into your long-term savings? The beauty of this system is that once you've removed your savings, you're free to spend the rest. Go ahead and have fun spending the rest of it.
- *Plan with your parents.* Here, we test your powers of entrepreneurship. How about turning to your parents and grandparents

and asking them to match your savings? Many companies do this with their employees—for every dollar the employee saves and invests, the company adds, say, twenty-five cents. Your family should offer you a similar plan!

Some parents match their children's savings dollar for dollar. Others put up fifty or twenty-five cents for every dollar saved. The net result can be awesome. For every $500 of savings you put away, you'll get anywhere from $100 to $500 in additional savings from your parents and grandparents. And if your relatives are worried about your putting them in the poorhouse by saving a ton of money, you can put a cap on their match each year. For example, they match you dollar for dollar up to $500 in savings each year.

> ## Famous Words
>
> *Good habits formed at youth make all the difference.*
> —Aristotle

One key here, though, is that you must commit that money to long-term savings. You must agree to save it for five to ten years or more. If you do, and they match . . . frankly, you'll be astounded by your savings power over time. And you'll almost guarantee financial independence in the middle of your life and beyond.

- *Spend less.* Here's a very useful exercise. Over the next month, make a note of everything you spend money on. Buy a CD, make a note. Buy a sweater, make a note. Buy movie tickets, note that, too. Buy dinner with friends, note it. Gather all those notes at the end of the month and add them up. Let's say you spent $325. Now divide the notes up into two groups: 1) Things I Needed, and 2) Things I Just Wanted. Let's say the breakdown is $125 for necessities and $200 for the desirables. Now look hard, real hard, at that second group of notes.

  The reality in America is that the average person is buying way, way, way too much from one month to the next. Stuff they won't use but a few times. Shoes, shirts, bags, CDs, videos, and so much more. Most of our houses in America are simply overloaded with unnecessary *stuff.* Look around your own house. Look at it all. Stuff everywhere!

  Obviously, we don't want you to root it all out. But really discipline yourself to not be wasteful. *Fifty dollars saved each month at the age of eighteen is literally worth hundreds of thousands of dollars to you in retirement.* You don't believe that? Well, an eighteen-year-old who saves $50 a month and invests it in the stock market at 11 percent per year will see that money grow to $800,000 by the age of sixty-five. Why not get started now with that measly monthly savings by cutting from the stuff you don't *really* need?

• *Consider the "opportunity cost" of purchases.* Here's our reinforcement of the point above. Consider the opportunity cost of your purchases. Opportunity cost is an economic term that applies to many parts of our lives. It essentially refers to the cost of giving up one alternative in order to act on another. Imagine that you can buy a CD for $15—or you can invest the money. If you invest for ten years and it grows by an average of 11 percent per year, that $15 will become $42.50. So your decision can be framed like this: "Do I want to pay a longer-term opportunity cost of $42.50 in order to have this $15 CD right now?" Sometimes the answer will still be yes, but we hope for your benefit that other times it'll be no. Because youthful opportunity costs can be quite high. Think about $50 tickets to a concert. Growing at 11 percent for ten years, $50 would become $142. Is the concert worth giving up $142 in ten years? Again, it may well be—though you should probably have a conversation with your twenty-something self! But if you're thinking of spending $4,000 this year on unnecessary shoes and clothing, consider whether that's worth the opportunity cost of $32,000 in twenty years or $260,000 in forty years. If it is, then shoes and clothing that you may not truly *need* are worth a lot more to you than to us!

Now remember, it's important to save, but it's just as important to spend, too. Don't begrudge yourself dinner with friends or a great movie or a CD or a shirt. Just make sure you know why you're spending and that you have some sense of the opportunity cost. A quick calculation: Using the stock market's average return and leaving out inflation for the moment, $1 spent today is equal to $8 in twenty years and more than $60 in forty years. For every $100 you spend today, you are forgoing $6,000 in forty years.

## Tips from Teens on Saving

Here are some more suggestions, from a bunch of teens and a few others fresh out of teenhood, on how to get into the saving habit.

- Ben Sheppard, 18: Don't carry too much cash, if possible.
- Clayton Smalley, 16: I used to be weak when it came to money. I couldn't go into a store without buying something. I'm glad I'm not that person now. I taught myself discipline by keeping a $20 bill in my pocket, walking around the mall all day, and not buying anything. Now I don't have any urge to buy stuff when I go into a store. It worked for me.
- Tacy Holliday, 19: When you buy something, use only dollar bills. If you buy a magazine for $3.25 and you pay for it with a $5 bill, you'll get back $1.75 in change. Put the dollar back into your purse (or pocket) and keep the seventy-five cents separate. Only spend the bills, not the coins. Put all the coins in a jar for savings. That way you'll always be saving a little. This works extremely well for me.
- Daniel Carroll, 16: Most teens would probably hate to give up a quarter of their earnings if they won't see the money again for many years. But they need to think about how saving now will help them in the future—for things such as retiring early, being able to go back to college and get a master's/doctorate, having enough money to support a spouse through retirement, having enough to pay for your children's education one day. I have a little bank that I put spare change and bills into. Whenever I have a significant amount in there, I either invest it or put it in the bank. It's important to keep a routine. Every time I get money, I put some away.

## Take It from Me

### Learn from Ex-Teens

When I was seventeen, I had two part-time summer jobs—one at a neighborhood bakery decorating cakes and one at a mall clothing store as a cashier. The clothing store offered 60 percent off their retail prices for employees. While it was great to buy clothes at a discount, I ended up spending almost all the money I earned on clothes and didn't have much left over at the end of the summer when I started college. I should have worked more at the bakery—it was easier for me to resist the doughnuts than a new sweater.—Duffy Winters, 32

## Take It from Me

### The Rewards of Saving

When I was about fourteen, I decided that I'd be proactive with money, so I got a part-time job at a local deli. With my first paycheck, I realized that I'd have to work awfully hard to make very little money. My supervisor had been making just above minimum wage for twenty years, and I knew I didn't want to spend the rest of my life working to death. Around the same time, my godparents took me to an investment workshop. Immediately, my eyes were opened to the power of compound growth in investing. I knew that this was a way to financial freedom. I left the workshop determined to make my money work *for me* instead of the other way around (which can get very tiring after a while).

Honoring what my mother had taught me, to share whatever I had, I donated a portion of my paychecks to raise money for breast cancer research and saved everything else to build up a large enough nest egg to open a brokerage account. Too excited to wait, I began reading everything I could about investing. With most of my life savings (which wasn't very much), I invested in DuPont, AT&T, Caterpillar, and International Paper. The pride in being a shareholder in a company, along with watching my stocks increase in value, fueled my desire to learn more. I went to three more investment workshops with my godparents and browsed books at the library.

I began with $4,000 in my account and have added about $2,000 since then. My portfolio is now worth roughly $12,000, five years later, having grown about 18 percent per year, on average. Some of my favorite holdings are Procter & Gamble and two biotechnology companies that I know a fair amount about because they're based near me.

In the years since then, I have experienced many moments of gratitude for discovering investing so early in my life. I'm in college now and plan to go on to medical school. And I know that thanks to investing, my road will be much easier. Not only have I taken a proactive step toward improving my long-term financial future, but I'm confident that I'll also be able to generously support the causes I believe in with more ease than I otherwise would have imagined.

—Tacy Holliday, 19

- Donald Hoang, 14: I deposit my money into a bank instead of my wallet, so the money is not there and I have to take an extra step to get to it.
- Jason Hart, 18: Take only what you *really* need for spending, and put the rest of it somewhere that's difficult to get to. Long-term certificates of deposit (CDs) work really well, and the money-market account I have works for me. Just making it inconvenient to get to your money might help you avoid the urge to spend it all. Also, set concrete guidelines once you get a regular job or allowance. Decide exactly what percentage you will spend and what you will save, and follow your own rules.
- Robert Morgan III, 17: Carry very little money at all times. You can't spend money if you don't have it. A candy bar would be nice, but without a dollar you can't get it. Little things like that really add up quickly. I like to see the number of shares of stock I own going up, too. That's a great motivator.
- Deborah Sperling, 14: When considering a major purchase, wait a week or so, at minimum. This will help you make sure you still want the item, and as an added bonus, the price might go down.
- Adam Kaufman, 15: Start with small amounts. When I first started saving to invest, I was saving $1–$2 each day, so by the end of the month I had $30–$60, depending on what kind of month it was.
- Jason Ramage, 20: I take advantage of automatic withdrawal from my bank account into my investment account, so that I'm always investing and I'm forced to make do with a slightly tighter budget.

### Your Saving Plan

Take a little time to think about and write down *your* saving plan. Perhaps you already have one that you stick to. But can you improve it? And if you don't have one yet, figure out what kind of arrangement would work best for you. What percentage of your money will you aim to save, and how will you go about doing that?

Writing this down now could be the first step toward living where you want, working where you want, and vacationing *when* you want.

_____

_____

_____

_____

_____

_____

_____

_____

_____

# ·STEP 3·

# Be Smart About Your Money

· · · · ·

Almost any man knows how to earn money, but not one in
a million knows how to spend it.
—*Henry David Thoreau*

**M**r. Thoreau is one of our nation's most clever philosophers. His writings are extraordinary. However, with this quotation he's just being cynical. There are roughly 275 million Americans today. We'll bet there are a lot more than 275 people who spend smartly. But if Thoreau was too negative, he wasn't absurdly wrong. Today, the average American adult has more than $5,000 in credit card debt. Most adults, you see, do not know how to spend intelligently.

Let's start with the obvious mistakes. Many people simply buy too much, from month to month. They spend beyond their means and end up having to borrow money to cover living expenses. There's nothing wrong with borrowing to buy a house—since over time a house gains in value. But too many adults borrow money to buy the latest-model car rather than a more affordable one. Too many go into debt to buy an entertainment center, a new set of golf clubs, the most expensive cosmetics. Each of these is likely unnecessary, and each loses value over time. When you borrow money to buy something that is unnecessary to you and that loses value over time, you harm your financial future.

Arguably, that last sentence is the most important one in this book. So let's say it again and break it apart:

When you 1) borrow money to 2) buy something that is 3) unnecessary to you and that 4) loses value over time, 5) you harm your financial future.

And because we can't hammer this point home strongly enough, now let's present it as free verse:

> *When you borrow money to buy*
> *Something that is unnecessary*
> *To you,*
> *And that loses value over time,*
> *You harm*
> *Your financial future.*

There is an enormous amount of evidence to support this, er, poetry. But let's just look at two scary facts that bear it out:

- According to the Securities and Exchange Commission's 1999 report, *The Facts on Saving and Investing,* "Two out of three households in America—an estimated 65 million households—will fail to realize one or more of their major life goals because they've failed to develop a comprehensive financial plan." The same report also noted: "More than half—55 percent—of all current workers have never even tried to figure out how much they need to save and accumulate for retirement."
- A 1999 Retirement Confidence Survey reported that "less than 1 in 10 American adults appears to be doing a very good job of preparing for retirement."

You can do better than this, much better. If you begin learning the art of saving and investing now, and stick with it, you'll change those statistics for your life and your generation.

We've reviewed at great length how to earn money and save it. Now it's time to discuss how to spend it wisely.

## Spending Smarts

Teenage years are when money matters start to get a little complicated. When you're nine or ten, maybe you just have an allowance to treat yourself to some candy or comic books or a video game. Your finances are pretty simple.

Teen years bring greater challenges. You want to look good, feel good, fit in. At the same time, you have more opportunities to spend your money. Sadly, though, you might not have much more money than you did when you were ten. Put it all together: You need more money than before; there are more opportunities for you to spend than before; and you may have essentially the same amount of money.

So, you have one of two choices. Either you recognize your limitations and plan accordingly, or you learn to spend recklessly and put yourself on a path toward borrowing and personal bankruptcy in your adult life. Choose carefully! We advise learning to make some tough decisions. Let's say you have a car and have to help pay for insurance. And there's gas to fill up the tank. Whoa there, you just got another flat tire. There goes more money. And now that you're driving, you're out with your friends much more. Shopping. Catching movies. Buying tickets to sports games and concerts. Eating out frequently.

Yes, you're having fun, which is great. But if you're not careful, that can all cost a *lot.*

One solution is a word that may send a shiver down your spine. Grit your teeth and get ready. Here it is.

*Budgeting.*

Poor budgeting—one of the least liked, most ignored words in the English language. Yet it's a bum rap. "Budgeting" is neither as painful nor as boring as it sounds. It can actually (really and truly) be relatively interesting. After all, it's all about showing you where your money goes.

## The Exciting World of Budgeting!

Okay, that exclamation point may be a bit over the top. But give us a chance to earn it!

Budgeting is something that can help almost every teen or adult, yet few ever do it. It's not something that you necessarily have to do forever. You might just create a budget every few years and find that you can stick to it without massive amounts of effort. Here's how to get started.

Okay, we're going to ask you again to write down all your expenses for a month, but with one new wrinkle: Add in how much you take in from work, allowance, gifts, and so on. Here's how.

Find a small notebook—one you can keep in your pocket or purse. Track all your inflows and outflows of money for the month. If you cash a paycheck for $85, jot it down. If you earn $25 baby-sitting, jot that down, too. If your great-granny writes you a holiday check for $100 (bless her heart), add that in.

Alongside all this incoming cash, store your outflows. If you buy a coffee at Starbucks for $2.75, write it down. If you go to the movies with your friends and pay $7.50 for the movie and $3.75 for a honkin' tub of popcorn, mark it down for no less than $11.25. Did you put $5 in the collection plate at church or deposit $30 into your savings account? You know what to do. For this exercise to be accurate and valuable, you need to be thorough.

Just for a month. Or even just for a week. Or you could even, ya lazy bum, just keep tabs on your spending for a single day to get started.

At the end of the period, put all the information together. Create categories for inflows and outflows and tabulate your results. Below is a sample list of categories you can use (with room for some of your own categories). We include a few subcategories that might apply only to older teens who are out on their own already. Don't worry about leaving many lines blank. Just make sure that all your inflows and outflows are recorded. (We'll explain the "Next Month's Plan" column in a minute.)

## My Money Inflows and Outflows

From _____ to _____

### INFLOWS

| Category | Amounts Received | Total Received | Next Month's Plan |
|---|---|---|---|
| Allowance: | _____ | _____ | _____ |
| Gifts: | _____ | _____ | _____ |
| Job 1: | _____ | _____ | _____ |
| Job 2: | _____ | _____ | _____ |
| Other: | _____ | _____ | _____ |
| Other: | _____ | _____ | _____ |
| GRAND TOTAL: | _____ | _____ | _____ |

### OUTFLOWS

| Category | Amounts Spent | Total Spent | Next Month's Plan |
|---|---|---|---|
| Rent: | _____ | _____ | _____ |
| Groceries: | _____ | _____ | _____ |
| Clothing: | _____ | _____ | _____ |
| Entertainment: | _____ | _____ | _____ |
|   Eating out: | _____ | _____ | _____ |
|   Movies: | _____ | _____ | _____ |
|   CDs/DVDs: | _____ | _____ | _____ |
|   Concerts/ events: | _____ | _____ | _____ |
|   Sports/events: | _____ | _____ | _____ |
| Books: | _____ | _____ | _____ |

| Category | Amounts Spent | Total Spent | Next Month's Plan |
|---|---|---|---|
| Hobbies/games: | _____ | _____ | _____ |
| Small impulse buy: | _____ | _____ | _____ |
| Personal care: | _____ | _____ | _____ |
| Gas: | _____ | _____ | _____ |
| Car insurance: | _____ | _____ | _____ |
| Car loan payments: | _____ | _____ | _____ |
| Car repairs: | _____ | _____ | _____ |
| Auto tickets: | _____ | _____ | _____ |
| Student loan bills: | _____ | _____ | _____ |
| Phone bills: | _____ | _____ | _____ |
| Utilities (heat, water): | _____ | _____ | _____ |
| Transportation: | _____ | _____ | _____ |
| Travel/vacations: | _____ | _____ | _____ |
| Gifts/treats for others: | _____ | _____ | _____ |
| Big buys (car, TV): | _____ | _____ | _____ |
| Charity/donations: | _____ | _____ | _____ |
| Short-term savings: | _____ | _____ | _____ |
| Long-term savings: | _____ | _____ | _____ |
| Investments: | _____ | _____ | _____ |
| College savings: | _____ | _____ | _____ |
| Medical/dental/ eye: | _____ | _____ | _____ |
| School expenses: | _____ | _____ | _____ |
| Other: | _____ | _____ | _____ |
| Other: | _____ | _____ | _____ |
| Other: | _____ | _____ | _____ |
| Other: | _____ | _____ | _____ |
| Other: | _____ | _____ | _____ |
| Other: | _____ | _____ | _____ |
| GRAND TOTAL: | _____ | _____ | _____ |

## Seeing Things as They Are

Now that you can see where your money is coming from and going to, you might be surprised. Perhaps you didn't realize that you were spending so much of your money on gifts for others. Maybe your car is eating up a lot more money than you thought. Maybe all that snack food is packing your waistline and unpacking your wallet!

## Comic Relief

### Six Things More Fun Than Budgeting

- Sleeping late.
- Eating birthday cake without silverware.
- Reading Greek lyrics.
- A good, old-fashioned food fight.
- Watching MTV for a ridiculous number of hours.
- Going for a hike (hey, it can be fun).

However, because budgeting can take just a few hours to do, why not do all of the above *and* budget?

## Keep in Mind

### The Millionaire Next Door

In 1996, Thomas J. Stanley and William D. Danko published a book called *The Millionaire Next Door: The Surprising Secrets of America's Wealthy.* It became a best-seller. It offered some big revelations. For example, the typical millionaire doesn't live in a posh mansion on a hill overlooking all the little people below. The typical millionaire does not drive a Jaguar, winking at the passersby and flashing a gold tooth. (Actually, many of these glitterati are hip-deep in debt, spend every penny, rarely save anything, and may even be on the brink of financial ruin.)

Instead, most millionaires live in ordinary neighborhoods and appear on the surface to be ordinary people. But they do have a few special habits. On average, they spend significantly less money each year than they can afford to. They also tend to drive older cars and eat out less than the average person.

### Making It Work: Next Month's Plan

Now that you've looked over your spending and saving list, it's time to think through each item. Where can you save some money next month and in the years to come? Remember, your goal throughout life will be to save more than 10 percent of your yearly salary. For now, though, with the allowance, the gifts, and maybe a job, we think you should be able to save more than 10 percent of the money that floats through your life. So go back to the lists above and plug in the numbers for "Next Month's Plan." Can you spend less on entertainment? Can you split some eating bills with your friends? Can you make more money at your job? Work hard at this for a few minutes and improve the numbers for the next month. Then track yourself and see how you're doing.

With your ideal earning, spending, and saving plan all set, now you just need to stick to it. If you need to keep tweaking, do so. The new plan may be hard to get used to, but you'll get good at it. Why? Because you'll be learning about a primary force in the lives of all creatures great and small: We deal with *limited means;* we must come to grips with our true *scarcity of resources.* And it is only when we do—realizing that we have limited time on this earth and limited money—that we can begin making smarter decisions about how we live our lives and how we spend our money.

If you learn to budget in life, even just loosely, you'll become better at a critical life skill: distinguishing between what you really *need* and what you really *want.* And you'll begin to pare back and eliminate expenditures of time and money on things you don't really need and may not even really, when you think about it, *want.* Here are some tricks to help you down that path:

- Don't carry much cash with you.
- Split food and beverage bills fairly between friends and family.
- Neither a borrower nor a lender be.
- Think before you buy anything that costs $10 or more. Do you really need and want it?
- Always save before you spend. Make that a part of your automatic thinking.
- Exchange stuff with friends. Trade books, CDs, and videos. (This can save big bucks.)
- Sell what you don't need. Hey, eBay is waiting for you to unload your stuff for profit.

Thinking about budgets and spending categories is helpful in all stages of your life. Here's one piece of advice from thirty-two-year-old ex-teen Duffy Winters: "When I was looking at colleges, I was eager to get far away from home—especially when my parents talked about my living at home if I chose nearby Northwestern. One thing I didn't take into account when I selected a school in Washington, D.C., is that I'd have to budget for plane tickets back to Chicago for Thanksgiving and Christmas. This was an expense I hadn't thought about, and it ate into my spending money. Perhaps I should've considered schools that were within driving distance—but not so close that Mom and Dad would visit all the time."

Budgeting is even more critical once you enter the real world. Imagine that you graduate from college and land a job that will pay you $32,000 per year. (Congrats!) Should you run out and rent a nice apartment that seems reasonable at $800 per month? Maybe not. A little budgeting can help you. If you end up paying about 25 percent in taxes, that means you'll take home roughly $24,000 per year, or $2,000 per month. Let's say you expect to have at least these expenses each month:

| | |
|---|---|
| School loans: | $200 |
| Groceries: | $150 |
| Eating out: | $200 |
| Car payments: | $200 |
| Car insurance: | $75 |
| Gas: | $60 |
| Phone: | $40 |
| Clothing: | $100 |
| Laundry: | $25 |
| Stuff (books, CDs): | $50 |
| Entertainment: | $100 |
| Travel: | $100 |
| Gifts: | $25 |
| Total: | $1,325 |

If you're making $2,000 per month and spending $1,325 per month, that leaves just $675 for rent—and utilities like electricity, which may or may not be included in rent. If you find a nice place for $675 with utilities included, you'll cut it. But you won't have any room for saving. That's not what you want. Ideally, you should aim to sock away 10 percent of your salary—which would be in the neighborhood of $200 or more per month. Maybe you'll have to start eating out less. Or buying

## Keep in Mind

### Your Life as a Ruler

Does all this talk of setting budgets and developing good habits have you exhausted? Are you having trouble seeing why it's important to you now? Well, find a ruler—one that's twelve inches long. Really. Do this. We'll make it worth your while.

Okay, welcome back. Now, do you see how the inches are divided into eighths? There are 96 eighths in twelve inches. Okay, think of that as the span of your life. Count each eighth inch as a year. If you're sixteen, two inches of your life are over.

But that leaves 80 eighth inches more! Those are eighty years where your money (the portion that you save and invest) could be growing. They're eighty years where you can be relatively secure financially—if you've developed good habits and, ideally, started young.

Now, look at the fifth inch. That represents someone who's forty years old. Or the seventh inch—someone who's fifty-six. Many people don't start planning and saving and investing until then or later. This is extremely dangerous, perhaps even disastrous. Allow us to say it again more forcibly. *This is potentially disastrous!* You need a head start on that. The choices you make now can affect your life for decades.

Okay, now if you haven't used that ruler in the past year, sell it on eBay.

---

fewer clothes. Or not spending so much on entertainment. Or you might be better off finding an even cheaper apartment or getting a roommate willing to sleep on the floor of the kitchen (and split the rent with you . . . now there's a deal!).

Though saving $200 a month might seem unduly painful, remember the power of compounding. These few hundred bucks per month in your youth are hundreds of thousands of dollars in your retirement.

### Banks

It's true that banks exist to serve our needs. But they're not doing so out of the goodness of their hearts. They're out to make money. Think about all the things a bank does. Two biggies are keeping your money for you and loaning out money to the people and businesses that need it. If you fork over $100, do you think your $100 is locked up in the vault for years until you personally need it once again? No sirree, Bob. As quickly as possible, they're looking to loan out that money to someone else so they can begin charging him interest. The key to a bank's profits is in that amount of interest . . . and the likelihood that it will be paid back. These go up and down from day to day and year to year, but the interest a bank pays you on your deposited money is always less than the rate it's charging borrowers.

Let's make sure we all understand that. Here's a simplified example: Picture First Federal United Bank (FFUB), the big stone building on the corner in town. Its employees wear blue suits. Its owner won the Good Samaritan Award in town last year. The bank has been in business for more than ninety years.

Okay, let's say that FFUB has 1,000 customers who've deposited a total of $10 million into bank accounts. The bank's paying them 3 percent interest per year. (That means the bank has to shell out about $300,000 annually.) Meanwhile, FFUB has made a bunch of FFUB loans to borrowers—small businesses, home owners getting their mortgage, car loans, school loans, and so forth. Typically, FFUB will have loaned out $8 million of that $10 million it has in deposits. If the bank is charging an average of 8 percent on those loans, it can expect to collect $640,000 from its borrowers for the year.

Now you see some of the profit in the bank. It pays out $300,000 in interest to its customers. And it takes in $640,000 in interest from its borrowers. That's the basic business of your local bank. That's the basic explanation of what happens to your savings when you deposit it.

Things aren't quite that simple, of course. Different loans are made at different interest rates. And different kinds of bank accounts earn different interest rates. Also, some loans "default"—they're not paid back; there, the bank loses money. Then again, most banks earn additional profit by charging fees, often *lots* of 'em. For instance, your mom and dad have probably paid hundreds or thousands of dollars in fees just to use cash machines (ATMs) over the course of their adulthood. Some accounts sport monthly fees. And if you bounce a check, there's a fee. If you need to wire money into the bank, there's a fee. At the same time, let's not forget the bank's operating costs, either. It has to pay for its staff, building, electricity, postage, and so on. Finally, consider also that the bank can't loan out all its money. It has to have some on hand in case you walk in and want to withdraw some of yours.

Come to think of it, that's a decent introduction to banking. You're ready for a banking internship!

## Credit Unions

Most of the above discussion about banks applies to credit unions as well. While a bank is created to make money and turn a profit, a credit union is a nonprofit organization that operates pretty much like a bank. You can deposit money in accounts there and can take out loans, too. Credit unions typically offer better interest rates, also—but not everyone is able to join a credit union. Some are restricted to people who work for certain companies or organizations; others are just for people in a certain neighborhood or religious group.

If you're in college, see if there's a credit union available for members of the college community. You can learn more about credit unions and search for one for you at www.cuna.org. Because credit unions usually charge much lower fees, they can make a great deal of sense for young savers in high school and college.

## What Your Bank or Credit Union Can Do for You

When you walk into a bank with a fistful of dollars, you can open one of several different kinds of accounts. Here's a rundown of the main possibilities you might consider:

- savings accounts.
- checking accounts.
- money-market accounts.
- certificates of deposit (CDs).

### Savings Accounts

A savings account is fairly simple. You deposit money, and it earns interest. You withdraw money whenever you want. The interest rate for the account may depend on how much money you keep in your account. Often, accounts with higher average balances will earn higher interest rates.

### Checking Accounts

A checking account is like a savings account. You can deposit money and withdraw money—and you can also write checks. But you may or may not earn interest on the money you keep in a checking account. If you do earn interest, the rate is likely to be lower than for savings accounts.

## Money-Market Accounts

A money-market account will pay you more than the typical savings account. It usually has a few more strings attached, though, such as requiring certain minimum balances. Some money-market accounts will let you write some checks, too, if you keep a relatively high balance.

## Certificates of Deposit (CDs)

A certificate of deposit involves handing over a certain amount of money and not being able to access that money for a specified period of time (several months or years). In exchange, you earn an interest rate on the money that's usually higher than with a savings account. Why? Because the bank can loan that money out for longer, earning more money on it. The longer the duration of your CD, the higher the rate you'll get. If you suddenly need to get your money out early, you can do so, but you'll be charged a penalty. So use CDs for longer-term savings that you know you won't need.

## A Comparison

Interest rates change all the time. You might earn 1 percent on a checking account one year and 5 percent on it ten years later. But your money will always earn less, on average, in a checking account than in a long-term CD. Here's how a bunch of rates might compare to each other in a given year:

| | |
|---|---|
| Checking account: | 1.55% |
| Savings account: | 2.05% |
| Money-market account: | 2.94% |
| 3-month CD: | 3.25% |
| 6-month CD: | 3.55% |
| 1-year CD: | 3.81% |
| 2-year CD: | 4.16% |
| 3-year CD: | 4.49% |
| 5-year CD: | 4.87% |

So what should you do with your money?

Well, it depends on many things, such as how much you have and what the minimum required balances are for the various options. It also depends on your plans for the money. If you have $1,000 and you're saving that for college in three years, you might put that in a three-year CD. If you want to be able to write checks on that money, forget the CD and consider a checking account (or possibly a money-market account). If you expect to withdraw money on occasion, but you don't need to write checks, then try a savings account. Look for the highest rate that you can earn, while still meeting your needs.

Wondering how a bank makes money on all this? Let's look at the other side of the business. Here are some interest rates that you might be charged for various loans:

| | |
|---|---|
| 30-year home mortgage: | 6.46% |
| 4-year car loan: | 7.83% |
| Personal loan: | 9.00% |

Notice how much higher these rates are compared to what banks were paying in interest at the time. That "spread" is where much of a bank's

---

## Keep in Mind

### Bonds, Savings Bonds

You may also want to consider parking some of your money in government savings bonds. A bond is essentially a loan. When you buy a government bond, you're lending money to the government. The government pays you an interest rate. Then the government uses your money for public projects, staff salaries, and so on.

There are a wide variety of government savings bonds, and they'll often pay you higher interest rates than a CD. Here are some basics on savings bonds. Some are tax-advantaged, meaning that they let you put off or avoid paying taxes on your earnings. Some bonds specify exactly what their interest rate is, while others have interest rates that fluctuate. Bonds typically have a life of thirty years, but you can usually cash out of them any time after six months. You will, however, frequently be charged a penalty if you cash out within five years.

You can learn more about bonds and whether they're right for you—at www.Fool.com/school/basics/investingbasics.htm. That's a long Web address to type in, but you can learn plenty there.

earnings come from. Does it sound criminal or "evil"? Listen, if banks couldn't do this, they wouldn't exist. Also, as consumers we can make them fight for our business by playing one off against another. They do compete.

By the way, have you been wondering why anyone would bother with banks and CDs and bonds when the stock market has historically increased your wealth by 11 percent per year? There's a good explanation: You can lose money on stocks, and stock market returns are not guaranteed. They're much riskier than bank accounts and government bonds and should only be where you park money you won't need for at least five (ideally ten or more) years. More on that later, though.

### Checking Out Banks

As we just hinted, it's smart not to go to just the first bank you see, but to find one that will serve your needs best. (Of course, depending on where you live and how easy it is for you to access various banks, you might have less choice as a teen.) Here are some questions you might seek answers to when you're shopping for a bank. Take this list with you when you go, and ask these questions:

- What are the interest rates on the different kinds of accounts the bank offers?
- What are the rules, restrictions, and fees for each of those accounts? Find out, among other things, what the required minimum deposit is to open various accounts and what the minimum balance is to avoid fees once the accounts are open. It's critical to learn about fees. You don't want to be paying $10 per month for an account with just $200 in deposits, as that money will disappear quickly. You also want to know if you're going to be charged an extra $3 per month whenever your account balance dips below a certain amount. Get the facts.
- What are the features of the different accounts? Which ones offer debit cards (or "check cards")?
- If you're looking at checking accounts: What is the per check charge? What is the charge for ordering new checks? What is the charge for a bounced check? How many checks per month will you be allowed to write?
- What fees are charged when you withdraw cash or make a point-of-purchase transaction (pay for groceries, pay for gasoline, and so on) with your ATM card? Are you charged a fee to speak to a teller rather than use the ATM for a transaction? Are you charged if you

use another bank's ATM, even if they are in the same "ATM net-work"?

- Can you have your paycheck direct-deposited? (That means that you fill out a short form and then your paychecks are deposited automatically into your bank account. This can save you the trouble of depositing each check.)
- Are there any special accounts for those under eighteen? (Many banks have these, and they usually require very low minimum balances, which is helpful.)

### Bring Backup

If your local bank doesn't seem eager to let you open an account because you're not yet eighteen, consider taking a parent in with you. Sometimes that can make things happen. If your parents are customers at that bank, it should be even more important for the bank to assist their customers' offspring. Also, always ask the bank if they have special deals or rates for teens.

### Facts on Checking

When you write a check, the person or company you give it to might not cash it for a few days. Some checks are *never* cashed. It's important to keep track of when each check you write is cashed. (A good way is to put a check mark next to the check number in your check register.) You might have $200 in your account, but if you've forgotten about a $300 check you wrote three months ago that someone hasn't cashed

## Checks and Balances

Here's what part of one page of your check register might look like:

| Check # | Date | Item | (-) | (+) | Balance: $744.25 |
|---------|---------|-------------------|--------|-------|------------------|
| 114 | 1/15/02 | Visa card | 76.11 | | 668.14 |
| 115 | 1/22/02 | Larry's Snack Bar | 15.00 | | 653.14 |
| | 1/26/02 | Paycheck | | 88.93 | 742.07 |
| 116 | 2/02/02 | Warthog sculpture | 110.00 | | 632.07 |

That's it! It's not terribly complicated. Just addition and subtraction.

yet, you may end up in trouble when she cashes it. One great way to keep track of all of this is through Microsoft Money or Quicken software.

If you fail to keep track of your checks and your current balance, you might end up "bouncing" a check. That's when someone tries to cash a check you wrote him, but you don't have enough money in the account to cover it. This usually results in your being charged a fee (sometimes $25 or more), a lot of headache, and some embarrassment. Keep excellent records (or at least good records)—and try not to flirt with a zero balance. (Also, check to see what your bank will do if you do experience a mishap and end up with a bounced check. If they do charge you a fee for one mistake, think about calling them, explaining what happened, and trying to get the fee waived.)

### ATMs (Automated Teller Machines)

ATMs are everywhere these days and are easy to use. If you have a bank account, you probably have an ATM card or some other kind of card from the bank that will allow you to withdraw money from an ATM. Using one is simple. Stick in your card, enter your "PIN" number (your personal identification number, or password), and answer the questions you're asked.

When you're done, you'll usually get a receipt that will show you your current balance. You might compare this with your check register, if you have one, to make sure it seems right. The numbers may not be equal, though. If you've written some checks that haven't been cashed, the ATM and your bank won't know about them yet.

It's usually free to use any of your bank's ATMs, which are probably

---

## Take It from Me

### Managing My Money

I put away all of my paychecks into my bank account. I spend what I have to, and the rest begins to build up. When I have enough money worth transferring, I send it to my E*Trade brokerage account, so that I can invest it in stocks.—Bryan Sims, 18

located all over town. (Sometimes you're allowed only a certain number of free transactions, though.) You can generally stick your card into the ATM of other banks, too, but you'll probably get socked with a charge for that. That charge can be as much as $2 or more—which can add up. So be careful. (This is one more area where many adults make poor decisions. It's estimated that Americans pay around $2 billion each year in ATM surcharge fees. Many of these fees could be avoided.)

## Your Paycheck

Another kind of check that can be confusing is your paycheck. You'll typically see that you earned a fair amount of money, but some was taken out for this and some for that, and . . . gee . . . what happened to all your earnings?

One teen confided to us that he earns $6.75 per hour and that on his last paycheck he earned $78. But $4.06 was taken out for "federal income" and $5.96 was taken for "FICA." He ended up with just $67.98. What were these items?

"Federal income" represents money that's being withheld for taxes. It's supposed to approximate how much will be owed in taxes from this paycheck. Having to pay a sometimes bloated Uncle Sam aside, this withholding does have its upside—it means you don't have to be saving money separately in order to pay taxes just once a year.

"FICA" refers to your payments into the Social Security "trust fund." Will you get this money back? Um . . . well . . . not exactly. Think of it this way: The money you're paying now is going to retirees who are drawing Social Security checks this month. When *you* retire and pass a certain age, you'll also be eligible to collect Social Security payments to help you get by. Um, maybe. With people living longer and longer, there will be more people needing their Social Security payments in the future. Simultaneously, there will be relatively fewer people to pay money into the system. So your skepticism about the whole thing is warranted. We do indeed encourage you to stay informed and get involved in this situation, because it's crying out for solutions, and the answers are dramatically going to affect your, and your generation's, financial future. Chances are that you, like us, will pay a lot of money into Social Security while getting relatively little out when you retire.

Phew! We're done with banks. If you don't find banks the most exciting things in the world, you're not alone. (They're certainly not as exciting as budgeting, right?!) Let's move on now, to some ways that you can spend your money more effectively.

# Marketing

### Be Aware How Companies Are Trying to Sell to You

One way to not overspend is to be a savvy consumer. This involves taking notice of how companies and advertisers are trying to manipulate you. Here are some examples:

- Supermarkets tend to put some items that most people want (like milk and bread) in the back of the store or at least far apart from one another. That way, shoppers won't be able to rush in and out. They'll have to cover a lot of ground, encountering many products and perhaps buying some items they may not have planned to buy. It's been estimated by researchers that about 60 percent of supermarket purchases are *not planned.*
- Supermarkets and other stores often put tempting, low-priced items—like candy and magazines—along the checkout line. They're hoping you'll buy something on impulse, as you stand there waiting. A lot of candy gets sold because a parent is waiting in line with a child, who begs for the candy he's staring at. (Similarly, cereals that appeal to children will likely be on lower shelves, not higher ones.) They're targeting you, as teens, too. Guaranteed they've got an aisle of magazines or knickknacks and they've lined up as much Britney Spears and Josh Hartnett stuff at eye level.
- Look closely at ads in magazines and TV commercials. Notice how many times the advertisers will associate their product with something that appeals to people. For example, a sports car might be shown with an attractive woman. This is meant to get men subconsciously to associate that car with pretty women. The suggestion is that if they buy that car, they date that woman (uhh, it doesn't always work that way!). Notice how happy people seem to be in many cigarette ads. The advertisers want you to subconsciously associate smoking with having a great time. (As utterly ridiculous as that is. In fact, if it doesn't seem ridiculous, visit some lung cancer patients at your local hospice. Not so fun.) Ads generally suggest that you'll earn more respect, more love, more success, and more happiness if you use their product.

- Watch out for "up-selling," too. Surely you've noticed how fast-food cashiers ask you, "Want fries with that?" When customers don't order fries, they probably don't want them. But when asked if they want fries, many will say, "Uhh, yeah, okay." Ka-ching! An extra sale for the restaurant. Other restaurants will do similar things, asking if you want dessert. They're trying to influence your decisions. Electronics stores will try to up-sell you, too, recommending service warranties that usually aren't worth it.
- Basically, think hard about what a company is doing as it sells its products or services. Most moves are very calculated, aiming to get your interest and make a sale.

## Shop for Bargains

If you're in the market for something, don't just rely on the advertisements you see. After all, no ad is going to say, "Our food's pretty darn expensive and it tastes like cardboard!" No company will promote: "We make the *third* best videocamera on the market!"

When you need to buy something, particularly something pricey, insist on objective information about it. One terrific resource is *Consumer Reports* magazine, published by the nonprofit Consumers Union. Each issue reports on a wide variety of offerings and tells you

- what to look for when you're shopping for a specific item.
- what to ignore in a product's claims.
- how its experts tested and rated competing products.

Consider checking out *Consumer Reports* for free at your local library. It makes for interesting reading that can save you a fortune. You needn't research each and every purchase. But how about learning how to get the best deal on anything that costs you more than $200?

## Cars

Cars are everywhere. Our roadways, crisscrossing every community, are littered with cars all hours of the day (the world wasn't always this way!). Few adults live without a car. Naturally, most teenagers are eager to get their own. And if you can't persuade anyone to buy you that

## Take It from Me

### Consider Giving Some Money Away

I read somewhere that if you have any money in a bank account and a little money in your pocket right now, you're among the wealthiest people in the world. Having gone to Honduras on a mission trip and seen the conditions that others live in every day, I see things from a different perspective here in the United States. It's amazing how much we have that just gets squandered on depreciating assets that really do not make one's life much happier.

I wish more people saved more, invested more, and gave more to charity. It certainly makes you feel better to have financial security, enabling you to direct some of your income toward a productive purpose. Sounds better than always using it to buy a nice DVD player or computer system that quickly becomes worth only pennies compared to what you paid for it.—Jason Ramage, 20

sleek, black Corvette 8000-ZX with automated sunroof and JetFire audio system, you'd be happy with the family's beat-up, fourteen-year-old Wagoneer with dog slobber all over the windows. Then it's roll down the windows, crank up the music, flip on the overpriced sunglasses, and get that Wagoneer to its peak of 47 mph. Baby, we were born to run!

But before that, let's think about the economics of our cars. Because by not doing so, you risk wasting literally tens of thousands of dollars in your life on the wrong cars at the wrong prices. To help you out, we turned to the denizens of The Motley Fool's on-line "Buying and Maintaining a Car" discussion board (boards.Fool.com), which we highly recommend. (May we interrupt for a brief commercial. . . . Fool.com hosts an on-line community of discussion boards. You can test-drive our service with a thirty-day free trial.) Now, back to our show. We asked everyone to share advice on cars for teens. Here are some of their tips.

1. Start by visiting www.Fool.com/car. We believe we can save you hundreds or even thousands of dollars with some basic negotiation tips. Here's a simple process that works: a) Test-drive cars

without any intention to buy. b) Pick the car you want. c) Do all negotiating by fax. Simply ask the dealer to itemize all features and costs. Fax out requests to all the competing dealers in your area. d) Work dealers against one another. For more details on this, visit us on-line at Fool.com.

2. We know it's not a real thrill doing so, but find out about the cost of insurance for you and the car you're thinking of buying *before* you buy it. You might not like what you learn. Insurance rates for teens can be as high as several thousand dollars *per year,* depending on various factors. (And to you guys out there—yes, your insurance *will* be higher. . . .) For more on the cost of your car insurance, visit www.Fool.com/car.

3. Don't sink a fortune into your first car. Believe it or not, new cars lose 20 percent of their value the moment you drive them off the lot, then 10 percent of their value each year. That's a lot of your money down the drain. Why lay down your future fortune on something that loses value so quickly? At the same time, don't set-

---

### Take It from Me

#### Sometimes Less Is More

When I was seventeen, I bought a 1969 Chevy Camaro—candy apple red with black racing stripes—with my life savings up to that point. A few months later, it was stolen from a mall parking lot. The police found it, stripped and lying in the street without any wheels and badly in need of a paint job.

With the insurance money, the car was restored and became quite valuable. Only then it was *too* nice and, with the prior theft, I was paranoid about leaving it anywhere. It was no longer basic transportation but rather an expensive headache. I sold it for a pretty good price, put the money in a couple of certificates of deposit at the bank, and then lived off that money when I was in graduate school some years later. Today you won't find me driving anything but dependable, economy transportation. The va-va-varrrrooooooms just aren't worth it.—Motley Fool senior editor, Bob Bobala, 33

tle for a car you don't like at all, either. If you like your car, you'll probably take better care of it. Thus, consider buying a fairly high-quality used car, preferably a heavy one, for your first vehicle.

4. This one might sound like a nuisance, but it could save you time, money, and maybe your life out on the road. Get someone to show you the basics of how a car operates. Just take an hour to learn what's under the hood, how it all connects, routine maintenance problems, changing a tire, and so on. Then have someone take a few hours to show you how to drive on the open road. Passing most state exams is, frankly, a joke. A little extra help from parents, aunts, and uncles may be the difference between a close call and an accident on the road. And once it snows, have a veteran driver take you to a parking lot with no obstacles (parked cars, curbed landscaping islands, pedestrians). Learn how your car will behave in the snow and rain. And learn how to recover from a skid.

5. Save up your money and go to a defensive driving school, where you'll learn to control a car. Driving is one of the most dangerous things you'll do in your life. All your favorite NASCAR drivers (you do have favorites, don't you?) have learned defensive driving. And the defensive driving instruction is comprehensive. Knowing how to drive carefully will save lives. It can also save you money. It can help you avoid costly damage to your car, reduce your insurance costs, and keep you from getting tickets. The www.carguys.com Web site is one place where you can learn more about this kind of training.

6. Find out if your state charges a property tax on cars each year. (Some states charge as much as several percent or more of a car's value, which can amount to hundreds of dollars per year.) If there is a car tax, find out who will pay it—your parents or you.

## Car Insurance

Car insurance can be the bane of the teenager's life. The folks who pay the highest insurance premiums are males under the age of twenty-five (sorry, guys). It may not seem fair, but it's based on the statistics—as is pretty much all of insurance, actually. The insurance price you're quoted will depend on many factors, including

- the insurance company.
- your gender, your age, how long you've been driving, whether you're a good student.

- your driving history (whether you've gotten any tickets or are a safe driver).
- the car (its type, age, mileage, and the like).
- where you live (city, suburb, and so on).
- how many miles the car will be driven per year.
- safety factors (whether the car has certain features, such as air bags, and whether you've had any special training).
- whether this insurance is being tacked onto your parents' policy or is a new policy.
- your credit rating (if you've not repaid loans on time, insurers may see you as an extra-risky person to insure).

As you can see, many of these items are out of your control. You can't do much about your age or where you live. But you probably *can* control, at least to some degree, what kind of car you get, how good a student you are, whether you pay your bills, and whether you get any speeding tickets. Speeding tickets themselves can cost as much as $150. *And* they'll drive your insurance premiums 15 percent higher (which can mean a few hundred bucks more each year). In fact, our

---

### Take It from Me

#### Look at the Big Picture

Maintenance costs and gas money add up. When I graduated from college, I bought the four-wheel-drive pickup truck I'd always wanted but could never afford. It turned out I still couldn't afford it. My twenty-six-mile commute each way every day cost 2.5 gallons of gas. That came to about $3.75 per day, or close to $1,000 per year—*just for getting to work.* I also didn't realize that my tires would wear out faster and cost a lot to replace.

I eventually sold the truck and bought a less expensive, more fuel-efficient, and more dependable car (a Honda Civic). Since I was navigating only the concrete jungle of the city, neither I nor my savings account really missed my four-wheel-drive. And now that I have a family and kids, I'm glad I have that savings.—Mark Andringa, 32

first cousin Garrett Lowe was hit with two speeding tickets on the day he got his driver's license! Gasp. Don't let that happen to you!

Consider this, too. According to the Mid-Atlantic Research Institute, the chance of death for someone who crashes at 70 mph or more is 100 percent. At 60 mph, it drops to 50 percent. Driving safely and within speed limits does save lives—and big insurance bucks, too.

You'll find many tips on driving and cars at www.teendriving.com and www.drivehomesafe.com.

## College

College. Ah, college. The autumn leaves. Spiral notebooks. Study groups. Football chants. The rush of love. No prevailing authority. Headaches on Saturday morning. Poor eating habits. And $5,000–$30,000 a year in tuition costs (depending on how much you think the brand-name schools are worth).

Many of us will go to college for four or more years. Those of us who do will, on average, strengthen our mind and improve our salary checks throughout life. But, unfortunately, we'll likely deal financially with our advanced schooling for many, many, many years before and after freshman orientation.

First, you and your parents might be socking money away for college for more than a decade leading up to enrollment. Then, at college, odds are you'll be trying to get by on limited cash. Ramen noodles. Midnight black coffee. Discounted shirts and socks and shoes and slacks and sweaters. And those $400 textbooks (what a heist!). You might need a part-time job to get through. Regardless, you'll be paying living expenses for four years at school. Then finally, after college, you might spend years paying off your college loans.

Oof!

Fear not, though. There's some good news. According to the College Board (www.collegeboard.com), as a nation, we're paying less than we thought for higher education. Even with colleges charging as much as $25,000 per year for tuition, that's not typical. Here are some statistics:

- More than 70 percent of college students attend four-year colleges where tuition is less than $8,000 per year.
- The average cost (tuition and fees) of a four-year public college or university is $3,510 per year.
- The average cost (tuition and fees) of a four-year private college or university is $16,332 per year.

+ More than 60 percent of full-time college students receive some type of financial aid.

As you save money for college (assuming you're doing so), make sure you know if your savings are short-term or long-term. If you're a precocious twelve-year-old reading this book, then you've got a full six years before you head to college (unless you're *so* precocious that you're already a college sophomore). If you're sixteen, though, you'll be tapping those college savings within a year or two. That means your money is short-term savings.

We consider any money you'll need within about five years to be short-term savings. It should not be placed in volatile or risky places, like the stock market. (Money-market funds and CDs are examples of low-risk options where your short-term money belongs.)

With money you won't need for a long time, you can afford to take greater risks, such as investing in stocks. If the market suddenly swoons, you'll have time to ride out the downswing and wait for a recovery. Of course, if you're risk-averse, you can still put your long-term savings in lower-risk investments.

We'll talk more of the joys and pains of the stock market in coming chapters.

---

## Keep in Mind

*People with a college degree earn 81 percent more on average than those with only a high school diploma. Over a lifetime, the gap in earnings potential between a high school diploma and a college degree (a BA) is more than $1 million.*
— The College Board

---

### Financial Aid, Scholarships, and Grants

Financial aid is worth considering while you save and invest. How much you and your parents have socked away can, to a significant degree, determine how much financial aid you receive.

Many financial aid/scholarship programs are based upon need. The more money you have, the less you need. A student is expected to contribute about 35 percent of his or her assets toward educational costs, while a parent is expected to contribute up to 12 percent, according to the 2001–2002 *Student Financial Aid Handbook*. Financial aid differs from state to state, so please check with your school's college admissions counselor to get the specifics on your situation.

Some people avoid saving and investing for college, thinking that it just means they'll then lose that much money in financial aid. Again, the more money they have, the less financial aid they'll receive. And that can be true. But since you never know exactly how much aid you'll get from the college you really want to attend, we still think it's better to save and invest. Why? Because it's better to have the cash than not.

You may even determine—like billionaires Bill Gates of Microsoft, Michael Dell of Dell Computer, and Larry Ellison of Oracle, all of whom dropped out of college—that a college education costs too much and offers you too little. Frankly, more of the unmotivated students on college campuses today *should* drop out (and return when they're ready). Regardless . . . please, please, please carefully compare the value of the school you're attending—the value of your learning—versus the costs you're paying. Admittedly, there's no clear way to assign a value to your education day by day. Intuitively, though, you should have a decent sense of its worth.

Finally, whether or not you're a candidate for financial aid, be sure to

## Take It from Me

### Spending in College

I honestly believe that 75 percent of the money I spent in college was on food and drink. While some of the best times I had were going out for dinner and celebrating with friends (wahoo!), I really wish I'd been more aware of how much I was spending on pitchers of beer, Starbucks Frappuccinos, and, of course, ahhhh, my late night Papa John's breadsticks.

I recommend paying for as much as you can with cash. Avoid racking up high monthly credit card bills that don't always get fully paid off. Also, avoid playing Sugar Daddy (or Sugar Mumsy, in my case) by footing the whole bill for groups when you're the only person with the credit card. I can't remember how many times I said, "I'll get this on my card and you can just pay me back"—like *that* ever happened!—Liz Cherry, 24

check out available scholarships and grants. Some are offered on the basis of need, but many are meant for students with particular skills, interests, backgrounds, or circumstances. And a good number of these scholarships go uncollected because no one applies for them! You may be able to earn much more in scholarships than you earned from jobs in the last few years.

### Financial Aid and Scholarship Resources (Check Them Out!)

Here's a list of Web sites where you can learn more about college planning in general and financial aid in particular:

- www.ed.gov (the U.S. Department of Education)
- www.ed.gov/prog_info/SFA/StudentGuide
- www.finaid.org
- www.Fool.com/pf.htm
- www.collegeboard.com
- www.petersons.com
- www.campustours.com
- www.mapping-your-future.org
- www.savingforcollege.com
- www.scholarshipcoach.com

Here are some Web sites where you can look up scholarships that are available. You may find a financial grant that funds your schooling and demands no repayment:

- www.finaid.org/scholarships
- www.collegeboard.com/fundfinder/html/ssrchtop.html
- www.fastweb.com
- www.uncf.org (the United Negro College Fund)
- www.hispanicfund.org (the Hispanic College Fund)
- www.college-scholarships.com
- www.collegescholarships.com (this is different from the site above)
- www.wiredscholar.com

And here are a few (of countless) books on paying for college and the college planning process:

- *Fiske Guide to Getting into the Right College* by Edward B. Fiske and Bruce G. Hammond

- *The College Admissions Mystique* by Bill Mayher
- *Get into Any College: Secrets of Harvard Students* by Jim Good and Lisa Lee
- *How to Go to College Almost for Free* by Benjamin R. Kaplan
- *The Government Financial Aid Book: The Insider's Guide to State and Federal Government Grants and Loans* by Student Financial Services
- *The Scholarship Book* by Daniel Cassidy
- *The A's and B's of Academic Scholarships* by Anna Leider and Ann Schimke
- *The Minority and Women's Complete Scholarship Book* by Student Services Inc.
- *The Black Student's Guide to Scholarships* by Barry Beckham
- *The Athletic Recruiting & Scholarship Guide* by Wayne Mazzoni

---

## Take It from Me

### $25 Per Week

In college, I wanted to be financially independent. I'd had a job the previous semester working at school. But in the spring, tennis season started and left me with little time to work. So I had to ask Mom to put money into my bank account. I hated doing this, so I asked for just $100 a month. With that little money, I was forced to budget. I started eating on campus more and found a deli nearby that offered inexpensive pizzas. Instead of going out to see movies, I rented them. And I happily took advantage of every free movie shown on campus.

Amazingly enough, my grades went up because I spent more time at home. I was getting work done. On top of that, the guy I was seeing at the time was pretty low-key. Our dates consisted of going to the supermarket, buying whatever was on special, and cooking dinner for ourselves. I had a great semester. I realized that some of my new habits cost less and were actually more fun, so it's helped me keep my spending down ever since.—Amanda Gearey, 19

### Keep it Simple, Fool (KISF)

We've thrown a lot at you. But let's remember the basics. Winning the game of finance demands little sophistication. Key back in to these timeless truths:

- Your modest savings can expand greatly over time through the power of compounding.
- You don't need to sacrifice all life's joy and pleasure in order to save.
- Many or most of your dreams are very reachable—if you plan for them.
- You can accumulate more wealth than anyone in your family ever dreamed of.

It's the classic KISF axiom—keep it simple, Fool. Oh, you've probably seen it elsewhere referred to as "KISS" (Keep it simple, stupid). We think that's clichéd, silly, and overwrought. The winds of change are blowing through your life and through this book: KISF.

# ·STEP 4·

## Avoid Financial Blunders

· · · · ·

Beware the Jabberwock, my son!
The jaws that bite, the claws that catch!
Beware the Jubjub bird, and shun
The frumious Bandersnatch!
—*Lewis Carroll, "Jabberwocky"*

Y ou've come a long way in this book, young Jedi Fool. We've learned together how you can put yourself in position to make your dreams come true through the power of compounded growth. We've tackled how you might earn and save more money. Put some or all of these ideas into play, and you'll dramatically improve your (financial) future.

Ah, but the only trouble is, the more you gather, the more you have to lose. As you wander down life's pathways, over its hills and through its valleys, you're sure to run into villains who'll try to separate you from your hard-earned money. These are the financial Jabberwocks and Jubjub birds and frumious Bandersnatches (and please note that even the Jubjub birds can be frumious on bad days).

Here's a handy field guide to pounding back these dastardly beasts (or at least skipping past them, furtively). Learn this chapter's contents well. You'll avoid plenty of grief if you do. Honestly, if you learn *any* of the following lessons well, you'll save fortunes.

### Smoking

Yeah, yeah, we could tell you how smoking's bad for your health. (It is, of course. Deadly, in fact. It'll take ten to thirty years off your life. And it'll throw coughing fits and emphysema into the good years. It'll interrupt your sleeping patterns. It'll subject you to more colds and flus than the average person. It'll burn holes in your clothes. It'll make your hair smell like the underside of a gum-stuck dirty bench in a college bar. And . . . well . . . we could go on.)

But this is a *financial* book, so let's just tackle together the *financial* side of smoking. Imagine that you're eighteen years old, you smoke one pack a day, and each pack costs you, on average, $3. Multiply three bucks by 365 days, and you're looking at an annual cost of $1,095. If you're a half-pack-a-day puffer, then $547 of your savings goes up in smoke each year.

If you spend $547 each year on cigarettes for most of your life (let's say from age twenty to eighty), you'll spend nearly $33,000 on cigarettes. But the price of cigarettes will go up, too. So you're more likely to spend at least $75,000 to $100,000 on your habit. If you smoke a pack a day (which is what many teen smokers will work their way up to), you'll spend more than $65,000 at today's prices. With price increases, you'll likely plunk down $150,000–$200,000 on cigarettes over your lifetime.

Extraordinary. No wonder big tobacco companies will love you!

But what if you saved and invested that money rather than paying it out to choke your lungs with noxious smoke? Imagine that you took the $1,095 you might spend each year on cigarettes, invested it in the stock market, and earned a market-average return. Well, after sixty years (from age twenty to eighty), you'd have an eye-popping $5 *million*. Yowza. And you'd have healthy lungs. And normal sleeping patterns. And, barring any basic hygiene deficiencies, you'd smell pretty good, too.

Smoking a half pack or pack a day throughout your lifetime will cost you anywhere from $60,000 to $5 million. And we hate to be detailed about this, but you haven't even begun to factor in the medical costs for regular doses of cold medicine, for scraping tar from your lungs, for removing a lung, for trying to suck tumors off your other lung, for replacing a kidney, for removing your legs, then putting you on oxygen for the last five years of your life. Horrifying, yes. But true.

If you're a smoker and you'd like to quit (which we think is one of the smartest decisions you'll ever make), tons of resources are available to you. And if you're not a smoker, consider sharing this information with a friend who does smoke. For some information and support if you're thinking of quitting, drop by our on-line "Quitting Smoking" discussion board at www.QuitSmoking.Fool.com. Other useful sites include www.quitsmokingsupport.com, www.quitnet.com, and www.quitsmoking.com. We believe we can help you quit and stay quit.

Finally, note that alcohol and other substance abuse can be as costly as smoking. Think before you submerge yourself in this stuff.

### Gambling

To understand why serious gambling isn't such a hot idea, picture Las Vegas. Miles of bright, wild, shimmering lights. Dozens of hotels and casinos, one taller than the next, one wider than the others. The main drag's lit up, frankly, like a cigarette. Those must be *some* electric bills, eh? Wonder who pays them?

The gamblers do, of course.

Casinos typically keep 5 percent of your "investment." So if you play twenty quarters, on average you'll get nineteen of them back. Then you'll play those and get fewer back. In fact, after fourteen rotations, you will, on average, have half your money left. It's amazing how willingly Americans give their money away. It's simple mathematics.

It's also basic psychology.

If you study psychology in college, you might hear of Dr. Stanley Mil-

---

## Keep in Mind

### What You Didn't Do

Many financial troubles or disasters stem from things that people did *not* do rather than what they did do. Many, for example, fail to buy necessary insurance coverage for themselves and their belongings. When disasters strike—major illnesses, prolonged or permanent disability, death, robberies, fires, floods, earthquakes, vandalism—they find themselves in dire financial straits.

For starters, please look into low-cost renter's insurance if you have anything of value in your college room or apartment. It costs on the order of $150 a year for the minimum amount, which is generally $25,000 in coverage. If you're like most students, that ought to be enough. But there's even greater benefit than just securing the valuables in your room. Renter's insurance usually includes up to $100,000 of personal injury liability coverage. If you can't afford the $150 in renter's insurance, talk to your parents. They should see the benefit in this.

gram's famous experiment with three groupings of caged rats. In one group, whenever a rat pressed a lever, it got a treat—a yummy pellet (can't you just taste it!). The rats kept pressing the lever, collecting their pellets, getting fat and happy. A second group of rats got nothing when they pressed the lever. As you'd imagine, they soon lost interest with the exercise of bar tapping. The third group of rats pressed the lever and got occasional pellets—either regularly (say, every third time) or randomly. These rats kept pressing the lever, wildly, hoping for rewards.

Then Dr. Milgram—dastardly fellow—stopped providing pellets.

Guess what happened. Well, the rats who weren't getting pellets didn't care. They'd long since given up. The ones who'd gotten a pellet for every press quickly figured something was wrong and stopped slapping the lever. The most fascinating part of this study concerned the rats who'd received their treats *randomly.* Poor blokes. They kept pressing and pressing and pressing.

And pressing and pressing and pressing.

And pressing, desperately pressing.

In fact, it took them a very, *very* long time to learn to stop.

Much as it may hurt our egos to admit it, we humans act a lot like these rats—and casinos bank quite a lot of money on that! Once you get a random reward or two, from a slot machine or a roulette wheel, you'll keep trying. You want those damn pellets! Even though there may be no more reward coming, you'll keep pressing and pressing and pressing.

And pressing. Maybe even desperately pressing.

Sometimes for a very long time. And just when you're ready to stop, you'll get another little pellet. Yum, yum. Somewhere along the way, you'll look down into an empty billfold or plastic cup and realize you've been paying out more money than you're getting back. Bad mathematics. Bad psychology. Bad trip.

Think about it. When you're old enough to gamble legally, be smarter than a rat. Don't do it.

## Lotteries

Lotteries make as little sense as serious gambling. Actually, far, *far* less. While casinos keep, on average, about 5 percent of every dollar you gamble, lotteries keep about *50 percent*—ten times more! That means it's ten times more financially lethal for its regular players. (Brought to you by your local state government! And you thought they were feeding, not *feeding off of,* many of the poorest and least-educated people in your home state.)

Many lottery players just buy a ticket every now and then, never many pellets, and they avoid financial ruin. But more than 80 percent of all ticket sales come from just 20 percent of all players. These people take their lever pressing very seriously. They spend more than $4 per day on tickets, more than about $1,500 per year. Bad mathematics. Bad psychology. Bad trip.

Unfortunately, these folks are also usually the ones least able to afford such a habit. According to an August 2001 article in *The New York Times,* lottery players are "almost twice as likely as the average adult both to have dropped out of high school and to have a household income under $10,000." The article also noted that lottery organizers have found that "reducing the chance of winning [can] actually *boost* ticket sales."

What do you want us to say here? We don't like the lottery. Its marketing hype. Its direction by officials elected to protect their citizens. Its careful targeting of those who can least afford to play. Its absurdly poor odds. Did we mention the marketing hype?

Be smarter than a very daft rat.

## Gullibility

Another beast preying on too many adults (and some teens) who don't know better is simple gullibility. Mix that with greed, and you've got a dangerous combination. The world is full of hucksters who profit by promising to tell you how to get rich quickly. You will hear them on the radio. You will spy them on late-night television. You'll read their adverts in the newspaper. You'll meet them at a seminar or conference. These are the sorts of folks who claim to be taking the stock market by storm with aggressive investment strategies—featuring monthly gains of 40 percent, for example.

Forty percent growth per month? Oh, my.

Sadly, most people don't realize that it's unheard of for anyone to repeatedly earn even 40 percent per *year,* not to mention monthly. Let's do a little math together. If you take a single dollar and compound it at just 20 percent monthly for fifteen years, you'll have $179 trillion. That's more than seven times the total market value of all goods and services rendered globally in an entire year. If you started with $5,000 and earned 40 percent monthly, you'd end up in just five years with around $2.9 trillion.

Do write us when you get there.

Most of the time, when you run into something that sounds too good to be true, just run some numbers. Think a little harder, research a little more. Be skeptical. Ask your friends and family what they think. Obviously, there are ways to make millions on this blue-green planet. Bill Gates and Warren Buffett have net financial worths in excess of $50 billion, in fact. But that doesn't come overnight. Gates has built Microsoft, plank by plank, for more than twenty-five years now. Buffett has invested his money for more than fifty years.

Think before leaping into a get-rich-quick scheme.

## Poor Purchase Decisions

We've talked smoking and gambling and huckstering. What a grim chapter! But we must go on.

Obviously, the most common way we waste money is through poor purchasing. Take the gal who earns $35,000 per year yet buys herself a $30,000 new car. Take the guy who makes $50,000 a year yet carries $14,000 in credit card debt at eighteen percent interest rates. The CD and DVD players, the new PC, the thrice weekly dinners out, the car and car loan, the Armani suits, the Versace ties—the life of a debtor.

None of the above represents an investment that makes money over time. In fact, all lose value the moment you purchase them and lose it progressively from year to year.

It's important to understand the difference between assets that gain value and assets that lose value. Most homes will gain value over time. Yet virtually all cars will depreciate or *lose* value from the moment you buy them to the moment you sell them. And that fancy stereo system isn't likely to increase in value over time. Neither is the CD player, the PC, or the silk suit.

But stock in a growing company like General Electric or Coca-Cola or Johnson & Johnson probably will. Buy a nice computer for $1,000 and within a year or two it will be worth just a fraction of its cost. Park $1,000 in a certificate of deposit and in a year or two it might be worth $1,100. Put that $1,000 in the stock market and it'll be worth thousands to your future.

This isn't to say that you shouldn't work to own *things* that will make your life more enjoyable. Just be aware of how you're allocating your money. Think before spending. Evaluate your budgets and stick to them. Spend what you can. But build a future you can look forward to—one where you can tell a bad boss to shove it or a great boss that you'd like to keep working for her forever. One where you can visit New Zealand. One where you can easily afford surgery or medicine. One where you can give savings away to help others. One where you can help pay college tuition for your children and theirs.

A future where you can afford to do what you want with your life.

## Adults' Dumbest Money Moves

How many really stupid things have you done with your money? Probably not many, if you're fourteen or eighteen years old. But your parents have been around longer. Your aunts and uncles. Your grandparents. Their friends. They've lived for *decades*. They've had a ton of time to blow it a few times, to make poor decisions about their money. Even Warren Buffett and Bill Gates can share some doozies with their kids.

That's right, your adult friends and family members have likely slapped their foreheads and shouted, "Doh!" numerous times. No matter how smart, no matter how successful, adults make financial mistakes. But remember—few of them were ever taught anything about money management or investing when they were young. Nearly all of them had to wing it.

You've got a significant advantage over them. So learn from them now.

Here's an interesting exercise. Pick four adults. (Heck, pick thirty— you'll learn even more!) How about one of your parents, one or two of your teachers, and the owner of the corner market? Ask them what one or two of their dumbest investments or money moves have been. For a long time in this country, there was a natural resistance to talking about money. This has contributed to our great ignorance. So begin now. Ask questions. Don't ask specifically how much money someone made or lost. But do ask them for lessons.

If they seem too embarrassed to admit to any, remind them that their pain will be your gain, that they'll be sparing someone else from making the same mistakes—in other words, point out how exceedingly generous they'll be. And make sure you also ask some adults you consider to be very successful—you'll find that everyone has at least a few regrettable moves. Record your findings for future reference.

**Adult #1:** _____

Their blunder(s): _____

_____

_____

_____

_____

_____

_____

**Adult #2:** _____

Their blunder(s): _____

_____

_____

_____

_____

_____

**Adult #3:** _____

Their blunder(s): _____

_____

_____

_____

_____

**Adult #4:** _____

Their blunder(s): _____

_____

_____

_____

_____

Don't let this exercise stop here. Continue asking adults politely about financial mistakes they've made. And join us on-line in our Dumbest Investment Mistakes discussion board (boards.Fool.com), where you'll find hundreds of blunders you can avoid. Learn this stuff now and improve your chances of early retirement, the beach house in Malibu, ownership of a minor league baseball team, or whatever dream of yours needs capital.

## Take It from Me

### Breaking Family Tradition

Here's a wonderful story from thirty-one-year-old Jennifer. She writes us:

We all have reasons why we're working our way out of debt and investing in our futures. My motivation is my grandparents. I love them, but I don't want to be like them.

Some of my earliest memories are of Saturdays spent shopping. My grandmother Ethel would drive by and pick me up, then pick up my great-grandmother, Aunt Doris, and Uncle Owen. We'd all pile into Ethel's *huge* (gas-guzzling) Buick and go shopping. This happened *every* Saturday. We'd start at the mall, or Kmart. We'd hit J. C. Penney, Sears, Montgomery Ward. Sometimes we'd go to three different malls on the same day.

When we'd stop for lunch, Ethel and I would play a game with her credit cards. I was just four years old when Ethel would hold up a series of credit cards and quiz me. I'd shout, "Visa! J. C. Penney! Sears! American Express! Diners Club! Maas Brothers!" I think I learned to read from those cards! She sure had a lot of them. I couldn't wait until I was grown-up and could have all those credit cards, too.

Ethel and Papa also liked to take vacations with the family. Sometime in the mid-1980s they discovered cruises. Since then, they've taken a cruise almost every year. They've been to Jamaica, Mexico, Bermuda, the Bahamas, Aruba. They've had a lot of fun.

Ahh, but they're paying for it now.

Ethel is seventy-seven years old, and Papa is eighty-six. Ethel *finally* retired last year but may end up working again soon. Why? Because they don't have any money. Each has a small pension and Social Security. That's it. Over the years, they've owned big travel-trailers and new cars and vans, but they've never owned a house. They have no savings. They have no investments.

Ethel has spent fifty years collecting unique teapots. Now she's selling them at minuscule prices in order to pay the bills. (She once considered them an *investment!*) They've rented the same house, a very nice place, for fifteen years and never even considered buying it. I asked them why, once. They told me that when the owner was willing to sell it to them, they couldn't come up with a down payment. The saddest thing is that Ethel worked in banking for thirty years and she didn't learn anything about money.

My mother learned her poor money management skills from these people, and I learned from her. I'm now in the process of *un*learning it all. I refuse to end up like them financially. I will be debt-free next year. I will buy a condo next year. I won't take vacations unless I've saved the money for them. I won't spend six years paying for vehicles that are more than I need. I *can* break my family's tradition of poverty.—Jennifer Wagner, 31

### Credit Cards

When people are living beyond their means, they're spending money they don't have. They're usually doing so with credit cards.

Credit cards are controversial. Do we love them or hate them? On the one hand, they bring great convenience to most people. On the other, they've also helped wreck the lives of many others. Teens are often warned—rightfully—to beware credit cards. But they're also sometimes told to steer clear of them and never use them. That's not the best advice.

Let's consider the good and bad of credit.

**The Good**

Credit cards can be a blessing. You can charge your expenses virtually everywhere, and each month you'll receive a statement from your card company detailing your expenses. These account statements can help a great deal when you're working on your budget. You have an automatic record of your spending, not so easy to keep when you spend cash.

Think with us about the process for a second.

When you use a credit card, you're borrowing money. You wander the walkways of the mall this weekend and buy four pairs of dark blue Diesel jeans and a $1,000 DVD player. You pay for it with your Visa card. Visa then pays the blue jean and DVD vendors for you. And at the end of the month, you get a statement and a bill for how much you must pay back to Visa. There it sits at the bottom of the page. You owe $1,189.93.

It's time to pay.

Back in the olden days, a few decades ago, you had to pay your monthly bill in full. No *ifs, ands, buts,* or *hey, can you give me a few weeks.* If you didn't come up with the $1,189.93, then some guy named Mac or Sal or Freddie Fat Fingers pulled you behind a Dumpster in the shadows of an alley and redefined the utility of the traditional crowbar. Maybe we're overdoing things a bit, but the point's made. When credit cards were first created, you had to pay your bill in full, on time, each month.

But then the credit card companies realized just how much money they could earn by extending loans with interest charges. If you didn't pay in full, they applied interest charges to your unpaid debts. Stiff interest charges. In fact, over the past twenty-five years, the card companies have consistently and significantly increased the rates they charge. Today, the average credit card levies backbreaking 18 percent annual interest rates on unpaid bills. Crowbars and all.

So, you have two choices.

The first is to pay off your bill in full at the end of the month. You'll avoid all financing charges. In essence, you'll have actually gotten away with using someone else's money for free for a few weeks. Good deal! You're playing this game with greater skill and insight than the average American. Really, this is a good deal. And it reminds us that credit cards can be very useful tools.

But then there is the second choice, which is unfortunately the more popular of the two. That is to make little or no payment on your bill at the end of the month. Your bill converts to a loan. That loan bears an average 18 percent charge per year. And as months turn to years, the total cost of those blue jeans and that DVD player rises. Significantly. In fact, if you make only the minimum monthly payment on the DVD player and blue jeans, get this, it will take you *nineteen* years to pay it off.

Ahh, but already we're crossing over into the *dark* side of credit cards. Halt! We're supposed to be singing the praises of credit. Okay. So what else do we like about credit cards? Well, they sure are pretty. When you get a new one, they're all shiny and sparkly. And they fit real snugly in a standard wallet. And boy, weren't those credit card salesmen friendly in the college post office? They were polite. Respectful. And we didn't even mention the free toaster they gave for signing up.

Credit cards. They give us the warm fuzzies.

## Take It from Me

### The Credit Card Death Spiral

Credit cards almost got the best of me during my teen/college years. I never realized just how important it was to pay them off until it was nearly too late. The lure of buying $100 worth of CDs and having to pay only $15 a month was just too great. Once I reached college, I spent hundreds of dollars on books and other school supplies each semester, nearly all of which went on my credit cards. By the time I made any significant dent in my ever-growing credit card bills, another semester would roll around and I'd have to charge more books and supplies. (And pizzas, of course!) My debt on my four credit cards soon topped $4,000, and I was paying 23 percent interest. (That's more than $900 per year just to pay the interest off, without putting a dollar toward paying the loan down!)

I eventually realized that I was throwing money away.

I asked the credit card issuers to lower my interest rate based on my years of loyal patronage (read years of financial slavery), and most of them did so, rather than risk losing my business altogether. I closed out the accounts for those issuers who didn't lower the rate and transferred that debt to friendlier (lower-rate) issuers. Once I was taking less of a hit on the interest rate, I could concentrate on paying off the balances.

It took me three years, but I finally managed to pay off every last cent of credit card debt. I'm down to one credit card and a check card linked directly to my bank account (which I use instead of my credit card when possible).

The moral of my story is simple. Credit cards are merely tools. Like any tool, they can be abused (try hitting your knee with a hammer). When used properly, though, credit cards are very helpful and convenient. You must pay them off promptly each month, though, or they are a misused tool (again, think about slapping that hammer on your knee).

To do the right thing here, all it takes is careful planning (using credit cards only when necessary and prudent), discipline (paying them off as soon as possible), and knowledge (of percentage rates, annual fees, and so on). Use credit cards to your advantage or pay an awful price. I did, for too long. —Michael Pomorski, 23

## The Bad

And now, the dark side.

Do you remember a few chapters back we talked about how banks work? They pay you a few percentage points in interest on your savings account. Then they lend your money out to borrowers for a few percentage points more, profiting off the difference. This is how banks make money off mortgages, car loans, small business loans, and the like. In recent years, they'd be making these loans in the range of 6–12 percent interest per year.

But banks have found far greater opportunity in their credit card business.

Why? Because they've taken interest rates on credit cards into the neighborhood of 16 percent to 18 percent to 20 percent—or more. Largely without resistance. They've done so because the average American consumer has little idea what to pay for short-term credit. Ask your adult friends. Many won't know what a fair rate is—13 percent? 17 percent? 10 percent? The average consumer is just happy to have the convenience of a credit card and the opportunity to delay the cost of buying stuff. Never mind how much interest he'll pay!

The net result is that Americans owe billions upon billions of dollars on their credit cards. The average household sadly carries more than $5,000 of credit card debt. And the majority of cardholders pay no more than the minimum monthly bill each month. No wonder, then, that more than a million Americans have been forced to declare bankruptcy in the past five years.

So, where are credit card companies naturally turning for their next growth opportunity? Well, of course, *to you,* dear teenager. Teens beginning college are mailed bagfuls of "preapproved" credit card applications, with the promise of easy money. And what strange bedfellows we have here. According to a March 2001 *U.S. News & World Report* article and a wonderful segment on *60 Minutes,* many colleges are making extra money by selling the mailing lists of their students to credit card companies. (Insert sound of Fools choking on our lunch.) Some colleges even take a cut for every dollar charged on student credit cards. (Insert sound of Fools gasping for air.)

That means that an increasing number of universities are in the ironic position of wanting their students to make poor financial decisions. Why? Because there's a fortune in it. Banks pay the nation's 250 largest universities nearly $1 billion a year for marketing rights. They do so because they expect to make billions more for *years to come* off teenagers trapped in credit card debt.

To understand just how dangerous it is to be young and stuck with debt at high interest rates, imagine that you're a twenty-three-year-old with $5,000 in credit card debt at 20 percent interest. You had a *great* time in college—apartment rental, new stereo, VCR, past due fees on movie rentals, a car, fuel, insurance, cardboard cutouts of your favorite *Simpsons* characters, and your assortment of Frisbees.

And now you're $5,000 in the hole.

At that 20 percent interest rate, you'll pay $1,000 per year *just on the interest* (not to mention what you actually owe). With your rent and living expenses and even school loans to pay, all of a sudden you find it's getting harder and harder to keep up. Worse still, your cat just got sick with Cushing's disease; the vet bill comes to $300, which you charge on your card. And then your worn windshield wipers served only to further blur your vision as you rammed a braking pickup truck in the middle of a rainstorm. That's another $500. Insurance defrays the rest of the costs, then raises your rates. All the while, since you're not really budgeting, stylish outfits, meals out, a few gifts for your sweetheart, and vacations are taking their toll on your finances.

At twenty-four, you have $7,000 in credit card debt.

By now, the bank providing your card really, *really* loves you.

You're great business for them.

They can't get enough of you.

Of course, you do mean to pay it all off, but you're still having trouble. This year you'll pay $1,400 in interest payments just to keep your debt level at $7,000. But, uh-oh! Your best friend in college, who lives on the other coast, is getting married. Wow, that's terrific! The problem is, now you have to buy cross-continent round-trip tickets, get a hotel room, buy something to wear, and find a nice gift.

At twenty-five, you have $9,000 in credit card debt.

Your bank is sending you love letters. (Or should be.) They can't wait for the year ahead.

This year, you'll fork over $1,800 in interest alone for this debt (just to hold steady at $9,000 in debt). That's $150 each month. And let's say that when you turn twenty-six, you start realizing something's wrong. So you pay off what debt you can. You get it down to $8,000. But you still owe another $1,600 in interest this year. All told, you've now paid $5,800 in interest over the past four years. That's more than you owed in the first place, but you still owe more now than ever before. And the interest keeps piling up. Sadly, you're paying for things you bought a long, long time ago. That $200 you paid for the cashmere sweater might end up costing you $400 or $600 in the long run.

And who are you paying all that money to? The bank that provided you the credit card (perhaps marketed to you by your own college).

That's how so many people get trapped. It's like quicksand. At Fool.com, we've got discussion boards where people share horror stories alongside numerous tips for getting out of debt. (Remember, we do offer a thirty-day free trial to check out our discussion board service. So come check them out!) Some people have $20,000 or $40,000 or $60,000 in credit card debt. It takes them *years* to dig out—difficult years pinching pennies, living way, way, *way* below their means. One Fool proudly wrote that it took him and his wife three and a half years, but they finally paid off *$84,000* in debt ($37,000 on eight credit cards, $14,000 in student loans, and $33,000 on two car loans).

Boy, did he regret running up those debts! It was even hard for him to remember what he'd really bought with all those loans.

Remember that credit card debt is pretty much the *opposite* of investing. If your money is in the stock market, it could grow by 11 percent per year. Conversely, if you have credit card debt, you're *losing* 12-22 percent per year. And therein lies the most prominent difference between the wealthy and the poor in America. The former are disciplined savers and investors. The latter are reckless borrowers and spenders. Not to say that there aren't many other issues at play in American poverty. But the primary one is that most Americans do not know how to save and spend their money (take a look at the Henry Thoreau quote that launched this section).

It's your choice: you can grow a mountain of wealth or cut a widening hole of debt.

## Smart Strategies: Debit Cards and Low Limits

There are two ways we see to enjoy the convenience of plastic without sinking your finances. The first is the debit card; the second is the credit card with a low limit.

Debit cards, also called check cards, don't extend loans to you like credit cards. Instead, they're linked to your bank account, from which they draw funds as you use your card. If you have $600 in your account, you can "charge" that much but no more. There is no bill for debit cards, but there are regular account statements (which help you with your simple planning and budgeting). You can get debit cards through most banks. We highly, highly, *oh so very highly* recommend them.

That's the debit card.

You might also consider getting a credit card with a low limit. Something like $500. That means you can't charge more than $500 on it. Of course, you *will* get charged the standard deafening and blinding rate

---

### Take It from Me

#### Enslaved by Debt

I spent my teen years trying to become independent. I didn't want my parents or anyone else controlling my life. But when I got into debt, I gave away my ability to live my life as I wanted. Some things may be worth going into debt for. Student loans expanded my ability to learn and to pursue my dreams. But a nice car? Electronic gadgets? Trips to the beach? Restaurant meals? Great clothes? Very few of those purchases were worth the debt. Most were forgotten long before they were paid for. Debt enslaved me for a while. Don't let it enslave you. —Ann Coleman, 50

---

of interest on any unpaid borrowing up to $500. But at least you'll limit the downside. You'll control reckless urges, like the impulse to pick up that $6,000 platinum tennis bracelet or the $1,200 on cosmetic surgery (skip that, we think you look great just as you are). Low-limit cards are a great way to develop good habits.

Whatever you do, take credit cards seriously. They have brought pain and misery to the careless, tens of millions of them.

#### Beware Credit Card Tricks

Your average credit card provider has gotten pretty good over the years at sneaking extra fees past you or tricking you into a poor financial decision or two. Remember, young Fool, credit card companies are in the business of making money off you. As much of it as they can. If they can zap you with a $25 charge, along with five hundred thousand of their other cardholders, they've just netted $12 million. This is a game they love playing. It's a strategic game that talented mathematicians and marketers at these companies stay up late pondering.

Here are some of their latest ploys—all of which you should avoid.

1. **They hit you low, then hit you high.** How? By marketing a low interest rate to you. You tear open their letter, and they're offering a new card with a *low, low 5.9 percent interest rate.* But look for the fine print. Usually that's just a teaser rate. After the

first few months, your rate will rocket to 17 percent, 21 percent, 24 percent.

2. **They give in order to take away.** How? By "rewarding" you over the years with more access to capital. You might start out with a low $500 limit. But after a period of charging, you open their letter congratulating you on your new $1,000 limit. Six months later it goes to $2,000. A year later, to $5,000. They give you all this money in order to take much more back from you in the years ahead.

3. **They surprise you with tricks dressed as treats.** How? You rip open another mailing from them (TIMBERRRRRRR!!!!—listen for the sound of another tree falling to supply all that paper), and they're offering airplane miles, or a microwave oven, or a T-shirt with the bank's logo (what an insult, really). Just sign up for their card and you get it. Beware, though. Any seriously valuable offering from them carries fine print with it. You'll often have to charge tens of thousands of dollars before you realize any major benefit with some cards.

4. **They like to play landlord.** How? Well, they charge you annual fees. They make you rent their card. Our advice? Avoid cards charging you annual fees or call your card provider to have these fees eliminated. Why pay $35 a year to use their card (from which they take cuts on every transaction from the vendors)? Don't.

5. **They bite your hand the first chance they get.** How? With late fees. A number of credit card companies will work to confuse you about when your payments are due. They prefer that you pay late. That way they can hit you with a $35 charge (even if you're a day late on just a $10 payment). Then they can start charging you interest on the late fee. Shylock would be proud.

6. **They get down on their knees and pray that you don't learn.** Why? Because they don't want you to realize you can negotiate lower interest rates. You can. The credit card industry is *very* competitive. There's always another offer coming. So threaten to move your debt to cards with lower interest rates. Most credit card providers will drop your rates during a single phone call. They're loath to lose your business. So negotiate your rates down. And keep threatening and negotiating all the way to your financial freedom (that is, your total elimination of all revolving credit card debt).

Of course, the biggest trick that credit card companies play is making it easy for you to pay a tiny minimum amount each month, leaving most of your debt just sitting there. That generates interest expenses *for you* and piles of profits *for them*. If you learn nothing else from our Foolish rantings and writings, please learn to carry no credit card debt from month to month in this life.

## Take It from Me

### Treading Water at $500 Per Month

As a college student, I fell into the trap of credit card debt. I used credit cards to pay for travel, clothes, even groceries. I knew full well I didn't have the money to pay off my bill each month. And I never even wore many of the clothes I bought. I think I just loved the idea of getting new stuff without needing my parents' approval (and money).

Harsh reality hit me in the face after graduation, when the bills kept coming. I was paying hundreds of dollars out of my low entry-level salary each month toward my credit card debt, and it wasn't making a dent in the mountain of debt I still had to overcome.

I finally paid off my debt. Now I'm committed to saving at least 10 percent of my salary each year. Even after I set aside my monthly savings, I still have the funds to pay the utilities and buy airline tickets or clothing as needed. It's amazing how much you can save—and how much further your dollar goes—by not having to pay $500 a month to a credit card company.—Siobhan Forde, 25

# ·STEP 5·

# Know What to Expect

•   •   •   •   •

*The noblest pleasure is the joy of understanding.*
*—Leonardo da Vinci*

Let's talk about understanding for a minute. Let's talk about understanding what to expect in your financial life. Why? Because how you set expectations primarily determines how much joy you'll get out of life.

Here's a simple example. Your friend Esmeralda tells you that Chris Rock's new movie is stupendous, amazing, a riot, outstanding. Thumbs-up. A guaranteed Oscar winner! It's a ten, she says. Maybe the best she's ever seen.

Well, it had *better* be. Because if it's anything short of completely amazing, you'll be disappointed. If it isn't one of the greatest films you've ever seen, you'll feel misled. If you didn't laughingly spit popcorn in your lap, if your heart didn't nearly stop, if you didn't stand up and shout in a crowded theater, "This is so freaking amazing!"—then you've been let down by Esmeralda's recommendation.

She set expectations too high.

Imagine, on the other hand, that your other friend, Gwendolyn, recommends the same movie with tempered language. Even though she completely loved the movie, she only says she *thinks* you'll like it, *she* enjoyed it, at least, it's kind of a fun movie. Given that, the chances are much greater that you'll really like Chris Rock's new movie. Why? Because your expectations were reasonable going in.

One of our favorite theorems at Motley Fool Global Headquarters in Alexandria, Virginia, is all about expectations. It proposes the following: Happiness equals reality divided by expectations. Think about that for a second. Look at it again:

$$\text{Happiness} = \text{Reality} / \text{Expectations}$$

For algebra fans:

$$H = R/E$$

And what does it all mean? It means that the lower your expectations, the greater your chance of happiness. And it means that the *higher* your expectations and the *worse* the reality, the less happiness you'll find. Got that? If you have the time, muse on it. Then consider our contrary and controversial point:

Paupers truly can be happier than princes.

To modern capitalism, that's a radical and revolutionary notion. But indulge us for a minute. Is it not true that a pauper who sets realistic expectations, who lives within his means, and who pursues what he loves in life will be infinitely happier than a prince who does none of these? A prince with unrealistically high expectations, who buys more than he can afford and has little idea of his own talents—will his life not be *less* satisfying than that of our pauper?

We don't want to go overboard with this idea. After all, we agree very much with legendary jazz singer Sophie Tucker, who said, "I've been rich. And I've been poor. Rich is better." But wealth, even extreme wealth, under sky-high expectations leads to misery. Even the wealthiest woman in the world, if she has unrealistically high expectations, is bound for disappointment. She may have $50 million. She may have six sports cars. She may have seven admiring suitors. She may have massage therapists, psychotherapists, homeopathic therapists, and physical therapists tending to her every need. But if her expectations are ridiculously high, she's in for trouble. If she believes she'll live *forever,* or will *always* be in good health, or will *always* have power and control over every aspect of her life, or will *always* be happy, she's bound for gloom and frustration.

As you might anticipate, expectations play a critical role in finances, too. You want examples? We'll give you examples.

Many new investors threw their savings into stocks believing that the stock market boom of the late 1990s would continue forever. Stocks were doubling. New Internet companies were born and rose to

$1 billion in value within three years. Everything was on the rise. Sadly, it didn't and couldn't continue. In fact, it reversed direction, harshly. And those with unrealistic expectations of the stock market were horrified when the Nasdaq, a measure of the performance of newer technology companies, fell 70 percent from its peak.

At the other extreme, many older adults in America chose never to invest in stocks because they lived through the stock market crash of 1929 and the Great Depression that followed. President Roosevelt tried to pull the country out of its funk but mostly couldn't and even, as some economists now argue, prolonged it. The Federal Reserve often did the wrong thing. And investors were burned badly for years. The stock market just kept falling, for years and years. Many investors decided never to return. Unfortunately, that meant they missed out on the best-performing investment vehicle available to them—for their *entire* lives.

If only they'd known what to *expect*.

If they had known to *expect* to lose on certain investments, they would've continued investing long-term savings into the stock market. If they'd known to *expect* the market to suffer through some very difficult periods, they'd have persevered as investors. They would never have risked money they needed in the short term. Yet they would never have stopped investing for their long-term future.

If they had only known generally what to *expect*.

They made mistakes—we all make mistakes like these—because they didn't have historical context. They didn't truly know how well the stock market had done over the long haul and yet how poorly it had done at intervals along the way. That lack of context significantly hurt their chances for financial happiness and security.

The rest of this chapter will cover various information that you'll need to understand before you jump at the chance to invest in the stock market. You'll be surprised at how simple success can be yet how complex the overall market is.

### *Expect* a Risk-and-Return Trade-Off

Some people avoid the stock market because *it's too darned risky*. Believe it or not, over your lifetime as an investor, it's riskier *not* to invest in the stock market. If you put all your savings under your mattress, and you're not making $20 million a year playing professional basketball, you probably won't have enough savings to sustain a long, healthy retirement. And if all your savings is in a bank account earning 3 percent per year, on average, then your money will gain no ground on inflation. A dismal circumstance.

So what are you to do? You may not want the wild risk of stocks, having seen the years 2000 and 2001 deal financial blows to your family and friends. Yet at the same time, you want your money to do *something* for you along the way.

Let's consider some of the alternatives.

First, a key concept to understand is the trade-off between risk and return. If you store all your savings money in a vault underground in your backyard, that money is close to 100 percent secure. But what return are you getting on it? How quickly will the money grow? It won't. In fact, every twenty-four years, the value or "purchasing power" of your savings will effectively be cut in half by inflation (prices rise 3 percent per year, historically). So the trade-off there is essentially 100 percent security for a negative 3 percent annual return.

Ugly.

At the other end of the spectrum are options like the lottery. With the lottery, you have a greater than 99.9 percent chance of losing the money you "invest" in it. But if, against all odds, you win the jackpot, you'll earn an incredible return on your "investment." Good luck. Don't bother telling us how you did. We can guess. And it ain't pretty. Playing the lottery offers the following trade-off: 0 percent security with potentially an out-of-this-world return.

Reasonable Fools should aim for something in the middle of a continuum, with the backyard vault at one end and the lottery at the other.

You should be willing to take on a little risk in order to make a decent return. Your safest options include bank accounts, money-market funds, CDs, and government bonds. Most bank accounts are insured (your bank is most likely protected by federal insurance). You'll earn anywhere from 2–6 percent per year from putting your savings in the bank. Government bonds are backed by the governments that issue them. They represent your making a loan to the government. So as long as you have faith in the nation, then U.S. bonds should be considered very safe. Unfortunately, for all the safety of the above options, you get very little in return. Historically, you will only marginally beat inflation each year.

We think that the best place for your long-term money is in the stock market. You *do* take on some risk with stocks. Some stocks, like Microsoft, go up. Other stocks, like eToys.com, go down. In fact, in the case of eToys, there was *no coming back*—it declared bankruptcy in February 2001. But over the long run, the overall stock market has gone up. And up. And up and up and up. In fact, the stock markets of the United States over the past hundred years have been among the great wealth creators in the history of the human species.

But that doesn't mean you'll always do well. If you look at a graph of the stock market's value over a short period of time, you'll see a pretty jagged line. Over any few years, the market can rise and fall wildly. But back up a few steps and look at an extended period. Take a look at a full decade, or two, or four. The line becomes a much smoother, upward-sloping one. Take a look at this graph.

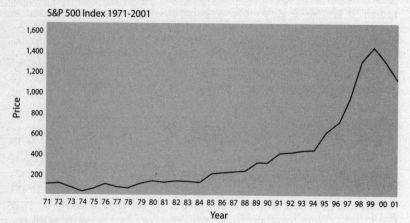

S&P 500 Index 1971-2001

Now, you are a teenager. You have many decades to invest. History suggests you should be putting your long-term savings into the stock market. Here's a summary of how various investments have performed on average each year, between 1926 and 1997:

| | |
|---|---|
| Stock market: | 10.6% |
| Long-term government bonds: | 5.2% |
| Short-term government bonds: | 3.8% |
| Inflation: | 3.1% |

Source: *Stocks for the Long Run,* Jeremy Siegel, 1998

If you invest in the stock market for just a year or two, don't expect to earn 10.6 percent. You might earn 19 percent, or you might lose 23 percent. Over the *long* run, though, the stock market has averaged just about 11 percent per annum—the best of all options out there.

### *Expect* to Own Pieces of Companies

Many people think of stocks just as pieces of paper that change in value from day to day. In fact, a share of stock represents ownership in a company. If you own a share of Abercrombie & Fitch, you literally own a piece of that company. If the company's cargo pants and multi-

---

### Keep in Mind

#### How You Profit with Stock

Imagine that you buy ten shares of stock in Old McDonald Farms for $25 each. You spend a total of $250. A year later, those shares are trading for $28 each. If so, your ten shares are worth $280, and you have a "paper profit" of $30 (actually, slightly less, owing to a small commission paid to your broker for making the trade). You can turn that paper profit into a real profit by selling the shares. Or you can hang on. A year later, the shares might be worth $32 each. Or maybe they'll fall to $27.

It's up to investors to decide which stocks (or other investments) seem most promising, which ones they want to buy, and when they want to sell.

---

striped fitted sweaters are in hot demand, then Abercrombie will make more money. And when it makes more money, it's worth more money to its owners (shareholders like you). If you own shares in Philip Morris, which is a major cigarette manufacturer, and a growing number of foreign governments outlaw cigarettes, the company will suddenly be worth a lot less, and so will your investment.

You can buy shares of stock in any company that is *public.* When you hear a company called "public," that means it has shares of stock that the general public can trade. When you hear a company called "private," that means that the owners have not sold any stock to the general public.

Almost every major company that you can think of is public—Coca-Cola, PepsiCo, Abercrombie & Fitch, Starbucks, Apple Computer, Dell Computer, Microsoft, Intel, AOL Time Warner, Ford, General Motors, Boeing, Nike, Callaway Golf, Wal-Mart, Home Depot, Scholastic, General Electric, General Mills, Kellogg, Viacom, Eastman Kodak, ExxonMobil, McDonald's, Johnson & Johnson, and many, many more.

#### Going Public

A company "goes public" when it has an "initial public offering" (abbreviated "IPO"). That's when it issues shares of stock to be traded in pub-

## Keep in Mind

### What Exactly *Is* a Ticker Symbol?

A ticker symbol is essentially an identification number for the stock of a public company. It's just shorthand, saving investors and the financial media from always having to refer to the company by name. Starbucks, for example, trades on the Nasdaq exchange under the ticker symbol SBUX. To get a stock quote at Fool.com, you need not type in the entire company name, just the ticker.

Companies that trade on the New York Stock Exchange, the oldest of our country's markets, have up to three letters in their ticker symbol. Those trading on the Nasdaq, as a general rule, have four letters. Here are a few examples.

| | | |
|---|---|---|
| Southwest Airlines | LUV | New York Stock Exchange |
| Anheuser Busch | BUD | New York Stock Exchange |
| The New York Times | NYT | New York Stock Exchange |
| Barnes & Noble | BKS | New York Stock Exchange |
| Microsoft | MSFT | Nasdaq |
| Oracle | ORCL | Nasdaq |
| Cisco Systems | CSCO | Nasdaq |
| Amazon.com | AMZN | Nasdaq |

Other, mostly older firms, have the prestige of a single-letter ticker:

| | |
|---|---|
| F | Ford |
| G | Gillette |
| T | AT&T |
| K | Kellogg |
| S | Sears |

lic stock markets such as the New York Stock Exchange or the Nasdaq. And that's when you and we can become investors in their business.

Consider our example, the inspiring story of Big Fat Pies Inc. (ticker: GOBL). Over the past five years, it has introduced the world to tasty honeydew melon pies. Stores can't keep the stuff in stock. The president wolfed down an entire pie at a public gathering on the White House lawn. Howard Stern talked about them, without vulgarity, on his national radio show. And Martha Stewart delicately and prominently featured them on her Thanksgiving Day TV special.

To meet the wildly growing demand, Big Fat Pies Incorporated has to make a heck of a lot more tarts. After all, they're baking in order to 1) make people happy, and 2) make themselves a lot of money. Just like most businesses, they want happy customers and happy shareholders (meaning, they need to make as much money as they can on their pies).

Now, in order for Big Fat Pies to fill all the orders coming its way, it'll have to hire more workers and build more factories and buy flour and sugar and melons on the open market. To do so, whoops, Big Fat Pies will need a lot more money than it has right now. The company isn't doomed, though. It has options.

It can borrow money from a bank. Or it can issue bonds (borrowing money from individuals or institutions and promising to pay the lenders back with interest). Or it could find a really wealthy person (Howard Stern?) or a well-heeled company to help finance it—maybe Sara Lee would like to own half of Big Fat Pies for $15 million? If so, Sara Lee would be counting on making millions of dollars off that investment in the decade ahead.

A final option for the management team at Big Fat Pies is to go public, issuing shares of stock to the general public (that's where you and we come in) to raise cash for the business.

Start-up companies often use many or all of these financing options. Many tiny companies rely on bank loans. If they're ambitious and move from tiny to just small, aiming to get bigger, they then frequently obtain venture capital funding. (Venture capitalists are wealthy people or investment firms that invest money into small companies early on, in exchange for a significant stake of ownership.) After that, the growing company will often go public, enabling those who invested early to get their money back at, it is hoped by them, a significant profit. That's a short life history of many public companies.

So let's say that Big Fat Pies, over the past five years, has gone through every option. It borrowed money from a bank at 13 percent interest. And then it received an investment from three venture capitalists. Since then, it has taken a $20 million investment from a large European food and beverage company. Throughout, it has funded its growth with outside investment while selling pieces of ownership along the way. And in the year 2002, it has decided to go public.

Big Fat Pies will need to hire an investment banking firm, which "underwrites" stock and bond offerings (examples include Goldman Sachs and Morgan Stanley). The bankers will study the pie industry and the business of Big Fat Pies: Are its pies sweet enough to bring back loyal customers?

Does it buy supplies inexpensively? Are its pies so good that it can charge more than twice what they're worth? And how about the management team? Are they honest? Are they smart about their money?

After answering all these questions and more, the underwriting firm will put a price tag on the business. In the case of BF Pies (their nickname), the underwriter has calculated that the company is worth around $150 million (five times their annual sales of $30 million and seventy-five times their annual profits of $2 million).

The company and banker then decide together that the company would like to raise approximately $15 million in cash to fund their growth. That means 10 percent of the business will be sold as new public stock (or "common stock"). If all goes as planned, the public will buy up the share offering, eager to get in on the baked honeydew melon business. And, for its expansion, the company will get that $15 million (minus fees to their investment bankers). They will issue one million shares of common stock priced at $15 per share.

Henceforth, the investment community will buy and sell Big Fat Pies shares on the stock market under the ticker symbol GOBL. Now every Tom, Dick, and Harriet can buy the stock (supposing they wanted to), and/or quote it on their Internet browser every passing minute just using the company's cutesy GOBL symbol. A new public company, a new stock, is born.

---

## Public and Private

While most major companies are public, the vast majority of American businesses are smaller, private companies. Fred and Bertha's Bait Shop down by the lake is a private business. So is Joey's Market on Route 1. The same too for Hysteria, women's apparel and accessories, here in Alexandria, Virginia. There is no open, public stock market via which you can buy shares in these businesses. They're not for sale.

Here are a few major companies that are private: Levi Strauss, Mars (the candy company), Publix Supermarkets, IKEA, Amway, Penske (a transportation/trucking company), Packard Bell NEC (a computer company), Hallmark, Borden, Domino's Pizza, Subway, and Hyatt. They have financed their companies with private market investments and their own profits.

Again, though, most of the major companies that we've all heard of are public companies.

## *Expect* Stock Prices to Go Up and Down

When you invest in shares of stock, expect the prices of those shares to go up and down. They will, every day, sometimes for understandable reasons, sometimes for no apparent reason. Here are some of the many reasons a stock price will move significantly up or down.

### Why Stocks Go Up

- Because people want to own it—more buyers than sellers drives the price up.
- Increasing sales and profits at the company.
- A great new executive is hired to run the business.
- An exciting new product or service is introduced.
- Additional exciting new products or services are expected.
- The company lands a big new contract.
- A great review in the media.
- Scientists discover a revolutionary use for product.
- A famous investor is buying shares.
- A Wall Street analyst upgrades the company, changing her recommendation from "buy" to "strong buy."
- Other stocks in the same industry go up.
- Most of the stock market is up.
- The company wins a lawsuit.
- The company announces a major global initiative.
- The industry is "hot"—people expect big things for good reasons.
- The industry is "hot"—people don't understand much about it, but they're buying anyway.
- The company announces it will be acquired by another business at a higher price.
- Rumors.
- No discernible reason.

### Why Stocks Go Down

- Because people don't want to own the stock—fewer buyers than sellers drives the price down.
- Profits and/or sales are slipping.
- Top executives leave the company.
- A famous investor sells shares of the company.
- An analyst downgrades his recommendation of the stock from "buy" to "hold."
- The company loses a major customer.
- A factory burns down.

- A high-profile peer company in the same industry announces bad news.
- The industry falls out of favor.
- Most of the stock market is down—perhaps in a temporary recession or bear market.
- Another company introduces a better product.
- A big lawsuit is filed against the company.
- Scientists discover the product is putting infant lives at risk.
- Fewer people are buying the product.
- The industry used to be "hot," but now another industry is more popular.
- Some new government regulations are hurting sales or profits.
- A powerful company becomes a competitor.
- Rumors.
- No discernible reason.

### *Expect* Growth

You can expect that your money, invested in the overall American stock market, will increase in value—over the long term. You can expect a long-term average annual return between 9 and 11 percent for the stock market as a whole.

> **Famous Words**
>
> *Buy right and hold tight.*
> —John Bogle, founder of mutual fund giant the Vanguard Group

You can expect your wealth to compound. With compounding, *expect* the growth to start out slowly, but then begin to snowball as the years go by.

So much of sound investing is about having the right *expectations*.

### *Expect* to Wait

With sensible investing, it usually takes time for you to see significant results. Don't jump in, see your holdings drop a bit or not move much for a while, then jump out in an impatient huff. Engage in long-term, not short-term, thinking. *Expect* to wait.

### *Expect* Volatility

One thing that often throws new investors for a loop is volatility. Volatility refers to how wildly a stock jumps in price from day to day or

# Keep in Mind

## The Problem with Stock Market Games

There's a good chance you've played a stock market game in school and/or on-line, where individuals or teams are given an amount of imaginary money to invest in some stocks. The point is to see whose portfolio (collection of stocks) grows in value the most over a period of time.

These games can pique your interest in the stock market and show you how investing works. To a degree. Following your holdings regularly, you learn how they go up and down in value. Ideally, you even do some research into various companies before "buying" any stock. It's an admirable aim at teaching investing. Stock market games are often run by teachers who operate outside of their standard curriculum in order to give you, the student, a taste of something important.

*But* there's a downside to these games. They're very much oriented to the short term. They usually run for a few weeks or months, until the semester's up. Please don't think that whoever wins this sort of game is the best investor in class (unless like me, Dave, you won it *all* in fourth grade, receiving as a prize a large Hershey bar from your teacher Mr. Hoskinson—in which case, if you share the same fate I did, you too owe it to yourself at regular intervals to remind your classmates of your brilliance).

Poor Dave—no humility.

Anyway!

Just remember that on the stock market, over such short time periods, anything can happen. You might invest in a few wonderful companies that will triple in value in the next ten years but whose stock prices don't move much during the clipped duration of the contest. And whoever wins might have picked some companies that ran higher quickly but went out of business in a few years.

Successful investing is a marathon, not a wind sprint.

If you'd like to try a stock market game, have a teacher check out www.smgww.org. Another offbeat alternative you can play on your own is the Hollywood Stock Exchange, at www.hsx.com. It's set up just like a stock market game, but you buy stocks and bonds in movies, movie stars, and other celebrities. It's a clever way to teach the basic philosophy of investing.

week to week. The stocks of some companies (often sleepy ones like cement firms or real estate trusts) tend to go up or down by a fraction of a percent on most days. They hardly move at all. More volatile companies (for example, smaller businesses in fast-changing and heavily technology-dependent industries) often see their stock prices move by multiple percentage points each day. Given that your bank pays you 3–5 percent *per year* to carry your deposits, those changes in a stock price in *one day* are dramatic.

Over a few days or weeks, a volatile stock might surge by 50 percent or drop by 40 percent. These are major swings that can frighten uninformed investors into premature selling. Look at the stock price of Microsoft over the years, for example:

| | |
|---|---|
| October 1989 | $1 |
| November 1990 | $2 |
| December 1990 | $4 |
| August 1994 | $7 |
| January 1995 | $7 |
| March 1995 | $9 |
| March 1996 | $13 |
| January 1997 | $26 |
| March 1997 | $22 |
| March 1998 | $45 |
| January 1999 | $87 |
| February 1999 | $72 |
| December 1999 | $119 |
| April 2000 | $65 |
| June 2000 | $82 |
| March 2001 | $50 |
| June 2001 | $65 |
| September 2001 | $56 |

(Hint: Don't look for great companies trading at $1 per share. Microsoft was never trading for $1. These prices are adjusted by stock splits. We'll explain this in greater detail later.)

Imagine yourself owning stock in Microsoft at various times. If you owned it from August 1994 to January 1995, and the stock wasn't gaining in value much, you might've sold (not *you*, you're a genius . . . some other bloke). If you did, you'd've missed out on significant future gains. Or if you'd bought Microsoft in February of 1999 at $72 and saw the stock rise to $119 and then fall to $50 in March 2001, what then? Sell? We don't think it's a good idea to buy or sell stocks based on the wiggling and waggling of their prices over a few months or even years.

Expect volatility with some stocks. Don't stress out too much about how much the share prices swing up and down. Get much more interested in learning how the business is doing. You'll have to learn how to evaluate a busi-

---

### Famous Words

*It will fluctuate.*
—J. P. Morgan, when asked
what the market will do

---

ness's performance; we think we can help. If the company isn't succeeding, then sell. But as long as you have faith in the company, its long-term stock performance is what should matter to you. Microsoft's stock has gone up and down a lot, but just about anyone hanging in for three to five years has made good money to date.

## *Expect* to Lose Some Money

This might be alarming or depressing to hear, but if you invest in the stock market, be ready to lose some of your money along the way. If you invest in the overall market and not in individual stocks, then over many years, if not a few years, you should come out ahead.

With stock in individual companies, though, you could lose money on some or even many of your selections. It happens to the best of investors. Even Warren Buffett, the greatest investor in American history,

---

### Take It from Me

#### Curses, Foiled Again

I've been investing for about two years. I started when I was fourteen. There's been only one stock I've lost money on, but boy, did I lose money. It was Egghead.com, and I was an idiot. I hoped that the stock was going to go from $12 per share to $60 in a few weeks, so I bought it. I sold it at $2.80 or so. Ouch. I lost nearly all my money. But I'm lucky I'm making mistakes when I'm young, so that I can learn from them. I've done much better with shares of Nike and Texas Instruments.—Daniel Watson, 16

## Take It from Me

### Dang!

After opening a brokerage account, I promptly lost 40–50 percent of my money and then decided I had better *really* figure out what I was doing. That led me to reading the wisdom of Warren Buffett, Benjamin Graham, and Peter Lynch. I believe that in order to see further, you must stand on the shoulders of giants, and as their records show, these are among the best investors ever. If you get interested in stock market investing, and why wouldn't you, definitely track down the writings of Buffett, Graham, and Lynch in your library (Lynch, in particular, makes for a very enjoyable read).

One of the first stocks I owned was Office Depot. I read about the company in the newspaper and bought some shares at $11 per share. Then it tanked and I bought more shares at the lower price. Unfortunately, not yet having learned the value of patience, I quickly sold at a significant loss. The kicker? About a year later, that stock stands at $13.50 and my idol, Mr. Buffett, recently purchased five million shares. My heart still aches. But I'm learning.—Brian Stutz, 22

has some regrets when he looks at all the stocks he's bought and sold over the years.

The more you know, the fewer losses you'll end up having. As long as your money is divided among a handful of stocks, and not parked just in two, you'll minimize your risk. If you own stock in seven companies and one or two tank, the others could gain enough to more than make up for your losses.

### *Expect* Conflicting Information and Advice

Be prepared to feel confused at the beginning. You'll run across people giving you conflicting advice. Some will tell you *always* to have all your long-term money sitting in stocks. Others will say that it's okay to keep a lot of your money in cash, waiting for the right time to invest it. Some will tell you not to buy more shares of a stock if it starts falling. Others will counter that if you still believe in the business, you might want to buy more shares, as the price is lower.

Don't let these and other contradictions throw you. Expect contradictory ideas, think about them, and invest in ways that make sense to *you*. The most valuable lesson we can teach, truly, is to learn from your mistakes as you go.

### *Expect* Work—And Fun

Investing can actually be quite simple. Yes, there are timeless mysteries to the market. There are deep complexities. They can wrinkle your brain and rattle your nerves at times. But, truly, to be an average investor and to earn the excellent returns of the stock market can be easy. We promise to prove this to you before you shut this Foolish book. But we'll warn you right now. If you want to do *better* than average, then you'll need to do some work. You'll have to invest

> ### Famous Words
>
> *Almost everything that is great has been done by youth.*
> —Benjamin Disraeli

in stocks to do that. And if you choose to do so, say hello to homework, baby! (But hey, it'll be homework you get paid to do.)

The good news is that it can be a lot of fun. Especially if you invest in companies that interest you. If you love Starbucks, how painful would it really be to learn how the company operates? If you're fascinated by airplanes, then studying Boeing and its competitors will be interesting, not boring. If Tiffany or Gucci sets your heart aflutter, learning their business should fascinate you.

In fact, you'll soon find that any interest of yours is actually supported by a public company. Whether we're talking piano playing, Frisbee throwing, reading, bungee jumping, eating, traveling, listening to music, or just plain sleeping—there's a public company that provides products and services to meet those needs.

Not only can researching the companies that serve your interests be fun—the investing can be, too. You'll get to watch your holdings grow in value. You might even compare how you're doing with friends or siblings. You'll follow how your companies fare over time. You'll root for your home teams—your companies. It's work, but it might not feel like it.

### *Expect* Some Obstacles

One of the teen consultants for this book, seventeen-year-old Robert Morgan III, offered some tips on obstacles that teen investors will face:

**Famous Words**

*Ninety percent of the people in the stock market, professionals and amateurs alike, simply haven't done enough homework.*
—William J. O'Neil

"First, starting to invest takes a tremendous leap of faith. It takes a lot for a teenage investor to get up the nerve to enter the investment world. We really don't know what to expect. To make matters worse, many times someone at a brokerage firm will make it extra difficult for you to open an account or will try to tell you to wait until you're eighteen. (You don't have to wait. You can open a *custodial account* with a parent.) Steep commissions can also be an obstacle, as it's not worth investing $30 if you have to spend $12 of that paying a broker to make the trade.

"So, teenagers must have a lot of confidence and not back down. Believe it or not, your age can work *for* you. I've learned that if you have the nerve to ask, a brokerage might waive its fees and lower its minimums for you. [*Gardner note: Right on, Robert—in fact, you'll find lots more stuff in life is negotiable than you would have thought. The trick is often just asking.*] You have to try. You also need your parents to help you open your account. That could present a problem for some: Many parents want to help and get overinvolved, which will prevent teens from learning. Teens have got to make mistakes to learn. (I have learned well. I held shares of Cisco as it dropped from $50 to $20 per share. Yowch!)

**Famous Words**

*Unless you can watch your stock holdings decline by 50 percent without becoming panic-stricken, you should not be in the stock market.*
—Warren Buffett

"Just get up the nerve to start investing. Teens are going to face any or all of the following: rude brokers, outrageous commissions, uncooperative parents, and high fees/minimums. And you're going to make mistakes. But you have to persevere and not be intimidated. The rewards of investing throughout your life will be substantial."

# ·STEP 6·

## Your New Friend:
## The Mutual Fund

· · · · ·

*In the book of things people more often do wrong than
right, investing must certainly top the list, followed closely
by wallpapering and eating artichokes.*
—*Robert Klein*

Most Americans doubt they could ever do well investing on their
own—deciding which companies' stocks to buy and when to
sell. Frankly, many Americans also don't know much about wallpapering a house or eating artichokes. Given that, what's the right approach?
Maybe you're thinking the following:

1. Steer clear of artichokes (a shame, really, because artichokes are
   healthy and tasty).
2. Hire a pro to wallpaper the house (possibly a good idea; it's backbreaking work).
3. Hire a professional to invest for me (dangerous, unless you know
   what to look for).

Imagine that you have $500 to invest. But you've read nothing about
investing and are too scared to start on your own. You have no confidence. You have no reason to be confident. So you shrug your shoulders, scratch your head, rub your ears, and park your money in a bank
account, earning very low interest.

Sigh.

But now imagine instead that you have twenty-five friends. And each
of you has between $500 and $1,000 to invest. Your total cash is

---

**Famous Words**

*One of the troubles with Wall Street is that people either feel investing is "impossible" or they figure it's "easy."*

—John Magee

---

$20,000. Further, let's say that one of you knows someone—let's call him Cartman—who loves stocks and investing. You could all decide to hand your money over to Cartman and have *him* invest it for you. Why would he agree to such a thing? Well, because you'll pay him to do so. So Cartman takes 2 percent of your money (or $400) and invests the rest of it.

Cartman determines when to buy and sell shares of stocks. And if he's good at what he does, your investments increase in value over time.

If you've ever wondered what a mutual fund is, well, you just learned. Instead of twenty-five investors with $20,000, most mutual funds have thousands of individual and institutional investors investing millions or billions of dollars. And while the average individual investor might own stock in eight to fifteen companies, the typical mutual fund will hold shares in more than a hundred companies—often several hundred. In fact, mutual funds are required by law to spread the money over *at least* a few dozen companies, to provide safety for their investors.

### Kinds of Funds

Once you start looking at mutual funds, you'll discover that there are a wide variety of them. Some buy stocks. Others buy bonds. Some invest in America, others only in Asian companies. Some buy just entertainment businesses. Others invest in everything from women's jewelry to doughnut shops to commercial airliners.

We are now going to share some of the many categories of mutual funds. Please, however, please do not get overwhelmed. At the end of this section, we're going to make things real easy for you. Here's the general list of some of the main types of mutual funds. Note that some funds fall in more than one of these categories.

- *Equity funds.* "Equity" is just a fancy way of saying "stock." Equity funds invest in stocks.
- *Fixed-income funds.* These funds invest in bonds. Remember that a bond is a loan to a company or institution that pays the lender— you, if you own the bond—a *fixed* amount of interest.
- *Money-market funds.* A money-market mutual fund buys CDs and bonds issued by the government or other companies. It sticks to

short-term, high-quality securities, is relatively safe, and offers moderate returns.

Note: Remember that you'll typically earn less money with money-market funds (the safest) than bond funds (the next safest) and less with bond funds than stock funds (the riskiest in the short term).

Here are some more specific distinctions between funds to let you sample the different flavors. You don't have to remember all these categories to be a successful mutual-fund investor. We just want to present you with the overview.

- *Income funds.* The managers of income funds aim to generate regular payoffs for their shareholders through dividends from stocks, interest on bonds, or both. Its investors should expect regular checks from these funds (which are taxable). These funds are often favored by retirees, who need regular income from their investments. Because of this very reason, they're not ideal for most teens. (You're investing for the future, *not* for this coming summer! You'll have enough fun this coming summer. . . .)
- *Growth funds.* Growth fund managers don't try to generate income checks for investors. Instead, they invest in growing businesses in hopes of stock price appreciation in the days, weeks, months, or years ahead. The value of your investments increases if the fund manager buys successful growing companies.
- *Value funds.* Value investing fund managers look for beaten-down stocks of companies that may not be growing much. They hope to buy when the price of a stock is considerably lower than managers think the company is worth. Remember, a stock price reflects the value of the overall business.
- *Balanced funds.* These funds are invested in a "balance" between stocks and bonds.
- *Sector funds.* These funds are invested primarily in companies that are in a particular industry or sector, such as restaurants, real estate, telecommunications, banking, or biotechnology. They're ideal if you believe in a particular industry's future but have neither the time nor the expertise to select individual companies.
- *Regional funds.* These funds are invested primarily or exclusively in particular parts of the world. One might invest in French companies, another might specialize in Russian companies, and a third might limit itself to Latin American enterprises.
- *Large-cap, medium-cap, and small-cap funds.* These funds are restricted to certain sizes of companies. A large-cap fund must stick

to very large companies—like General Electric, Wal-Mart, and IBM. A small-cap fund must stick to small, usually unknown companies.

• *Index funds.* Each of these funds mimics an index. An index is a special group of companies. For example, there is the total market index fund—which buys shares of the five thousand largest companies and thus matches the return of the overall stock market. Alternately, the S&P 500 is a group of five hundred of America's leading firms in leading industries. An S&P 500 Index fund would invest in those exact five hundred companies, in the same proportion as the index itself.

And here are two final general distinctions between mutual funds.

• *Actively managed funds.* These funds hire money managers to do research and make numerous investment decisions. Mutual fund shareholders are counting on these professionals to provide above average returns for the additional fees they'll pay.
• *Passively managed funds.* There isn't much brainpower needed to run these funds. With an S&P 500 Index fund, for example, no one has to deliberate about which companies to invest in. The fund simply buys and holds whatever is in the index. And if the S&P 500 replaces a failing large company (like Polaroid) with a newcomer (like eBay), then the managers just make the appropriate adjustments. No brainpower needed; no high salaries needed; no high fees passed to the shareholders; yet also no chance of above average returns.

There are still more categories of funds. Why? Because in America today, fer cryin' out loud, mutual funds outnumber stocks! (We'll explain why in a bit.) Some mutual funds are, for example, "focused," aiming to hold stock in as few companies as possible, instead of hundreds. Others refer to themselves as "socially responsible," avoiding, for example, tobacco companies or firms with poor environmental records. (This is much easier said than done, though. You can find something socially objectionable in virtually every company—in every person, for that matter.)

There are even mutual funds for young people. If you're curious, look up funds like the Stein Roe Young Investor Fund (ticker: SRYIX; phone 800-338-2550). It has very low minimum investment amounts. And its annual write-ups are designed for young readers. It's not the best-performing fund out there, but it can be a fair starter.

---

## Keep in Mind

### The Scoop on Funds

You can learn much more about mutual funds in general at

- www.Fool.com/school/mutualfunds/mutualfunds.htm
- www.ici.org
- http://personal.vanguard.com/educ/inveduc.html

And you can dig up valuable information on various mutual funds at

- www.morningstar.com

Just as with stocks, do your homework before you buy. A little digging will tell you what a fund's fees are, how well it has done in past years, what kinds of investments it holds, and much more. An hour of research can generate tens of thousands of dollars over your lifetime.

---

If this huge variety of mutual funds has your head spinning, chill. Put your feet up. Breathe!

Because we're about to make it all very simple.

You see, there's really only *one* kind of mutual fund that we at The Motley Fool favor. . . .

### The Problems with Most Mutual Funds

Mutual funds do have their advantages. They're certainly convenient—especially if you don't know too much about investing. They give you instant diversification. You own hundreds of companies, making your investment less volatile. It would be risky to have all your money invested in just one or two companies.

There are some considerable disadvantages to mutual funds, though. You need to learn these problems and never forget them.

1. Not long ago, we mentioned that actively managed mutual funds employ professionals in an attempt to better the market averages.

Sadly, though, most funds underperform the market's average. Over the past one-, ten-, and twenty-year periods, more than 75 percent of stock mutual funds have done *worse* than the stock market's average. If the overall stock market rises a total of 34 percent over three years, the vast majority of mutual funds won't have done that well. *Bad news.*

2. Many mutual funds are too big for their own good. A bunch have more than $10 billion to invest. Imagine being the chief manager of one such fund. Maybe you've found ten amazing companies that you'd like to put most of your money into. That means you'll have to invest around $1 billion in each. Many companies aren't that big—you can't spend $1 billion on a $500 million company. Further, the Securities and Exchange Commission, the regulatory arm of the financial services industry, requires that you never invest more than 5 percent of your fund into any one company. That means all mutual funds must own a minimum of twenty different businesses. All in all, the bigger the fund, the less nimble it is. And the less it can focus its assets on just the best of the best. We pity those handsomely paid managers: it's truly difficult for them to provide market-beating performance to their customers.

3. Most mutual funds are too diversified to do well. Imagine managing a mutual fund where you're invested (in roughly equal amounts) in a hundred companies. Let's say that one or two—or even five—of them do really, *really* well. Their stock prices quadruple. Cowabunga! (Aren't we glad that craze is over?) Now, getting all that growth from a few companies should make your mutual fund's value skyrocket, right? Well, no. Those are just a few of your holdings. Their returns are just a drop in the drink. The dozens of other investments will likely bring these few outstanding returns down to a very average annual return.

4. Most mutual funds charge *significant* fees, which really hurt performance. Some of these fees you pay up front as a onetime "load" (basically a commission payment rewarding the salesman who sold you the fund). Other fees come out of your fund, out of your money annually, paying the operating expenses of the fund, things like salaries, administration, and advertising. These fees are assessed as a percentage of your investment, the percentage being called the "expense ratio." So if the expense ratio was 1 percent (the industry average is 1.25 percent), you would have 1 percent of your holding removed near the end of each year from your account.

Let's make it all too real with an example.

Say you begin by putting to work your $5,000 of savings earned during high school summers. You choose a mutual fund. That fund has a 5 percent load, paid up front (a "front-end load"). So straight out of your $5,000 that fee will come to $250 (ka-cha-cha-ching!), rewarding the person who sold you the fund. So now you're investing only $4,750. (By the way, have we mentioned yet that our favorite funds are "no-load funds," and you can probably guess why?) At your present value, by the end of the year you'd be paying about another $50 in annual expenses (about a 1 percent expense ratio). Perhaps you're getting the message: Watch the fees! Fees can really delay your financial independence! Watch the fees! Don't get nickel-and-dimed! You are getting the point! We're hammering it home by using exclamation points for every closing sentence of this paragraph! Investor, know thy fees! Before ever paying them!

5. Most funds do a lot of buying and selling. In fact, on average, they do far too much buying and selling. That's called turnover. It's bad because each time you (or a mutual fund) buy or sell something, a commission is charged. Those costs add up. If you have a brokerage account in which you pay $10 every time you make a trade, look out. If you trade a hundred times during the year,

---

## Take It from Me

**Regrets? You're Darn Right, Regrets!**

As my fiftieth birthday approached, I wondered what—if anything—I should have done differently to prepare for retirement. It was obvious. I should have started planning for this all-too-imminent stage of my life when I was back in my twenties. Darn.—Linda Purdy From, 50

I only learned about the magic of compounding interest in my twenties, but I believe it's something so important that I'd like my daughters to be familiar with the concept when they're teenagers—at the latest! They'll think I'm the most boring dad around when I begin teaching them. But I'm sure that one day they'll be very grateful.
—Patrick Coppens, 34

that'd amount to $1,000 in fees. Oooof. The same effect can hurt a mutual fund's profitability. In addition, if the fund is selling stocks on which it's making a profit, then it generates capital "gains," which get taxed. (Guess who pays those taxes? Look in the mirror.)

### Fees Matter

Imagine that you've invested $1,000 in a fund that charges a hefty 2 percent annual expense ratio. If that fund earned a 12 percent annual rate of profit, you'd subtract your two percentage points to arrive at an actual rate of return of 10 percent. Over thirty years, that investment would become $17,400. If the fund carried just a 1 percent fee, in thirty years your money would grow to $22,900. That's a $5,500 difference! Fees matter. A lot.

### Evaluating Funds

When you're researching a mutual fund, find out what its fees are and if it charges a "load." By now, you can probably shoot an arrow blindfolded and still hit the general rule spot-on: The lower the fees, the better. Oh, and make sure you get what you're paying for. This begins with a comparison of the fund's performance to a benchmark. If it's a stock fund, compare how it does *after fees are taken out* to the stock market's average return (as measured by the S&P 500). If a fund has lost an average of 3 percent over the last two years but the stock market has fallen 7 percent, then the fund is actually doing better than the market.

### The Solution to Underperformance?
#### *Try Index Funds*

Too many investors buy mutual funds without understanding the fees or performance of those funds. Most grown-ups, in fact. By a wide margin. *Why*, we ask, would they ever want to buy a mutual fund that charged high fees while consistently underperforming the market's average return? The unperplexing answer to that perplexing question is simply that they themselves don't even know that. They haven't checked. They haven't, in many cases, educated themselves enough to *know* to check, or to know *how* to check.

Do you remember that total market index fund we mentioned? It's the one that buys shares of five thousand different companies and in so doing duplicates the stock market's average return. The one that hires no expensive managers. The one that, via the Vanguard Group, charges just 0.2 percent per year in fees (80 percent lower *per year* than the average mutual fund).

Yes, we think you can avoid most of the problems tied to mutual

---

## Keep in Mind

### Index Power

A thousand dollars invested in a stock market index fund that earns 11 percent on average per year will double every 6.5 years. If that doesn't sound great, picture your money doubling, then doubling again, then again, then doubling again, and again, on average every 6.5 years. Your $1,000 investment will grow to $13,585 in 25 years. And it'll grow to $184,565 in 50 years. A mere $500 invested *every year* will, at the stock market's historical rate of return, grow to $8,400 in 10 years, $57,200 in 25 years, and more than $830,000 in 50 years.

Our final and favorite illustration is the twenty-one-year-old college graduate who gets a magical, whopping $10,000 tax-free gift from her grandparents. Rather than buying a car or splurging at Gucci, she decides to put it all away until her retirement. After all, she wasn't even expecting that money. Well, here's what happens to her $10,000 at 11 percent per year.

| Age | Investment Value |
| --- | --- |
| 21 | $10,000 |
| 30 | $25,600 |
| 40 | $72,600 |
| 50 | $206,200 |
| 60 | $585,600 |
| 70 | $1,662,700 |

She will pay for a very substantial portion of her retirement with that single investment at age twenty-one. And unlike so many baby boomers today, she won't be deathly afraid of Social Security not paying enough of her bills. The simple investment in an index fund made our college graduate's life that much sweeter, that much simpler.

funds by investing in just that sort of fund—an index fund. It's true that with some digging and research, you might be able to uncover a few mutual funds that outperform the market averages over long periods of time. But truly, there are very, very few of them.

The Motley Fool recommends index funds for just about anyone who can afford the risk to be in the stock market. Why? Here are some reasons.

1. While the vast majority of mutual funds do worse than average, index funds are precisely average. Given the alternatives, that's pretty good.
2. While the typical mutual fund charges you 1.25 percent per year, index funds usually sport extremely low fees, in the ballpark of 0.20 percent.
3. There's little turnover within index funds. They just hold stock in whatever companies are in the index they mirror.
4 They're simple. Investing in index funds will take very little of your time or mental energy. Once you're invested in them, you can forget about them (er, except for adding money periodically to them!). Investing for the long term in just index funds will put you financially way ahead of the average American adult. And heck, why not? You're already, by this point in the book, by far better educated about finance than the average American adult.

There are many different indexes that track groups of companies. These are the three most famous:

- *The S&P 500.* As we stated earlier, this is an index of five hundred leading companies in America. Just about any major company you can think of is in the S&P 500. (Examples: Ford, Motorola, Dell, Cisco, Hershey, Black & Decker, Maytag, Hasbro, Marriott, Chevron, Gillette, Wendy's, The New York Times, CVS, Radio Shack, Safeway, Kroger, American Express, Staples, Toys " Я " Us, Sprint, Merrill Lynch, and many more.) The S&P 500 is often used as a benchmark for the entire stock market. In other words, if the S&P 500 rises 5 percent, people will fairly generalize that the overall market has risen 5 percent.
- *The Wilshire 5000.* This index is an even better benchmark for the entire stock market because it actually contains the vast majority of stocks traded in the United States. At one time there were five thousand such companies, which is how it got its name. Today the index contains more than six thousand companies. This is often re-

## Pop Quiz

### Pop Quiz!

See if you can identify the following companies that are in the Dow Jones Industrial Average. We've thrown some challenging ones at you. Do the best you can.

1. _____ I'm a major telecommunications giant, and one of my initials stands for "telegraph."

2. _____ I was founded in 1837. Some of my 250-plus brands are Tide, Crest, Folgers, Mr. Clean, Cover Girl, Ivory, Pepto-Bismol, Pantene, Pampers, and Bounty.

3. _____ I've made and sold everything from light bulbs to dishwashers to aircraft engines. I even bought NBC.

4. _____ I've made a lot of money since 1923 with a couple of mice, a few ducks, and now ABC broadcasting.

5. _____ I was founded in 1886. Some of my best-known brands include Band-Aids, Tylenol, Motrin, Neutrogena, Mylanta, Reach, and Acuvue.

6. _____ Founded in Arkansas, I employ more than a million people in more than four thousand superstores around the world.

7. _____ My spokesman is a big clown.

8. _____ I'm one of the world's largest photography firms, selling more than $10 billion of products and services in more than 150 nations.

9. _____ Founded in 1908, I'm the world's largest vehicle manufacturer. I sell more than eight million Chevys, Pontiacs, Buicks, Cadillacs, GMCs, Saturns, Hummers, and Saabs in more than two hundred countries.

10. _____ Don't leave home without me.

11. _____ Based in Atlanta, I sell 3 trillion ounces of beverages each year, and plan to increase that number.

12. _____ Known mostly for my software, I'm one of the most valuable companies on Earth.

**Answers:** 1. AT&T 2. Procter & Gamble 3. General Electric 4. Walt Disney 5. Johnson & Johnson 6. Wal-Mart 7. McDonald's 8. Eastman Kodak 9. General Motors 10. American Express 11. Coca-Cola 12. Microsoft

ferred to as the "total market" index. It is the basis for the Vanguard Total Stock Market Index Fund, which we greatly favor.

- *The Dow Jones Industrial Average.* This is an index of thirty of America's biggest companies. It's a famous index, often referred to as "the Dow." It's also the oldest index, at more than a hundred years old.

You can invest in a mutual fund tied to any of these indexes. We recommend contacting Vanguard in Valley Forge, Pennsylvania, at 800-871-3879 or via www.vanguard.com.

Why do these indexes exist? Well, they make it easy for people to read how a group of companies is doing, without having to make numerous calculations. There are more indexes than those we've listed. But we've given you the primary ones. If you buy shares of an S&P 500 index fund, you instantly own a tiny chunk of each of its five hundred companies. Your holdings are weighted from largest to smallest. So you'll own a lot more Microsoft (the second largest company in the world as of this writing) than you will of Kellogg's (the dominant maker of breakfast cereals, but nonetheless a lot smaller than Microsoft).

Owning shares of funds based on indexes such as the S&P 500 and the Wilshire 5000 is in many ways like owning a piece of all American business. If you have faith that over the next ten, twenty, or thirty years America's economy will flourish, then consider investing in an index fund. It truly is our favorite stock market investment.

If you want to try to beat the 9–11 percent annual growth we think the market will offer over the next forty years, then you need to learn more about investing in individual stocks. That means more work, but it can also mean greater fun, more satisfaction, substantial intellectual reward, and more growth of your savings. If you choose to start and end with just index funds, though, you'll do very well. In fact, you'll do better than most professional investors!

[A personal apology from the Gardners (yes, this is called for): We really don't like to overuse the exclamation point. You've heard the same thing from your writing teacher. People! Who overuse! The exclamation point! Bore you! And over time you can't take their hyperbole! Seriously! Yeah, yeah, we know . . . we took the same classes. We agree with these teachers. But this chapter has been so steeped in irony—indeed, more shocking skullduggery at every page turn—that we would not be doing these truths justice if we were to punctuate them with . . . mere . . . periods.]

So this is another of our cardinal points. We've made a couple of others. Summed up, they suggest that you should:

1. pay down all credit card debt at the end of the month.
2. save 5-20 percent of your annual salary.
3. invest those savings in a total market index fund for five years or more.

Done throughout your life, you should be able to pursue your dreams, retire early, and dance a mean jig.

---

## Take It from Me

### My Investing Life—So Far

Three years ago, I opened an account with a discount brokerage. I was instantly in the stock market game. Drunk on power, I felt like a major player in the financial markets. With a point and click, I moved hundreds of dollars from stock to stock: Papa John's Pizza, Indonesian Telecom, 3Dfx, Analysts International. The titans of Wall Street trembled at the mere mention of my name.

Day trading was soon an all-consuming passion of mine. I snuck out of classes to check my stocks and pulled the trigger on companies just for the thrill. Unfortunately, I was losing money. Trading five times daily simply didn't work. Even with my brokerage's low commissions, I was paying $10 each time to get both in and out of positions. Factoring in taxes on any gains, I found my meager profits evaporating.

So I smartened up and settled on the traditional method of value investing espoused by the old guard—some of the world's greatest investors. I would take my time and invest in only the sturdiest of businesses.

After extensive research, I selected five solid companies that would make my fortune. And so my life continued, placidly, until that fateful day (oh, misery) that my cousin David called. A big-shot investment banker in Miami, David's the type who wears $900 Gucci sandals and cements deals on a fifty-foot yacht. "I have an amazing deal for you," he promised. Some global satellite company called Iridium was trading at $14 per share, down from a high of $75. Confident in its imminent turnaround, he apparently had half a million shares in it. (Run the numbers on that; that's a ton of money.)

At that moment, I pitied all those old ladies and their investing clubs. *They* couldn't get the kind of information *I* could from my yacht-steering, sandal-wearing all-star. I liquidated all my other positions, sat back, and waited for Iridium Satellite to make me rich. And waited. When it fell from $14 down to $7 or so, I placed a call to my cousin, who assured me that it was about to skyrocket. When Iridium declared bankruptcy, he persuaded me again that things would be fine. He called it a *formality.* Its billions of dollars of debt were apparently no problem, either.

Well, now the stock is worthless, and my life savings are gone. I'm not kidding about this. It's true.

The moral of the story? The professionals don't always know as much as you think they do. You can invest well on your own with proper research and due diligence. Me, I just stick to index funds now. With the miracle of compound interest and fiercely disciplined savings on my part, I hope to retire at age thirty and buy a beautiful house.—Alexis Neuhaus, 18

# ·STEP 7·

# Actually Invest!

• • • • •

Making money is a hobby that will complement any other
hobbies you have, beautifully.
—*Scott Alexander*

At this point, you really do know the basics of money management
for the rest of your life. It's a simple song sheet off of which to
sing. It goes something like this (okay, so we're *not* songwriters):

*Pay down credit card debt, and don't let
any bank or card provider persuade you
to carry loans from month to month at
10 percent–plus interest rates.*

*Hallelujah! Hallelujah! Hallelujah! Hallelujah!*

*Regularly put away as much money as
you can from month to month and year
to year. Ideally, you'll save in excess of
10 percent of your salary each year.*

*Hallelujah! Hallelujah! Hallelujah! Hallelujah!*

*Push as much of that savings as you can
into Vanguard's Total Market Index Fund
for five years or more. On average, you*

*will double each dollar you invest every*
*seven years.*

*Hallelujah! Hallelujah! Hallelujah! Hallelujah!*

*A sixteen-year-old who scraps and scrapes and*
*saves and invests $5,000 for her retirement*
*can anticipate seeing that grow to more than*
*$800,000 by age sixty-five.*

*Hallelujah! Hallelujah! Hallelujah! Hallelujah!*

That's the song. Okay, so it has no rhythm. Okay, so it won't be sung in church or on VH-1. Okay, so it wasn't even really a song . . . just a few paragraphs rearranged to look like one. That said, you can master the general concepts of it, yes?

Good.

And don't let any of the simple steps intimidate you. When you begin saving and investing out of habit, your life won't change significantly. Yes, you'll save more money than you once did. But only 5–20 percent of your salary. That'll leave plenty of additional cash for you to enjoy. And investing won't take any significant time. None of it will, actually (expect for growing dependably rich, which when it comes to investing is best done more slowly and more surely). So please say the following with us in your best robotic voice: "Carry no credit card debt. Save 15 percent of my salary. Invest it into the index fund." Seriously, stand up where you are and say it like a robot. Do the robot dance while you do:

"Carry no credit card debt. Save 15 percent of my salary. Invest it into the index fund."

You can do that easily. You can turn 'em into automatic actions. You can complete that stuff in your sleep. And now that you have a good sense of what to do, let's talk about *how* to do it.

### Are You Ready?!

We make no bones about our intentions with this book. We believe your generation should be the first to stop the horribly negative American trend of credit card debt. We believe you can and should learn to methodically save some money each year. We believe you can, without tedium or even any real intellectual effort, get the market's average return each year through indexing. Finally, we believe there's substantial historic evidence to support taking these actions.

But don't let us tell you what to do. Keep learning. Understand your decisions and feel comfortable with them. Take your time. Even if you're an eighteen-year-old now and you take two years to start investing, you'll be far, far ahead of most adults. Heck, you could start at age twenty-five and still succeed wildly. Of course, though, if you can start at fourteen, you'll have an eleven-year advantage on that twenty-five-year-old.

Don't begin until your ready. Don't begin until you have reasonable *expectations* (there's that word again). But once you're ready, yes, please *begin*. Let's figure out the best way to do so.

---

## Keep in Mind

### Follow Your Heart—By Investing

As you move into and through adulthood, you'll always have choices to make about what to do with your life. Perhaps your dream is to be a dancer, teacher, social worker, newspaper reporter, or actor. If so, people have probably warned you that you'll never make a lot of money at it. Well, if you feel torn between a career that offers you a higher salary (lawyer, accountant, doctor) and one that you'll love more, investing can help you out.

If you begin investing early and continue saving and investing for the rest of your working life, you'll build a financial cushion that can make your life easier. Most actors struggle to make ends meet. But if you're an actor with a stock portfolio worth $100,000, you're in a much better situation. If you want to buy a home, you may actually be able to afford a down payment.

Investing can make it possible to get by (and even to flourish) on a small salary. And if you're lucky enough to be an investor with a job you love and a high salary—well, then, the world's your oyster! Crack it open!

---

## Famous Words

*Youth! There is nothing like youth. The middle-aged are mort-gaged to Life. The old are in Life's lumber-room. But youth is the Lord of Life. Youth has a kingdom waiting for it. Every one is born a king, and most people die in exile.*

—Oscar Wilde

---

### Minor Details

*Okay, so how can you open an investment account?*

Well, legally, you're a minor if you're under a certain age. (Depending on where you live, it's usually between eighteen and twenty-one.) That means you aren't allowed to enter into legally binding contracts. You'll need adult supervision to buy a car, to make a will, to sign a blockbuster movie deal, to add a six-album major music deal . . . to ink any contract. Oh, and more relevant to our discussion, you'll need adult sponsorship to open a brokerage account.

When you sit down with Mom or Dad, or your grandparents, aunt, uncle, or legal guardian, they can help you open what is called a "custodial account." The account is thus named because the adult is a custodian (defined in this case as one who guards, not one who sweeps).

There are a variety of ways to oversee a custodial account, depending primarily on the relationship you have with your parents or guardians. If your custodian trusts you ("C'mon, Mom, you *completely* trust me, right?"), you might be permitted to use the account largely as you wish. If, however, Mom's a little bit more conservative ("I love you, dear. But *complete* trust is earned over time"), you'll need to get her okay every time you want to access the account.

### Brokerage Accounts

A brokerage is a firm that facilitates the buying and selling of securities (such as stock) while charging fees (called "commissions") for its services. Some fairly well-known brokerages include American Express Brokerage, Ameritrade, E*Trade, Fidelity Investments, Merrill Lynch, Quick & Reilly, Charles Schwab, Morgan Stanley Dean Witter, and TD Waterhouse.

Millions of Americans invest through brokerage accounts, which are no tougher to set up than bank accounts (piece of cake). In fact, these days many brokerages also offer banking services. TD Waterhouse, for example, is both a brokerage and a bank. Open an account there and your money will earn some interest; you can write checks on the account; and you can invest some or all of your money in stocks and mutual funds.

There are three simple steps to opening a brokerage account:

1. Read up on a few different firms at their Web sites.
2. Find one you like and fill out an application (with help from a legal guardian if you're a minor).
3. Deposit cash into the account and prepare to invest.

When you're ready to invest, just call up your broker or log on to your account on the brokerage's Web site. To buy a stock or mutual fund, just specify what you want and how much of it you want and provide any other special instructions. Here are two examples:

### Scenario One

Yes, hello, James, thanks for taking my call. My account number is 99-8-77-66-5. . . . Yes, that's it. Okay, I'm going hunting for bargains this month. I've done my homework and I'm feeling good about this one. I want to buy ten shares of AOL Time Warner, but only if the price is below $30 per share. . . . Yes, that's right. A *limit* order, only if the price goes below $30. . . . Excellent. Thanks for your fine service, chappy.

### Scenario Two

Hey, Melanie. Yeah, it's me, Tony. Hey, how are ya? . . . Ah, great, great. Glad to hear it. Hey, my account number is 11-2-33-44-5. . . . I'd like to buy twenty-five shares of ExxonMobil at the current price. Sound good? Ya think I got a winner here? . . . Okay, let's make the trade. Hey, while you're at it, let me ask you, would you ever be interested in having dinner with me? (Loud coughing sounds.) Whoops, sorry. Way out of line by me. My apologies. Did my trade go through?

Excellent job in both scenarios—though phone flirting with your broker is ill advised. Try to keep your investment and personal lives separate.

After you've bought some stock, the shares will appear in your account (if not immediately, then within three days). Let's say you had

$1,000 in your account. You bought $500 worth of Krispy Kreme at $50 a share. And you paid a $10 commission to your broker to make the trade. When your account statement is mailed to you, you'll now see ten shares of Krispy Kreme, the $10 commission, and $490 cash remaining in your account.

You can add money to your account at any point. And you can withdraw money, too (if you've got the cash in the account). You'll usually receive monthly statements in the mail from the brokerage, detailing the value of your account or portfolio. Once a year, you'll also receive an annual report from each company you hold stock in.

## Shopping for a Brokerage

When you're shopping for a brokerage, there are at least five key factors to consider:

1.  Is it just an on-line brokerage, or does it have brick-and-mortar branches?
It's perfectly fine to use an on-line-only brokerage. But if you're just starting out, you might enjoy dealing with your broker in person. Schwab, Fidelity, and TD Waterhouse are some brokerages with lots of local branches.

2.  Is there a minimum amount you need to open an account with?
You'll typically see minimums anywhere from $100 to $2,000. How much you have to invest will help you eliminate a bunch of brokerages from the beginning. We encourage you, however, to let any broker know that you're a minor with a custodial account. Then ask them if they can cut you a deal on account minimums as well as fees. Seriously, please try this. It's a way to save important money for you early in your investment career. (For instance, $100 saved today and invested at 11 percent per year is worth more than $18,000 in fifty years. Sounds absurd, but in fifty years it won't.)

3.  How much does the brokerage firm charge to invest?
"Discount" brokerages, which The Motley Fool has long recommended, often charge you a fee, or commission, of as little as $8 per trade. That's a good deal. Others can charge you $10–$40, while offering you additional services. Old-fashioned "full-service" brokerages (such as Merrill Lynch or Morgan Stanley Dean Witter) will typically charge you more than $100 per trade.

Your main concern should be to avoid paying too big a percentage of each investment's value in commissions. For example, let's say you want to buy $100 worth of stock in Chocolate Heaven Confectionary Inc. Well, if you're charged $20 to do that, you just paid out 20 percent of your investment in commissions. That's terrible. It means you've essentially *lost* 20 percent from the outset. Bad idea.

Try to spend no more than 2 percent in commissions when you buy or sell stock. That can be tough. If your brokerage charges $10 per trade, you'll have to buy or sell at least $500 worth of a stock or fund in order to hold commissions down to 2 percent of your investment. Again, we encourage you to play the "minor card" and get them to lower their rates for you—to get you started as a potential lifetime customer.

4.  Can I buy mutual funds through my broker?
You certainly can. Most brokerage firms today offer an extremely wide selection of mutual funds, thousands of them. Remember to check the fees on the funds, though—since you'll now be paying a brokerage commission *and* an ongoing management fee to the mutual fund family. Fees can really add up.

Last chapter, we talked a great deal about the total market index fund and the S&P 500 Index fund, two of our all-time favorite investments. They can provide all the ballast your investment portfolio will ever need. Please know that you can purchase either of these through your broker or you can call Vanguard and order their fund directly at 800-662-7447. Other firms offer similar funds, but for anyone looking to keep fees down we'll continue to favor Vanguard, until others charge you as little as Vanguard does.

5.  Where can you get more information?
At www.broker.Fool.com, you can learn a lot more about how to evaluate brokerages. You can also order more information and account applications from a bunch of brokerages. Another good resource is http://brokerage.getsmart.com/broker. You can learn the brokerage lingo here, in our glossary: www.Fool.com/dbc/glossary.htm. (There are some terms you should learn that will help you when you place an order—such as "market order" and "limit order.")

## Take It from Me

### Me and My Brokerage Account

I knew I wanted a discount broker. My dad was using TD Water-house, so I just picked it and sent away for information and an application on their Web site. I deposit money by mail, keep all my statements together in a three-ring binder, and track my account online. I use my parents as middlemen for deposits. I'll give them a wad of cash, and they'll write a check out to the brokerage for me.

I had to start out with a custodial account because I was seventeen, but that doesn't really mean anything. My parents gave me total access. If I want to, I can invest or I can write checks out of it.
—Ben Sheppard, 18

### IRAs: Traditional and Roth

Okay, yes, there's even another approach to all this. We know this doesn't make for the *most* enjoyable reading. But focus again here. IRA accounts could put you in your dream home someday.

An IRA account is designed to hold investments for your retirement years. IRAs are *tax-advantaged* brokerage accounts. You'll significantly reduce your tax costs by investing in an IRA.

Teens can open IRA accounts with banks, brokerages, mutual fund companies, and other financial firms (again, through a custodial account with a parent or guardian). There is one hurdle with an IRA, though. You can only put money into an IRA account if you have *earned* income. That $500 you got for your bar mitzvah or from Uncle Fester won't work. You'll have to have a job of some sort—mowing lawns, tutoring, baby-sitting, selling stuff professionally on eBay, and so on.

You should also know that as of 2002, the maximum amount of money you can put into an IRA is $3,000 of earned income per year. We very, *very* highly recommend taking advantage of IRA accounts if you have the income and can willingly put away money until you're fifty-nine. It's a long way off—but if you start working toward your retirement now, even in very small ways, you'll almost certainly retire in style. (Maybe we'll all meet up as beach house owners in the Seychelles in 2050; since we're already in our thirties, though, please forgive our probable inability to party much past eight-thirty.)

There are two main kinds of IRAs. They are:

### The Traditional IRA

A traditional IRA is for *pretax money*—that is, your money goes straight from earned income (in other words, what you make at work) into the IRA without first being taxed. And once that cash is invested in the IRA, you won't get taxed for any capital gains made from year to year (capital gains are the profits you make on an investment once it's sold—capital losses are what result if your sales price was below your purchase price). All taxes on a traditional IRA are deferred until you're fifty-nine years old. Let's say you make $3,000 this year by setting up a small business and selling, in your neighborhood and on eBay, everything from old Pokémon dolls and Sega Dreamcast cartridges to a refurbished ten-speed bicycle and some golf clubs. You could then put any or all of that money into a traditional IRA—eliminating the income tax on that money. Plus your investment would grow tax-deferred until your retirement. Very nice indeed.

### The Roth IRA

Even better for teens, with a Roth IRA you invest *post-tax money* and ever afterward never have to pay (capital gains) taxes again. Here's how it works. Let's say you earned the same $3,000 above and chose to invest any or all of it in a Roth IRA. You'd first report the $3,000 in income and pay a minor tax on it; you don't get an up-front tax break, as you would with the traditional IRA. However, after you've paid the income tax, you'll pay no taxes on investment gains, spread out over a forty-year period. The Roth IRA is investment gold for teenagers.

Let's consider an example. We'll take a twenty-year-old. Her name's Amanda. She's a sophomore at Brown University. She likes skating on frozen lakes, sleeping late on Saturday, the taste of raspberries melting in her mouth, and anything to do with actor Josh Hartnett. She dislikes whiners, drivers who weave on the highway, smoking, and the way Britney Spears dresses. She's a standout history major with a minor in Russian literature.

To top it all off, this year she's decided to begin an important habit. She will henceforth invest $1,000 each year into an IRA account. However, being new to the subject, she's not sure whether to go with the traditional or the Roth IRA. Let's help her. If Amanda puts $1,000 away each year and earns 11 percent annual growth, either way she'll end up with $582,000. If that money is in a traditional IRA, she'll pay $145,000 in taxes (at a realistic tax rate of 25 percent). If, however, she can put $1,000 of *post-tax* money into a Roth IRA, she'll keep the full $582,000 for her retirement. Big difference.

And what a great habit this is for an ice-skating, raspberry-slurping, late-sleeping, Josh Hartnett groupie.

Obviously, though, this may all seem pretty out-of-this-world to you. What the heck?! Invest for your retirement? Plan for your sixties? Put your money away for decades? Ya gotta be kidding me?!

Well, it may be hard to imagine life in your retirement years. And that may make it largely uninteresting for you to begin preparing today. But please remember that we're not suggesting you sock every spare penny you get into an IRA for your retirement. You can grow literally hundreds of thousands of dollars for your future by investing a relatively measly $500 a year.

There's more to learn about IRAs. You can read up on them all over the Internet, including at www.Fool.com/taxes and www.Fool.com/retirement. Note that some banks and brokerages aren't eager to set up custodial IRAs for minors, so you might have to shop around. Don't let anyone tell you that a minor isn't allowed to start an IRA, though. As long as you have a legal guardian and earned income, you can have an IRA account at any age.

---

## Keep in Mind

### Index Funds Are Enough

Although this chapter is all about brokerage accounts, remember that you can generate all the money you'll ever need for your future by sticking with just an index fund. You can buy index funds via a brokerage account or you can just order them direct from Vanguard. Indexing is the great opportunity that too few of your parents and their friends learned about in school. Many of them have yet to know the beauty of passive index funds versus actively managed funds. Keep it simple, Fool (KISF).

## Newfangled Brokeragelike Things

In recent years, there have emerged some companies that operate very much like traditional brokerages, but with a few twists. Two examples are www.sharebuilder.com (866-747-2537) and www.buyandhold.com (800-646-8212). These firms offer the opportunity to buy and sell stocks for as little as $4 per trade.

How can they offer that when discount brokerage firms charge $10–$40 per trade and full-service firms will charge as much as $200 or more per trade? Well, these very deep discount firms will execute your orders as infrequently as just once a week, to keep their costs down. This shouldn't matter if you're a true long-term investor.

If you're interested in these companies, call them or check out their Web sites. Make sure you get educated about their process before you sign up. Ask any questions you didn't find answers to, such as whether they'll let you set up a custodial account with a parent and how much they'll charge you monthly and/or per investment.

## Drip, Drip, Drip

Can you believe there are so many different kinds of investment accounts? Sorry to throw them all at you, but we wanted to ensure you have a sense of the breadth of offerings out there. We plan to be quick about this—but, yep, we have another option to present to you.

One effective way for teenagers with limited funds to invest is through Drips. That's the nickname for "dividend reinvestment plans" ("DRPs"), or direct investment plans. If a company offers a Drip plan (and more than a thousand major companies do, companies like Coca-Cola, General Electric, and IBM), it means you can buy shares of stock directly from the company, bypassing brokerages and their commissions. Even though brokerage fees have come way down in past years, using Drip plans can be extremely cost-effective.

Another huge benefit of Drips is that you can automatically reinvest dividends. If you get $15 in dividends from a stock that's currently trading around $30 per share, the Drip plan will buy you half a share of stock for your account with that $15. Yes, Drips provide you with an opportunity to buy fractional shares. Essentially, what you're doing here is using the stock market like a bank. You're methodically able to add small bits of savings along the way. This can be a wonderful option for young investors.

You can learn more about Drips and which companies offer them in

## Take It from Me

### A Dripping Teen

I became interested in investing when I got my first job as a waiter. I'd saved money and wanted, like my parents, to buy stocks. When I turned sixteen, I opened an account with my mom at a local brokerage. I then bought my first two stocks: $200 worth of General Electric and $200 worth of Abbott Labs, a pharmaceutical company. I picked these companies using information I gathered from books and on-line discussion boards.

After buying my first stocks, I gained confidence and wanted to keep investing. It was as if I'd been on a swaying bridge and had finally set foot on solid ground. I continued to learn more and kept putting money in my brokerage account. I then bought stock in several other well-known companies, including AT&T, Cisco Systems, Intel, Pfizer, and WorldCom. As I learned more, I sold my first shares of GE and Abbott Labs, reinvesting the money in a Drip (dividend reinvestment plan) with Pfizer. Dripping is my favorite way to invest, because it's so inexpensive.

I pick my stocks using the principles of Warren Buffett and Peter Lynch. I like companies that steadily increase earnings and have high profit margins, with room to grow. I also like to see little or no debt. I prefer companies whose products are used by everyone, products without which the world would be different. Can you imagine the world without medicine and computers?

I've had many good stock picks and a few bad ones. My best has been my Pfizer Drip, which has grown steadily. Another good one has been AT&T. I invested $380 into AT&T; it's now worth $510. My worst pick has been Cisco Systems, which I bought at $50 per share and watched go all the way down to $15. You have to take the bad with the good, and I am not worried. After all, I'm only seventeen.

—Robert Morgan III

our book *The Motley Fool's Investing Without a Silver Spoon: How Anyone Can Build Wealth Through Direct Investing* by Jeff Fischer (who began investing as a teen). You can also get the latest scoop and more info at www.Fool.com/School/DRIPs.htm.

### Savings Accounts for Education and College

Okay, we've only got two more account-based considerations for you. But these are particularly relevant to you; they're accounts designed for saving and investing toward a college education.

### Qualified Tuition Plans

Qualified tuition plans (QTPs) are also known as "Section 529 plans," or just "529 plans." These investment accounts are offered by most states. They let you park money in the account but then offer you just a few investment choices. Further, you must pay a penalty fee if you plan to withdraw the money for reasons other than educational expenses. The great thing about these accounts, though, is that you (and your parents, or anyone) can sock away a lot of money in them. Then when you withdraw the money to pay for school, it's all tax-free. There are no capital gains taxes, even if your money has tripled in value.

Learn much more about these plans at www.savingforcollege.com.

### Coverdell Education Savings Accounts (aka Education IRAs)

Coverdell education savings accounts, formerly called "education IRAs," are also attractive. Your Coverdell savings account can have up to $2,000 invested in it per year. It's very much like a Section 529 plan, except that you have a lot more choice about how you invest the money in the account. You can invest it in whatever stocks or bonds or mutual funds you'd like. You can open a Coverdell savings account through most brokerages and other financial institutions. When you withdraw money for qualified education expenses, it's tax-free.

◆ ◆ ◆

Learn more about how to save for college at www.Fool.com/pf.htm.

# ·STEP 8·

# Learn Together
· · · · ·

*Real knowledge is to know the extent of one's ignorance.*
*—Confucius*

We hope that the horrors of credit card debt, the power of compounded growth, and the beauty of the U.S. stock market is compelling you to take action. You are feeling the urge to save and invest. Now that you know how to open an account, you can get started. Oh my, and once you do, you'll be building your financial house for all time. You can already see the numbers of geometric growth spinning wildly higher, from decade to decade, as your personal wealth expands.

You'll be able to buy that cabin in the Rockies. You'll be able to afford that change of career when you're forty-six. You can afford the health insurance you'll need. You can pay for food and shelter without concern. You can afford tickets to the U2 concert, because you've budgeted for them. Someday you'll be able to cover costs for your children to head to the very best college in the land. And you'll still have plenty left over to make charitable contributions each year.

As you begin to enjoy the comfort of financial security, we encourage you also to exercise your brain and vocal cords. We want you to practice your leadership skills. We ask of you two things.

**Learn Together**
If you've derived any value from this book, if you think it makes sense, if you believe it can make a real difference in your life, then tell others

about it. Loan a copy to a classmate. Poke around www.Fool.com for free with a friend. You might even open the eyes of your parents or teachers or other adults.

Do so and you'll end up with a finance and investing network. What one person learns can be shared with another. The more you talk with friends and family about saving and investing, the more help you'll get as well. Consider starting or joining an investment club, even a very informal one where you just share ideas and research over dinner once a month.

Oh, and, anyone you turned on to saving and investing is now a disciple of yours. He or she must, forever, continuously praise you for getting them started.

Not bad.

## Please, Keep Learning

There are plenty of ways you can extend your education as a saver and investor. Keep at it and your results will improve dramatically throughout life. Of course, you're bound to make some mistakes, some terrible ones, along the way. Getting down on yourself or sulking when you lose some money won't help you improve. Committing yourself to learning from your mistakes *does*. When you fall, rest for a second, make sure you haven't turned your ankle, then get up and press ever onward.

Finally, among the best ways to keep learning is to read and ask questions. There are so many good finance and investing books out there. Peter Lynch, for example, is a wonderfully accessible writer and thinker about investing. His lessons are timeless, and his examples remind us that the very best companies to invest in are right in front of our eyes. Pick up a book of his. And join us at our discussion boards on-line, where tens of thousands of people meet each day to improve their financial standing. The Web address is http://boards.Fool.com.

## Do You Dare?

Believe it or not, you've reached the end of this book—in a sense. No kidding. You can stop right here. You've learned enough to set aside money and drop it into index funds. It's a startling truth that doing so would put you ahead of 90 percent of the American public when it comes to sound financial habits and money management.

In fact, the challenge for you henceforth is not to battle ignorance. It's simply to build discipline and character. You're armed with the knowledge you need. Now the only question is, will you do it? Will you save? Will you set up your brokerage, IRA, or Drip account? Will you add money to it each month? Will you then be able to kick back and enjoy the best available investment vehicle for long-term savings, the simple average return of the U.S. stock market?

Speaking of which . . .

Do you want to try to do better than that?

Because if so, the bonus sections that follow are written for you. To earn a better return than 10.6 percent per year, you might search through mutual funds (though their fees and taxes can really hurt your chances). Or you can invest some of your money into individual stocks. You can do very well investing in companies familiar to most people. Take a gander at the following table that shows the average annual stock growth rate for a bunch of companies. (The overall market grew by almost 16 percent over these two decades. It was a period of above average growth.)

### Twenty-year Average Annual Returns (1980–2000)

|  |  |
|---|---|
| Wal-Mart | 31% |
| Coca-Cola | 21% |
| Schering-Plough | 21% |
| General Electric | 20% |
| Merck | 20% |
| PepsiCo | 20% |
| Pfizer | 20% |
| Sara Lee | 19% |
| Disney | 18% |
| Johnson & Johnson | 18% |
| McDonald's | 18% |
| Philip Morris | 17% |

So $1,000 invested in General Electric stock over that time would have grown to $38,000. And $1,000 in Wal-Mart would have grown to around $222,000. These amounts don't even include dividends. Pretty amazing. Two decades might seem like a long time to you, but are small investments not worth these sorts of rewards?

Okay, so should you rush out and put all your money into Wal-Mart stock? Well, it's a great company, but no, we don't advocate knee-jerk investing. The next two decades might be very different from the last two for these firms. That's why it's important to develop some skills in selecting companies. During the same 1980–2000 period, the average annual growth rate was just 9 percent for Sears, 8 percent for IBM, and *negative* 4 percent for Xerox. A well-known name is not enough.

If you dare, read the rest of the book. It's all about investing in the stocks of individual companies. There's no commitment, so you'll do well to keep reading even if you don't think you're interested. The worst that'll happen is that you'll miss an episode of *Everybody Loves Raymond.* The best that'll happen is that you'll become savvier about investing and more knowledgeable about the world around you.

Ahh, but before we move to the bonus section, it's time to learn from other Fools and time to give you a chance to win $1,000.

# ·STEP 9·

## Win $1,000 Being a Fool

* * * * *

Winning isn't everything—but wanting to win is.
—*Vince Lombardi*

Frankly, our number-crunching statisticians, trusted advisers, and high-powered image consultants have determined that we've talked enough for now. We do hope you've valued our advice thus far. At this point, however, we thought you might enjoy hearing from some of the more than three million people who visit Fool.com each month.

We asked The Motley Fool on-line community to share its best money advice for teens. We were inundated with great ideas for you. Grandparents, lawyers, teachers, doctors, Australians, parents, sewage haulers (honest!), and many others shared their suggestions and stories. The contest was run by Fool staffer Rex Moore; Rex is hopeful and optimistic that his own children (Patrick, age twelve, and Kristianne, age ten) will take the advice that our community provided.

We were so pleased with all of the contributions that we've decided to do two things.

First, we're sharing the very best with you in this chapter of the book.

Second, because of the great writing of the group, we've decided to launch a $1,000 annual grant for the next five years for the most eloquent and effective advice on personal finance, investing, or business offered by a teen submitted to us. It could come from you, could it not? If you'd like to compete and learn from others, then contribute (as many times as you like) your best financial thoughts on the Teens and Their Money board at http://teens.boards.Fool.com or via e-mail to contest@Fool.com and take a chance at winning $1,000 for being a talented communicator of financial advice. (Remember, we offer a thirty-day free trial to check out our boards. So don't delay. This could be the first $1,000 you invest for your future.)

And now . . . for the greatest contributions from our community (identified by their Motley Fool screen names) to you.

### How to Save Money: Matching Funds
### By houghton32

Saving and investing are wonderful ideas! In fact, investing money early and often can lead you to millionaire status far sooner than you think. But where does the money come from?

As a teen, your most likely sources of income are 1) part-time jobs, and 2) your parents. Jobs can really extend your income stream, but they're a lot of work! While I recommend going for a job, I also think it's much easier to get your parents to pitch in. The question is—how?

**First,** you need to convince *your parents* to provide a steady stream of income (aka allowance). To do this, keep track of what they give you for a few months and where you spend it. Then, ask Mom and Dad for that amount of money and make it clear that you'll take responsibility for your own expenses from then on. Most parents would rather hand over $35 per week than be pestered for $5 per day.

**Second,** now that you have income, you need to save what you can. Remember that $5 saved per week is $260 per year. But go further than that. How? Well, one way your parents save money is by getting their employers to match their savings. For every dollar they save from their salary, many employers offer them 50–100 percent of additional money. Unfortunately for you, you don't have a corporate benefits program.

Ah, but you *do* have parents.

Propose to your mom and dad that they help you learn about savings and investing. ("Hey, Mom . . . Dad . . . can you help me learn about saving and investing?" It's just that easy.) Ask them to match every dollar you're able to save and invest. If they agree, you can quickly turn that $260 of savings into $520. The beauty of this is that some parents won't believe you'll actually save money. So they'll go along with your plan!

**Third,** in addition to the regular savings, add gifts from your next most likely source of income—grandparents, aunts, uncles, and so on.

So, when Grandma sends a check, bank it. Then your parents will match it. Let's say you get $100 for your birthday and $100 for Christmas. Your parents match them both. That's $400. Added to your $520 above, now you have $920.

**Fourth,** since you're showing such responsibility, your parents will start to trust you and you can try another trick. I call it "Money for A's." Usually parents are willing to reward for good behavior, so how about some cash reward for good grades? Let's say you convince them to pay you $10 for each "A" each semester. If you take sixteen classes and ace them all, that's $160. Then you save it, and they have to match it with another $160. That's $320 more.

You now have a grand total of $1,240.

Okay, maybe this sounds like wishful thinking. Totally unrealistic. Eh? You may be asking, how do I know what I'm talking about? Well, I do have firsthand experience. You see, *I'm the mother of just the sort of enterprising avid saver above.* She's somehow turned her allowances, gifts, grade money, and matching program into over $20,000 in mutual funds at the age of fifteen! And since she recently started a part-time job, $2,000 is already in her Roth IRA. At age fifteen!

### Learning to Live Below Our Means Together
### By americanmadeSC

After my divorce, my teen daughter saw what frugality meant for the first time in her privileged young life. Shopping at high-dollar boutiques and malls was replaced by combing the racks at the off-price stores and consignment shops. There, she found clothes and outfits that were a fraction of what we would have spent previously but, truly, still looked like a million dollars.

We had to do this, out of necessity. We learned to buy and sell at auction on-line, turning some people's "trash" into cash and getting great deals on things we really needed and wanted.

Then there are *coupons!* Ah. She learned to watch for them in magazines, newspapers, and in stores. She organized them all, using them when and where they'd be doubled.

The great news is she still does all of the above now. She lives in an apartment on her own in college at the tender age of nineteen. Along the way, she even learned to (no kidding) change her own oil and filters in her Jeep! And, most important, she learned how vital it is to save and invest so that you have a *cushion* for emergencies. We would have never made it otherwise.

The moral she's taken is: It doesn't hurt a teen to have to work, scrape, and save for what he or she wants. And it actually does teens more good than anything to see their parents doing the same.

## Credit Cards and the Coveted Stereo
### By tarsym

When our son was thirteen, he badly wanted a new stereo. It cost $600. We explained to him that we couldn't afford it. And he retorted, "You all have a credit card. Just charge it." He didn't understand the value of a dollar and the cost of debt.

After my wife and I discussed it, we decided we'd buy the stereo on a credit card that had no balance. In exchange, our son agreed to pay for the stereo himself over time. He put $100 down with us; we bought the stereo on the credit card; and he agreed to pay down the balance, plus interest.

In the first month, he used his allowance and earned some money on the side to make payments. When the bill came, we tallied up the situation. He expected to see a $500 balance (with the $100 already paid on the $600 stereo). Against that, he was going to pay $50, leaving a $450 balance.

Imagine his surprise when he found that the 18 percent interest rate on the card added $7.50 to the total bill. Instead of his $50 counting toward the principal, only $42.50 did. He needed to use $7.50 to pay the interest. He realized, immediately, the uphill battle of debt and paid off his stereo as quickly as he could.

He was thirteen at the time. He's now twenty-nine. He has no credit balance that he can't pay off monthly. The only thing that's changed is that now *he's* trying to teach *his new wife* the same lesson!

## Spending a Fortune on Nothing
### By ksp0711

Can you learn from others? Yes, you can. You can learn from me right now. I've set a bad example for you. Learn from it.

Today, I make plenty of money at work. Plenty. However, I spend a ton of it on . . . *nothing!* That doesn't make sense, does it? Let me explain.

When I was in my twenties, I started using credit cards. At first I was careful. Soon I was finding things I felt I needed but didn't have the cash to cover. After all, starting out on your own can be hard. I continued to spend and rack up debt—gradually—on things I didn't really need. Soon I viewed my balance of available cash as a combination of my checking account plus my available credit. If I had enough credit, then I could "afford" it. Dinner, movies, furniture.

Not good thinking.

Now I'm stuck.

Let's do some math together. Today, my $30,000 of credit card debt at 18 percent annual interest demands payment of about $450 per month. Just to cover the interest! And what do I get for that? You guessed it—*nothing!*

I owe $450 a month for nothing.

Hey, I know you'd never get into this trap. You can't imagine anyone silly enough to do it. Neither could I, but here I am. Lower interest cards are not the solution. Promising to keep the balance "low" is not the answer. My only answer for you is to avoid the trap in the first place.

I'd be living much more comfortably if only I hadn't run up such large debts. Learn from my mistakes. Be a Fool, not a bank's fantasy.

## How Debt Crept Up
### By penniethewoo

Okay, you've heard the advice that everyone gives you. Budget, save, invest, spend wisely, and don't get into debt. That's all good advice, but let's get real here. Financial responsibility is a difficult thing to master. That's especially true, since many parents don't know exactly what to teach, and schools don't teach it at all. And even when someone does try to help you, it's mostly a live-and-learn experience.

When I was a freshman in high school, my parents set up a checking account with me. They showed me all the things that I needed to know, stuff like how to balance the account and not live beyond my means. I did fine on all of that *until* I reached college and was bombarded with the offers for credit cards (and free T-shirts and soda just for applying).

I would have done fine with those cards except I let someone else talk me into spending more money on the card than I could pay off at the end of each month. This started the downward spiral of debt. Living on a limited budget and financial aid got me through college. But my husband and I graduated with $55,000 in financial aid debt and another $20,000 in credit card debt. No, don't doubt it; those are the *real* figures.

We had enough credit cards and store credit cards that we could have made an interesting plastic car out of them. Now after almost four years of very, very hard work, we're getting everything under control. We've just begun building a house. It's been possible only because my husband is paid very well.

The long and short of this story is that you should always remember that financial responsibility is just that—*a responsibility.* You really do have to know the difference between needs and wants. You have to know what you really can afford. Above all, *do not* be afraid to ask for financial advice from people in the know. Don't wait until you're in deep trouble to ask for help.

Finally, remember that creditors will allow you to spend much more than you make. They'll encourage it, since that's how they make money. Don't give in. Spend with care and live well.

### The Rule of Thirds
### By GWestley

Most children today, from an early age, are bombarded with the latest movie, fashion item, CD, or toy from various influences in their lives. Learning to filter out *wants* from *needs* is a challenge for all of us. From an early age, our child understood that all she had to do was ask for what she wanted, and we bought it for her.

Then we decided to stop that. We developed a system of saving, investing, and spending for our daughter so she'd understand how money worked and how to control it to get the things she wanted. We wanted to prepare her for the rest of her life, where money is finite. The goal was to let her have her own money so she would develop a sense of saving and growing money. We wanted to teach her how to set aside money for future necessities, like clothing.

First, we gave her an allowance and explained that one-third of it was to be used for daily spending on necessary food items and such. Second, she had to save another third of it for the future, when she was older and needed something important. That went into a savings account that didn't get touched. And the final third of the money was put aside for a strategic buy, such as a new piece of clothing, a game, something she absolutely had to have. This was available for unexpected emergencies as well.

We implemented a twenty-four-hour waiting period to discuss the importance of the strategic buy. We wanted her to understand what she'd be giving up in the future if she spent all her money today. More often than not, we averted the impulse buy. With time to think about what she really wanted, she often didn't buy. At times, though, we chipped in with her to get things she really wanted that we wanted her to have. The money lessons were important to us.

Our daughter has learned to invest, save, and spend. At the same time, she has learned to spend money on the things that she really needs and to make rational decisions about the consequences of her spending decisions. She even has monuments in her room as a reminder of spending excesses (the three-foot-tall dinosaur she *had to have*) as well as some reminder of the really great buys (her digital camera).

We truly have some great memories of the times we spent teaching her the value of money and the importance of saving and spending wisely.

## The Envelopes of Financial Freedom
### By dduct

I had $0 when I left graduate school with a degree in business, an MBA. Think about it—$0 to my name. College had been a financial struggle. Now I was done with graduate school. I was smart and ready to earn. But I had no money. I wanted savings, a home, and long-term security.

As my work salary climbed in the years ahead, though, my friends (many of whom skipped college to "earn money") were pulling on my sleeve to spend what I was earning. To figure my situation out, I decided I needed a plan. I spent some time and created a budget.

Honestly, budgeting was hard. It was painfully obvious that my goals of saving, home ownership, and financial security were years away. If I didn't control my spending, I might never get there. Right then, I established a spending plan. I knew my goal and I refused to be kept from achieving it.

Here's what I did.

I labeled three envelopes: "Food," "Car," and "Discretionary." Those three items were the only ones where I used cash. Everything else was automatically put into savings and checking. When I went to the supermarket, I pulled out the Food envelope for money. I never spent more than was in the envelope. When I needed to pay for gasoline or an oil change, I went to the Car envelope. For my discretionary expenses (dating, clothing, sports, and entertainment), I went to that envelope. What I found was that I was willing to spend less on food and my car in order to protect my discretionary money!

All my other cash went into checking, savings, and investment. My savings money initially funded an emergency fund. Then it funded the down payment on my house. Soon after that, I was buying stock and joining dividend reinvestment plans. The amounts were small, but it was a start.

How did my free-spending friends view my envelopes?

There might have been a snicker or two in the early years. What you come to realize, though, is that *everyone* wants savings, a home, and financial security. The snickers vanished. But while my friends praised my goals, they ignored my method. They understood my aims but chose not to mimic. How did they react when they wanted to do something on Saturday night and I told them, "Sorry, discretionary is gone for this week"? Nothing. Everyone understands "no money." No person ever suggested that I take money away from my goals to go to Tahiti (yes, I really did have to pass on that).

Over the last thirty-three years, with increasing frequency of late, all my friends have asked the following at some point:

Where did you learn about the envelopes?

Why didn't you get us to save?

How did you afford to do so much?

Here are the answers. The envelopes were a manifestation of my budget. Money in a wallet didn't create a visual of what I'd set out to achieve. Separating the money into envelopes did. It made my financial life easy.

Furthermore, there isn't a person who knew me who didn't know about my budget. They all knew I was saving and why. I encouraged all of them to "get a plan." For many, though, it seemed like too much work. Unfortunately, without a plan, dollars go unallocated. Everything seems affordable in the right setting. Truly, if you don't have some kind of a plan and method, you can't know if something's affordable or not.

After thirty-three years at this, I now own my home and owe no money to anyone. I'm working on a very comfortable retirement. I've always been optimistic about life because I've always been working to reach a goal. I knew my aim and when I was going to get there. Pleasant surprises, like raises and promotions, were also a time to rebudget.

Think about it. It makes sense that my financial life has actually been easy—right from the moment I realized I had dreams yet $0 in my account to afford them.

## Hot Wheels, Baby, Hot Wheels!
### By BoSpelman

My first car was a 1981 Monte Carlo that I bought for $2,500. I borrowed to buy it and still owed a little when I upgraded to my 1986 Grand Prix LE. Wire wheels, gloss black, power everything, and a 305 V8 4-barrel purring under the hood. A friend of mine called it a "chick machine," but the only girlfriend I had while driving that gas guzzler broke up with me.

Anyhow, I didn't get out of that cycle of car-buying debt until almost ten years later. Along the way, I maxed out my credit card to buy the latest electronic toys and paid only the minimum each month. I finally woke up from my financial slumber and worked very hard to become debt-free for the first time since high school.

In hindsight, I have calculated that if I'd put my $1,000 life savings into Microsoft in the 1980s, I would've been able to pay cash for my first house in 1999 and still have plenty left over. Obviously, few could have known to invest in Microsoft back then, but I would gladly have given up the luxury of driving that so-called chick machine just to get the market's average return in an index fund.

By the way, I met my beautiful wife while driving a 1977 Buick Estate Wagon with vinyl seats and an AM Delco push-button radio. She told me later that she was impressed that I didn't feel the need to own an expensive, fancy car like other guys. I guess that says something about love.

I was foolish before I met her. Now I'm a Fool.

## The Great Map of Your Future
### By aromadot

I'm fifty-six years old, which is pretty old from a teenager's point of view. I know because my nine-year-old grandson thinks I'm very, very, *very* old. When I was young, I also thought about "old" people but never imagined that one day I'd be one.

As a teenager I thought I was invincible. I thought everything in my life would be perfect. And my life has been very good, really. But it's also zipped on by, and now I'm struggling to prepare financially for retirement. Why? Because I didn't consider retirement when I was young.

Now that I'm older and oh so much wiser (trust me, as a teenager you think you'll never say those words, but you will), the one financial thing that you should look at, study, look at, and study again, is a "compound interest chart." This chart will clearly prove to you why you need to start, right now, saving and investing. The younger you start, the more time and money works for you. You cannot have back the years that you waste. Get one of these charts and look at it right now. Tack one up on your wall. Look at it every day. And know you can either waste that day or make it count. I say, *make it count.*

### Setting Up an IRA Account at Sixteen
### By PosNetWorth

I know that IRA accounts don't seem sexy. Retirement is a long way off when you're a teenager. My uncle sat down with me when I got my first job, and he told me to start saving for retirement as soon as possible. "Interest makes the money grow over time," he said. "And the more *time* the *better.* If you don't put the money into an IRA now, you won't necessarily get the chance to make it up later. There's a limited amount you can put in each year."

Sure, I saved some money. I used it to buy pizzas and textbooks and other stuff in college—and I was grateful for those. But nothing went into an IRA account. I didn't know how to do that. It seemed unnecessary. I didn't want to figure out how to invest. And somehow, over the course of a few years, all my savings money from work just disappeared.

Now I'm in my twenties, and I'm starting to think I made a mistake. Think about it. Even if I'd saved only 5 percent of my money, I'd be better off. Really, even if I'd just parked it in a CD, I'd have a lot of money. I really didn't need to know everything about stocks, bonds, and mutual funds to start investing in my future. All I needed was enough insight to know that, in the long run, saving would make a big difference.

If you save faithfully, retirement might not be so far off (if it seems decades and decades away now). Imagine retiring while you're still young enough to travel the world and have some fun. You won't have to get a job you don't really like when you're seventy, as some have to, to supplement the Social Security check (if you even believe Social Security will exist when you qualify).

Saving in an IRA when you're sixteen might not seem sexy. But you're gonna be pretty darned happy later in life when you have no anxiety about your finances. Time to go put more money in my IRA. Even if it's just a small amount.

### Absolutely the Best Job Ever
### By drewchmiel

Given the chance to relive my teen years, I would not—I repeat, *not*—even consider the more popular teen career choices. Stuff like being a drive-through attendant or grocery bagger (that was my personal choice).

Instead, I'd walk—nay, *run*—to the nearest private golf club. Sure, you start out wiping off golf cart seats at five-thirty A.M. Ouch. Tough wake-up call! But soon enough, you work your way up to club cleaner or caddie. The pay is excellent. Most teens can make an easy $600–$800 per week via tips and salary.

A second benefit is the use of the course at specified times. It never hurts to be a good golfer. The people you'll meet on the course, and the lessons you can learn from them, are very valuable. Many of the members are business owners or executives of large corporations. You'll see these people week in and week out.

Then, when you're pounding the pavement after college to find your first job, who better to call than the member who's known you for the last four years? Just ask for their advice. What you'll find is that if they trusted you with their clubs, they most certainly will initially trust you with their accounting books, computer networks, or whatever type of business they run. From there, you'll have to earn their respect with hard work and integrity. But you'll most certainly get a chance to prove yourself.

Working at a private golf course . . . great pay, free use of the course, and a growing network of interesting people. It's too good to be true.

### A Life's Work (and a Smoky Mountain Gain)
### By Henny Bulten, mother of an overachiever

My father advised me on looking for a job. He said:"Keep bugging them until they get sick of you and hire you or figure out that you're serious." It usually worked.

My children never had trouble finding a job, though. They followed the basic rules: dress nicely, smile, be conscientious and honest and hardworking. You may not always like your boss, but you'll learn valuable life skills regardless. Be the best you can be at work.

My eldest daughter used work as a wonderful way to see the world. In high school and college, she landed a different job each summer. She worked at a cookie store and learned to decorate pastries. She worked in the Smoky Mountains at a gift store during the week, while leading church services on Sunday for campers. She was a waitress at a Michigan golf resort. She worked in a pet store in south Florida. She was a cashier at a buffet restaurant. She was a summer camp counselor. She worked in press relations at school in Indiana. And she took a mission trip to Mexico. And yes, she also worked at that famous fast-food chain where the Hamburglar runs free and where *you deserve a break today.*

Through these varied careers, she had the advantage of making friends all over the country. She ate for free, got great discounts on gifts for Christmas and birthdays, learned new work and life skills, and figured out what she really wanted to do with her life. And because of her varied experiences, the family benefited through her networking. One evening, her younger sister was stranded with car trouble on a trip through Tennessee. Fortunately, it was near a town where her elder sister had made friends through her summer job in the Smokys. We called the friends, and they put her up for the night and found a mechanic.

If you don't want to change jobs yearly, at least find a job in the food industry. You can feed yourself for free or at a deep discount (one of your primary costs in life). And if you don't enjoy the job, stick it out long enough to learn people skills and new occupational skills. Then you'll know what you *don't* like doing. You can try something else until the shoe fits.

When my daughter graduated from college, she still changed jobs frequently, but she enjoyed new challenges. Today, she's a full-time stay-at-home mom with two toddlers. She still does everything well, as far as her mother's concerned.

### Six Ways to Build Your Future
### By mweaner

These are my top six lessons. Some were learned early, some late, and some I'm still trying to master.

1. **Learn to read a financial statement.** Learn the difference between assets and liabilities, income and expenses. It won't take long to learn this stuff. Employers think most young people know little or nothing about money, accounting, or finance. Why? Mostly because, in my own experience as an employer, they don't. Learn these things early; apply them to your work whatever it is, and your employer *will be impressed* because you'll stand out from your peers.
2. **Treat your financial life like a business.** For years, I never worried about my personal checking account; it took care of it-

self every couple of weeks when I tossed the paycheck in. I had no savings to speak of. I only read my credit card statements to see what the minimum payment was that month. It wasn't until I started paying close attention to my cash, my debts, and the cost of those debts that my financial life improved. I put my life on a balance sheet and income statement. I wasn't making any more money necessarily, but I was *keeping more* of it, which is just as good. A business that consistently pays out more than it takes in will eventually be bankrupt; the same is true for all of us as individuals. Avoid doing so!

3. **Understand the real risk of credit cards.** Credit cards are every bit as addictive and deadly to your financial well-being as drugs are to your physical well-being. It's *easy* to run up $5,000 in charges for pizza, books, concert tickets, dates, gas, clothes, and music. I know. I did. And more. At 18 percent interest, the one-year cost of $5,000 in charges is almost $1,000 if you pay just the minimum due. In effect, you're renting those things you bought, and wow, the rent is high. *Paying the minimum on a $1,000 debt at 18 percent interest will take you nineteen years to pay off!* You wouldn't go into Sam Goody and pay $30 for a CD that is priced at $15, would you? But when you charge that CD and then take four years to pay it off, that's what you've done.

4. **Start saving for the big things and the rainy days, *now*.** Even if you can save only a little. The habit is more important than the amount. 'Nuff said.

5. **Start saving for retirement, *now*.** Even if you can save only a little. The government (Social Security), your family, and your employer aren't responsible for your comfort in your old age. You are. Retirement saving today is an investment in yourself. The return is being able to enjoy the last half of your life without having to work unless you want to.

6. **As soon as you have an income, start giving some of it away.** Even if you can give only a little. Just dropping the loose change from your pocket into the Salvation Army pot during the holidays counts. Being charitable feels good; it's the right thing to do; it makes our world a better place.

### Be Your Own Boss
### By may1ta

Many teens today have marketable skills that people are willing to pay good money for. Rather than work at McDonald's making $6 or even a whopping $8 per hour, wouldn't you rather work for yourself? You certainly can make significantly more money; you'll determine your own schedule; and you'll learn the many aspects of running a small business.

When I was sixteen, I started my own venture. I called it Computer Doctor. The whole concept was prompted by of one of my high school teachers after fixing his computer. I then relied on word of mouth, newspaper, and local industry magazines for my marketing. I would walk into a customer's home, fix his computer, install hardware and software, and train him on how to use it.

For this service I charged $35 per hour (much better than my buddies or even my older brothers were making). I carried this business with me to college and provided my services for fellow students. My business helped carry me through college.

Now, you might be thinking, Hey, I don't know how to fix computers. That's fine. I'll bet you know how to operate a rake, a lawn mower, a snowblower, and so on. Or perhaps you have a specialized skill or talent you can use. Perhaps you can make decorations, fix furniture, repair cars and small engines, or just about anything else. There are endless numbers of products and services you can provide with less than $100 in start-up costs.

In short, don't think the only way to make money out there is through those typical teenager jobs. Be creative and use your smarts to learn the rewards of self-reliance early in life. You can generate substantial money, and even greater amounts of pride, in starting up your own venture.

### And Now, Back to Your Regularly Scheduled Programming . . .

We hope you enjoyed these contributions as much as we did! What a bright group of writers, thinkers, and helpers. Our heartfelt thanks goes out to these members of The Motley Fool community for sharing valuable ideas and colorful stories.

Help like this is available every day of the week on our Web site at Fool.com, particularly in our Young Fools section. Just type

www.teens.Fool.com

into your browser. Click around and learn more about earning, saving, investing, and yes . . . spending money Foolishly! And learn with some of the great contributors here.

Finally, we'll look for you in our $1,000 yearly contest. Share your greatest financial ideas at www.teens.boards.Fool.com, send your e-mail to contest@Fool.com, or regular mail to Teen Contest at:

The Motley Fool
123 North Pitt Street
Alexandria, VA 22314

No purchase necessary. Void where prohibited. For a complete list of rules, please go to www.Fool.com/folly.

Now back to the book!

# PART II

# THE SEARCH FOR GREATNESS

# Bonus Section: The Search for Greatness

• • • • •

I never wanted to be famous. I only wanted to be great.
—*Ray Charles*

We'll start in late November 2000. The company is Enron.

With tens of billions in annual sales, Enron is the seventh largest business in America, providing open electronic networks over which a wide variety of commodities can be traded. Whether you want to buy or sell gas, electricity, bandwidth, or water, Enron provides the digital platform to do so. Based in Houston, Texas, the company has more than twenty thousand employees.

Enron is trading above $75 a share. The stock has risen five times in value over the preceding five years, making its shareholders extremely happy: $5,000 invested in Enron in 1995 is worth $25,000 in November 2000. The price tag on the entire company, obtained just by multiplying that $75 share price times the number of total shares outstanding, is an awe-inspiring $60 billion. Wall Street loves the company. The financial media loves the company. One of us brothers (that would be Dave) has put the stock in one of his young children's accounts.

Enron is the envy of every great business.

Now, flash forward just one year with us. It's late November 2001. Enron is gasping for air. The stock is down to just 40 *cents* per share. The business, worth $60 billion a year earlier, is virtually worthless. Thousands of people will lose their jobs—many more have already lost their invested money. Enron is headed into bankruptcy; its auditors and executive team have confessed that the company inaccurately over-stated its performance; the leadership of Enron is disgraced. The federal government's securities police, the Securities and Exchange Commission, announce they will investigate the business for fraud. The Senate Commerce Committee holds exploratory hearings.

Enron shareholders have lost everything.

As you turn these pages and read on, you begin a never-ending journey. The stock market is an adventure with surprising twists and hairpin turns. It's a world where those that appear the very best can crumble in a year. A world where underdogs can rise up, win for a decade, then fall apart publicly and painfully. And come back five years later! A world where fortunes are most likely to be made by the patient, persevering, and thoughtful. And a world where fortunes are lost every day by the impatient, despondent, and thoughtless. It's a world that may just fascinate you.

It is the world of public business and common stock.

Let's rewind to winter 1994. This time the company is America Online.

With fewer than five hundred thousand subscribers, AOL is a largely unknown on-line service. It's smaller than Prodigy; it's smaller than CompuServe. And as a company, it's not yet making any money. AOL's advertising costs are prohibitive. They shovel truckloads of free sign-on disks across the country. They drop inserts into magazines and run flashy television ads. Before AOL ever turns a dollar of profit, it will have spent more than $300 million on marketing and advertising. Even when it does turn profitable, the conventional wisdom holds that larger competitors, like AT&T and Microsoft, will eventually smother America Online. The tunnel looks dark. The company is valued at $100 million.

Flash forward seven years. America Online is the now largest on-line service in the world, with more than thirty million members, each paying over $25 per month to sign on to AOL. At this point, America Online has also acquired Time Warner, the largest media company in the world. Its overall business is now valued in excess of $150 billion. Five-year owners of America Online stock are unthinkably happy; the stock is up more than a hundred times in value: $10,000 invested in the company is worth $1 million.

Now let's pick up where we left off. . . . As you turn these pages and read on, you begin a never-ending journey. The stock market is an adventure with surprising twists and hairpin turns. It's a world where those that appear the very best can crumble in a year. A world where underdogs can rise up, win for a decade, then fall apart publicly and painfully. Then come raging back five years later! A world where fortunes are made most dependably by the patient, persevering, and thoughtful. A world conversely where fortunes are lost every day by the impatient, despondent, and thoughtless. It's a world that may just fascinate you.

# ·STEP 10·

# Finding Great Companies

· · · · ·

*All there is to investing is picking good stocks*
*at good times and staying with them as long as they*
*remain good companies.*
—*Warren Buffett*

America's greatest investor of all time, Warren Buffett, makes it sound easy. It isn't always so. Although investing in individual companies doesn't carry the sophistication of performing brain surgery, it does take work. Not high-level calculus. Not obscure theoretics. But, yes, you'll need common sense and a brain. Warren Buffett has been putting his noodle to work in the stock market for decades. In fact, he got started very young. Younger probably than you. *Before* he was a teenager.

Many people don't yet know who Warren Buffett is, but they're likely to hear of him frequently in the decades to come. If you care about the lists (we don't) that come out each year ranking the world's richest people, you'll find Warren Buffett's name very near the top. Worth more than *$30 billion*, he's usually one or two spots below his friend Microsoft founder Bill Gates.

Buffett is an inspiration to many investors because he didn't get rich quick. He didn't win the lottery. Instead, he's made a fortune over his entire lifetime. It started with a newspaper route and has led to remarkable wealth. Throughout, Buffett's been saving money and investing it. Where? Into carefully chosen companies whose businesses he knows thoroughly well.

But let's introduce you more formally to the man you'll probably want to emulate, if you plan to buy the stocks of individual companies.

## Meet Warren Buffett

Warren Buffett was like any middle-class child. He was born and raised in Omaha, Nebraska, to hardworking and honest parents. Early on, he began to distinguish himself as a fine mathematician with an eye toward finance. His fascination for the stock market grew each year. He began reading every book he could find related to money, the business world, and the stock market. At age eleven, he bought his first shares of stock.

Buffett made mistakes and lost money along the way, as every investor does. But he kept learning and applying the new wisdom. And it seems as though every investment experience he had informed him more about the world of business. Why did a company succeed when others failed? he asked himself. What made for great managerial leadership? How did a business maintain its competitive edge?

Buffett was involved in businesses throughout his childhood. He bought bottles of Coca-Cola and delivered them to friends at a profit. He read books about horse racing and published a racetrack tip sheet that he sold to subscribers. He was a newspaper carrier and also found time to hunt for and sell recycled golf balls.

While at Woodrow Wilson High School in Washington, D.C., Buffett and a friend bought a reconditioned pinball machine for $25. The two of them formed the Wilson Coin Operated Machine Company and struck a deal to put the machine in a barbershop. At the end of the first day, the coin box in the machine had $4 in it. "I figured I'd discovered the wheel," Buffett said. Eventually, the pinball business was netting the boys $50 per week. Buffett had $9,000 in the bank by the time he graduated from high school. (Adjusted for inflation, that's like having more than $66,000 at high school graduation today.)

These days, Buffett heads up a company he bought and built. It's named Berkshire Hathaway, headquartered in Omaha, Nebraska. He likes to refer to it as a painting. He and his close partner, Charlie Munger, are the painters, dipping their brushes and stroking the corporate canvas with color. They've been doing this for thirty years. Berkshire Hathaway today is a collection of many smaller companies that Buffett has bought in their entirety.

Berkshire Hathaway owns Dairy Queen, GEICO (insurance), Benjamin Moore (paint), Borsheim's (jewelry), See's Candies, Executive Jet,

FlightSafety (pilot training), Nebraska Furniture Mart, Dexter Shoe, and the *Buffalo News* (a newspaper company). He also owns big and small chunks of many other companies, having accumulated their stock over time. As of 2000, for example, Berkshire Hathaway owned 11 percent of all of American Express, 8 percent of Coca-Cola, 9 percent of Gillette, 18 percent of the Washington Post Company, and 3 percent of Wells Fargo.

How has Buffett done?

Well, he started with his own small savings, and he's invested so well that his company is now worth more than $100 billion (a tenth of $1 trillion). Remember how the stock market on average has grown by about 11 percent per year? Buffett's company has grown by nearly 24 percent per year, on average, since 1965. He has been twice better than the market per year—one of the greatest reflections of market outperformance in the history of public markets. In fact, if any of us had been around all the way back in 1956, when the then twenty-five-year-old Warren Buffett formed his first partnership, we could've done even better. Had we given him $1,000 to invest for us then, that amount would be worth more than $20 million today.

Buffett is the da Vinci of business and investing.

There's a lot more to learn about and from Warren Buffett, but for now, draw one key lesson. Buffett has done shockingly well not by investing in obscure companies, but by avoiding them. Not by hoping some fantastic and highly technical discovery might make him rich. Instead, he has stuck to what he understands, knows, likes, and has faith in. Hamburgers and soda pop and paint and jewelry and insurance.

With the discipline, the fervent interest, and the drive, anyone can be successful as a stock market investor. You may not accumulate quite the same amount of wealth as Warren Buffett. His net worth exceeds more than $30 billion as of this writing. But how about trying to do 1/30,000th as well as he has? That would make you a millionaire.

### Where to Find Companies

So how do you get started at this?

First, you'll want to think about what it is on this earth that fascinates you. Is it woodwork? Or the piano? Travel? Is it style and grace and fashion? Or is it military defense and aerospace? Is it the mind, the psyche, and the soul? Or maybe banking and commerce?

Whatever your interests, companies feed them. The over ten thousand public companies in America, ones whose stock you can own, supply products and services relating to all of the categories above and thousands more. As you learn more about business and more about the world around you, you'll come to recognize that there's really nothing in America that isn't tied to public business.

If you start with what businesses interest you and stick with your interests, you'll dramatically improve your chances of being 1/30,000th of Warren Buffett. You'll already be well ahead of a great number of investors—investors who make the mistake of buying a stock because they heard someone else bragging about it, or saw it mentioned on financial television, or read a short article on it in a business magazine. Don't do that. Don't feel you have to invest in *other* people's interests or beliefs in order to do well. Stick to your knitting.

Do you fit any of the following groups?

1. Are you a computer wizard? Then focus on companies that make computer equipment and software that you understand and respect: IBM, Dell, Gateway, Sun Microsystems, Microsoft, Intel, Oracle, and so on.
2. Do you love video games? Look at Electronic Arts, Activision, Sony, and other competitors. Start thinking about which ones are the leaders of the future.
3. Do you enjoy hanging out at the mall with friends? Focus on retailers, then. Check out Abercrombie & Fitch, the Gap, Bebe Stores, The Limited, American Eagle Outfitters, Ross Stores, Pacific Sunwear, and the like.

---

## Take It from Me

### Focus on What You Know

I bought Wal-Mart stock because one of their stores popped up in my neighborhood two years ago. I noticed a lot of people went there to shop, including my parents, because of the cheap prices and good quality. I buy most of my CDs there because I can get four CDs for $60. (Over at the mall, it's three CDs for $60.) And every time I go to Wal-Mart, the parking lot's full and the stores are crowded. Wal-Mart also owns a chain called Sam's Club that is a lot like Costco. Lots of people go to both Costco and Sam's Club. So I decided to invest in Wal-Mart.—Donald Hoang, 14

4. Do you love the world of media and entertainment? Focus on newspapers, TV networks, cable networks and channels, movie studios, magazines, publishers, and more. Learn more about companies like AOL Time Warner (which owns HBO, *Sports Illustrated,* and *Time* among many other things), Viacom (which owns CBS, Showtime, and MTV among many other things), GE (which owns NBC among many other things), Walt Disney (which owns ABC and most of ESPN among many other things), and others.

5. Are you a fan of eating? There are loads of food and beverage companies, restaurants, and supermarkets to follow. Think of Coca-Cola, Pepsi (which also owns Frito-Lay), McDonald's, Starbucks, Krispy Kreme, Wendy's, Safeway, Sara Lee, Heinz, Hershey, Tootsie Roll, Wrigley, Whole Foods Markets, and more.

From there, look around your home and your life. Open the fridge. You'll find products made by a variety of public companies. Open your closet. You'll find more. Open the medicine cabinet. Johnson & Johnson and Pfizer will peek up at you. Then look around outside. Check your mailbox. There might be something from FedEx or UPS. On the street, you'll see Ford and General Motors and Chrysler, fueled by companies like ExxonMobil and Texaco. Overhead roars a Boeing 767. Then look down at your feet and you might see Nike, Reebok, or Timberland. Once at school, look down at your notebook. There's Mead. In your hand, a Bic pen. In math class, a Texas Instruments calculator.

Remember that the ordinary can be extraordinary. While so many adults search for what they think are hidden gems—the gold-mining business in Uzbekistan, an unknown gizmo company, a something-my-uncle-Harold-told-me-about company—you can instead be quietly and

---

## Famous Words

*Even the amateur investor who lacks training and time to devote to managing his investments can be reasonably successful by selecting the best-managed companies in fertile fields for growth, buy[ing] their shares and retain[ing] them until it becomes obvious that they no longer meet the definition of a growth stock.*

—T. Rowe Price

gradually getting rich by holding shares of companies like Home Depot or General Electric.

## What Companies Are You Familiar With?

Let's do some brainstorming, people. Stop reading for a half hour. Open your minds up. Let's see what companies you can come up with. Take a walk around the house. Open up your knapsack. Think about your hobbies. Rest your eyes, dream, and remember. We're asking you to come up with more than twenty-five companies here, companies whose products and services you use and like. That's a piece of cake.

Company Name                                          Ticker Symbol

What I wear:

_____        _____

_____        _____

_____        _____

_____        _____

_____        _____

_____        _____

Where I shop:

_____        _____

_____        _____

_____        _____

_____        _____

_____        _____

_____        _____

What I like to eat:

_____        _____

_____        _____

_____        _____

_____        _____

_____        _____

_____        _____

Where I eat:

_____        _____

_____        _____

_____        _____

_____        _____

_____     _____
_____     _____

My hobbies:

_____     _____
_____     _____
_____     _____
_____     _____
_____     _____
_____

My interests:

_____     _____
_____     _____
_____     _____
_____     _____
_____     _____
_____

Products and services I use and like:

_____     _____
_____     _____
_____     _____
_____     _____
_____     _____
_____

Once you've got the company names listed, circle the five to ten companies that interest you the most and that you believe in the most. Now your task is to go find their ticker symbols.

You may have discovered that a company is private (or "privately held"), meaning that it doesn't have stock that the public can buy, doesn't have any ticker symbol. If you wrote down Mars Bars, that's owned by Mars Inc., a wonderful but privately held business. You may also find that a business you're interested in is actually owned by another company. For instance, if you wrote down HBO because you like to sink low in the couch and watch movie after movie, then you'll find out that HBO is owned by AOL Time Warner. The ticker symbol for the company, appropriately, is just AOL on the New York Stock Exchange.

We are asking you now to find the ticker symbols of all of the companies (or their parent companies) you've circled above. You can

look up companies and their ticker symbols at www.Fool.com and
http://quote.Fool.com.

### Build a Watch List

Now that you have a list of companies you know and like, it's time to
focus on them. Some of them are decent companies. Others are outstanding. And frankly, some of them are weak, *very weak.* Let's do our
best together to try to avoid the weak ones. They can cost you a lot of
your hard-earned savings over time.

For starters, though, we'll just
begin to watch all of these stocks.
Set up a portfolio on-line. Or simply track the performance of your
companies by following their
ticker symbols and price moves in
the newspaper. You needn't list
out all twenty-five; perhaps pick
your favorite ten. This is your
*watch list.* A watch list is helpful
for several reasons:

> ### Famous Words
>
> *It only takes a handful of big
> winners to make a lifetime
> of investing worthwhile.*
> —Peter Lynch

- It helps you track and remember companies that interest you—regardless of whether you've invested money in them.
- You'll learn to follow these businesses and see how they react to
  good and bad news. Maybe you're fascinated by Whole Foods Markets, offering organic food across the nation. As they open new
  stores, you can track how those new stores do each year while following the company's stock price.
- Out of the longer list, you can create a short list of companies you
  really think will succeed. If you keep these lists for a long time—
  let's say a year—you can follow how well the companies are doing.
  Perhaps you're enthusiastic about the food business but notice that
  many of your restaurant stocks have tanked (not unusual since running a restaurant is a very tough business). This can help frame
  your thinking as an investor for the rest of your life.

# ·STEP 11·

# Tracking Your Companies
· · · · ·

*We want the business to be 1) one that we can understand,
2) with favorable long-term prospects, 3) operated
by honest and competent people, and 4) available at a
very attractive price.*
—*Warren Buffett*

Warren Buffett's approach to investing, as he points out above, is surprisingly simple. We think we can make it even simpler. When you're trying to decide whether to invest in a company, ask yourself these two questions:

. Is this really a high-quality company?
. Is the price attractive?

It all hinges on *quality* and *price*.

If you focus just on one or the other, you can get into trouble. Imagine the Tattoo Advertising Co. (ticker: YOW). Perhaps you've studied it quite a bit and you're really impressed. It's clearly a top dog in its industry, and you see it knocking the socks off all its competitors. Any way you look at it, it's a high-quality enterprise. So you buy a bunch of shares, and within a year the stock has fallen 60 percent. YOW indeed! The problem might have been that *everyone* at the time was overenthusiastic about Tattoo Advertising. Its stock had been bid up to outrageous heights.

Even the very best companies can trade at prices higher than they deserve.

Similarly, you may have stumbled upon an old wicker stand down in the basement of your house and started to research the company that made it. It turns out the stand was made by the One-Legged Chair Company (ticker: OOPS). You search around for information and begin comparing OOPS with the stocks of other chair companies. You've come to the conclusion that the price looks pretty cheap. It's trading at one times its total sales, while its two leading competitors are trading at three times their total sales. Here, look at the examples:

| Company Name | Annual Sales | Price of the Company | Multiple of Sales |
|---|---|---|---|
| One-Legged Chair Company | $45 million | $45 million | 1x |
| Big Al Dog's Furniture Company | $100 million | $300 million | 3x |
| Reading Chairs Incorporated | $29 million | $87 million | 3x |

You're asking yourself, as you gaze adoringly at your old wicker stand, "What the heck is happening here?" Big Al Dog's and Reading Chairs Inc. are both being priced at three times their annual sales. It stands to reason, you think, that someday the One-Legged Chair Company will also trade for three times its sales. That would make it a $135 million company and would triple every dollar invested into it today.

You're about ready to sign on to your custodial account on-line and invest your savings from your summer job into the One-Legged Chair Company.

But wait! The game of pricing companies can be much trickier than this. What if One-Legged Chair Company is actually losing fifty cents for every dollar of sales, whilst the other two companies turn a profit on their sales? Or what if the One-Legged Chair Company has fifty-seven class-action lawsuits against it for actually selling one-legged chairs to unsuspecting consumers with banged-up and broken limbs today?

In either of these examples, simply taking a multiple off sales to value a business is focusing too much on numerical pricing and not enough on the analysis of business quality. Ignoring a company's quality and focusing just on its price is a mistake that too many people make. You need to evaluate the price of the stock *and* the quality of the business.

We can show you some ways to do so.

## Signs of High Quality

Here are some factors related to quality that you should consider whenever you're investigating a company.

## Industry Leadership

Is the company a leader in its industry? With many industries, you probably know the answer off the top of your head. For example, in the newspaper industry, Gannett (parent to *USA Today*) is top dog. The top dog usually ends up being worth the most money, often by a long shot.

## Future Growth

Is the company growing? Are its products and services becoming more relevant or less? What do you think about the five years ahead—will its pianos or Popsicles or sunglasses or reading lamps be in greater demand or less?

## Executive Leadership and Morale

What do you know about the leadership of the company? Have you read about their CEO? Have you learned some of the history of the company? Does the company have core beliefs and a philosophy of honesty and service? You can search out articles on your company and its leadership at Google.com and Yahoo.com. And how about talking to an employee at the company? Do they seem to have competitive spirit and a real interest in their employer? You really can get free information about this on the Internet easily. And isn't it worth asking these questions if you're going to invest your own money?

## The Competitive Landscape

Who are the company's leading competitors? Have you tried the competition's offering? Is it better or worse than the company you're following? How about the price of the competing products? How about the convenience of ordering the competitor's products? When you look for the leader in an industry, do not just assume that the biggest company is the leader. Instead, think about which companies make better products at better prices. Think about which companies make it very *easy* to buy from them. The leader in an industry is often a rising star, like Dell Computer, which certainly dominated Compaq, the one-time giant in the world of personal computing. It did so by offering quality computers at lower prices that could conveniently be ordered over the phone.

## The Business Model

How does the company make money? Think of the differences between Amazon.com and eBay. Both are in the business of on-line commerce. But they have very different business models. Amazon is more like a traditional retailer. It stores tons of books and CDs and toasters

## Pop Quiz

### Pop Quiz!

See if you can name one of the top companies in each of these industries:

_____ Soft drinks
_____ Athletic shoes
_____ Internet retailers, Internet commerce
_____ Fast food
_____ Film (for cameras)
_____ Discount stores
_____ Express delivery
_____ Toys and games

Answers:
• Coca-Cola, PepsiCo
• Nike, Reebok
• Amazon.com, Office Depot, eBay
• McDonald's, Tricon (owner of Taco Bell, Pizza Hut, and KFC)
• Eastman Kodak, Fuji
• Wal-Mart, Kmart
• FedEx, UPS
• Mattel, Hasbro

and garden hoses in massive warehouses across the country. When someone orders from Amazon, the company can quickly fill the order from one of these warehouses.

Meanwhile, eBay also helps people get the goods they want. But they hold no inventory. They just set up a Web site for auction trading between buyers and sellers, taking a profit from each sale. eBay doesn't buy products and store them. eBay doesn't build enormous warehouses across the country. It just provides an electronic platform on which others may trade.

Now, one of these companies, as of this writing, has not turned a profit (Amazon). The other has been profitable since it started (eBay). This is not to say that both can't be profitable and successful someday (though eBay does look like the favorite at this point). Amazon has to spend a lot more money to stay in business, employing warehouse employees, buying or leasing lots of real estate, and paying for products that sit on the shelves until they're sold. eBay just facilitates the trades of auctioneers and thus has lower expenses as a business.

It's important to know how your companies make their money.

### Protection

What's the up-front cost of doing business in your company's industry? Think of this as a moat around the castle of its business. If it takes a lot of money to get started, that can keep out would-be competitors. For example, it's much easier to enter the lawn-mowing business than the semiconductor equipment industry. The first just needs someone with a lawn mower. The second requires factories, expensive equipment, and highly specialized knowledge.

### Great Economics

Does the business model work for or against your company over time? This one's a bit trickier to figure out, but think through an example

---

### Comic Relief

#### Ten Signs You're Looking at a Low-Quality Company

1. The annual meeting presentation is done on an Etch-a-Sketch.
2. Your call to the company is greeted with, "If our product made you violently ill, please press one. If you're planning to sue us, please press two."
3. New line item introduced to the income statement: "Potential Revenue."
4. The company is named Planet Hollywood.
5. The very mention of its ticker symbol brings a chorus of laughter from co-workers.
6. The business, www.eMeringue.com (check it out), is based on selling pie meringues on-line.
7. One of the business costs mentioned in the annual report is "Bail."
8. The CEO reports that profitability depends on whether "23 45 83 54 9" hits on the Super Lotto next Saturday.
9. Revenue is reported in pennies.
10. The CEO has a red ball on his nose, rainbow-colored frizzy hair, and size twenty-four shoes.

with us. If it costs a company less the more it produces something, the economics of its business are excellent. Let's go back to the example of eBay. The company spent a lot of money designing and setting up its back-end infrastructure to serve its first auction customers. But now, adding millions more customers is relatively inexpensive. Is the same true for Amazon.com or not?

## Switching Costs

Are there high switching costs for customers? This is an important question. Is it easy for customers of your company to switch to the next best offering if they feel a need to? Imagine that you have an on-line account with America Online, where you've received e-mail for a year. Maybe you've set up a buddy list on AOL. Maybe you check your stocks and sports scores there. If so, you'll probably think twice about switching to another provider. And guess what that means? It means America Online can raise prices on its customers, regularly. Not surprisingly, that's exactly what AOL has done for years running.

## Brand Value

How well-known and strong of a brand name does your company have? If a company has a household name, it can be a profitable tool. New products introduced under the brand name will be much easier to market. Consumers generally go for familiar, trusted names. People are more likely to try a fancy new Nokia phone than one by Johnson (an unknown company). The values of the brand names at Coca-Cola, Microsoft, Disney, and Nokia have been estimated at more than $10 billion each.

◆ ◆ ◆

There are lots of other indicators of quality, such as a company's past performance, how much it spends on researching and developing new products and services, and how well it saves money from year to year. But, as you might expect, judging the quality of a company can be a bit like judging the quality of a person. You want to invest in honest people. You want to invest in smart people. You want to invest in interesting people. The same is true of the best companies.

## A Quality Worksheet

Here's a worksheet you can use to evaluate the quality of a company. Photocopy this page as needed (our lawyers give you permission this time!).

Company/industry name: _____

Is the company a leader in its industry? _____
_____
_____

What's the company's growth potential? _____
_____
_____

What's the company's competitive position? _____
_____
_____

What is the company's "business model"? How, exactly, does it make its money?_____
_____
_____

What are the company's competitive advantages? Does it enjoy any of the following:

Threat of entry: _____
_____

Great economics: _____
_____

High switching costs (meaning customers don't want to switch to another brand or service): _____
_____

Brand value: _____
_____

Other factors you feel are worth noting: _____
_____
_____
_____
_____

## What a Stock Price Means

A company's stock price is ultimately tied to the amount of cash it's expected to generate over its life. Think of young companies such as Amazon.com, which were valued in the stock market at many billions of dollars when they were still unprofitable. That's because investors expected that in the long run the companies *would be* profitable. In fact, many investors felt Amazon.com might well become *the* dominant retailer in the world.

If over the course of 2001 you witnessed the company struggling to make its first dollar of profit, and watched Amazon's stock price drop considerably, you no doubt recognize that many people lost confidence in Amazon.com's ability to dominate the retail future. The stock price is often a reliable advance indicator of a company's fortune or misfortune, even when in many cases you can't figure out *why* a given stock has been going up or down.

---

## Keep in Mind

### Bulls and Bears

In financial-speak, there are two terms you'll often run across: bulls and bears. A "bull" is a person who is optimistic or bullish about the future of the stock market or a specific company. A "bear" is someone less enthusiastic about the future of the stock market or the value of a particular company.

For most of the past century, the *bulls* have been right. The stock market has doubled in value, on average, every seven years.

Conversely, most companies in the public market do not meet with long-term success. *Bears* have won the day when we look at the overall performance of individual companies. Most don't succeed.

The general market rises dramatically because of the *minority* of public companies that are *truly special,* truly sustainably profitable, truly valuable. Thus, we advise that you be optimistic about the overall market's future but decidedly skeptical when you research individual companies.

### Evaluating a Company's Price

There are two pricing factors to consider when you evaluate any company: 1) its current price in the stock market; and 2) its intrinsic value. Take, for example, Yuckie Yogurt Inc. (ticker: YUM), trading on the stock market for $25 per share. And let's say that there are one million total shares of Yuckie Yogurt's business.

So, $25 is the current trading price of a single share of its stock. If you wanted to buy four shares of YUM, you'd pay $100 (along with a $10–$20 commission to a discount broker). The stock market has priced every share of Yuckie Yogurt's one million shares at twenty-five bucks.

But is it worth $25? Well, maybe not. The world of investors may have miscalculated the value of the business. Yuckie Yogurt may be heavily in debt, with no new stores coming and no sales growth. And the CEO might be losing respect at Yuckie corporate headquarters. If it seems ludicrous that investors could miscalculate the value of a business, hey, reflect on how we misjudge people in society. Someone with a hard-top convertible Mercedes *looks* rich. But what if he borrowed $20,000 to buy the car, has $28,000 in credit card debt, and just got laid off from work?

> **Famous Words**
>
> *Everything is worth what its purchaser will pay for it.*
> —Publilius Syrus
> (first century B.C.)

Looks can be deceiving. And the general market (and each one of us as investors) is prone to rely too much on how things appear at first glance. Our challenge as business-focused investors throughout our lives will be to understand how to evaluate a company regardless of its surface appearance or its stock's recent zigs or zags. We will want to learn to determine when a company's stock price is way too high or way too low.

Determining quality and price is the real challenge for great investors, smart consumers, and the world's business leaders.

Obviously, when a company's intrinsic value—or true value—is much higher than its current market value, you're looking at a bargain. Conversely, when a company's current price is way above its intrinsic value, look out below. Things could get nasty for investors.

Now it's time for us to provide you with some bad news. Perhaps you've expected this. So here it is. Dear reader, there is *no* way to look up a company's intrinsic value. There's *no* definitive answer to the question. There are opinions. There are debates. There are public analyses. There are loud proclamations, "Yuckie Yogurt stock is worth $35 a share. Today, it is priced at $25. I recommend a buy." But no matter how much is said, and no matter how many agree or disagree, there is never a definitive, clear, fair price to a business. Nor is there ever a completely predictable future justifying or invalidating today's quoted price.

No sure thing.

Now there are two pieces of good news to this problem.

The first is that if you ever get bored, restless, or frustrated with the challenge of valuing individual companies, you can always fall back to the total market index fund. Again, earning and protecting your financial independence is, frankly, not much more difficult than 1) always paying down your credit cards, 2) saving 10–20 percent of your salary, and 3) investing your long-term savings into the Vanguard Total Stock Market Index Fund.

KISF! (Keep it simple, Fool.)

The second bit of good news is that if you *are* interested in stock investing, you can learn ways to assess whether a stock's price is generally on the high or low side. Doing so successfully will take an open mind on your part and a willingness to learn new tricks and to admit you're sometimes wrong. It'll take your curiosity. It'll take your willingness to work through some numbers. As much as all of these, it will require your interest—indeed, even sometimes your love—for the businesses that you are studying. Finally, and most important, it will take perseverance. You will make mistakes. You will lose money on some of your investments. You will have to accept as your investment mantra: "Live and learn."

Is there any other way to live?

## When High Is Low and Low Is High

One critical mistake many make when valuing a company is focusing too much on just the stock price itself. Some will look at a stock trading at $4 per share and think, Oooh, that's cheap! Let me buy some of that! Or they'll see a stock price of $188 and gasp, thinking, Oh, my, that's far too rich for my blood!

Believe it or not, the $188 stock might be a bargain and the $4 stock may be horribly overpriced. In fact, more often than not, we'd say that's probably the case. The $188 stock would generally indicate a solid company (the stock had to get there in the first place, right?) that may be headed to $500 in five years, up more than 2.5 times in value. The $4 stock, on the other hand, may be headed to zero—zero, like the stock of

Enron, the company we cited at the outset of this chapter. We are not citing extreme cases here. These sorts of scenarios play out all the time on the stock market.

In March of 1997, one share of stock in the Washington Post Company cost about $350. That seemingly high price frightened away some investors. But just one year later, the price had risen past $500. Conversely, in July of 1999, one share of Xerox cost $50. Two years later, it fell all the way down to $9.

Analyzing a company's stock price per share on its own is a waste of time, because it's meaningless. As you'll soon see, the price per share is dependent simply on the number of shares available. Analyzing the price per share in the way we've criticized in this section is rather like saying one lottery or roulette number is better than another. This will make more sense in just a few pages.

To truly understand a company's stock price, you need to give it context, to compare it to something other than just the dollar number. In the chapters to come, we'll focus on things like the company's sales and earnings growth. How much cash a company has. How much debt it has. And what its market capitalization, or "market cap," is. A company's market cap is a much better indicator of its value than is its stock price. We'll explain why.

Read on, read on.

### The Market Cap

We may have just confused you with that last line, "A company's market cap is a much better indicator of its value than is its stock price."

Hey, how can that possibly be true when so many investors focus on the stock price from hour to hour and day to day? Well, quite frankly, our answer is that most people are looking at the wrong price. The stock price matters less to business-focused investors (those of us who believe a thorough knowledge of the business is your single best advantage as an investor) than does a company's market cap.

Let us explain.

Calculating a market cap (short for "market capitalization") is a quick way of approximating the price tag of an entire company. Simply multiply the current stock price by the total number of shares of a company's stock (the total ownership). You can find both numbers in many on-line stock quote services. Go to quote.Fool.com, type in the company's name or ticker symbol, then click on Snapshot. You'll find the information you need there.

So here's your calculation:

$$\underline{\hspace{4cm}} \times \underline{\hspace{4cm}} = \underline{\hspace{4cm}}$$
$$\text{Current Stock Price} \quad \text{Shares Outstanding} \quad \text{Market Cap}$$

As an example, let's look at Big Cars & Trucks Inc., a nationwide dealership of the biggest gas-guzzlin' driving machines known to man. The company's stock is trading at $40 per share. You dig around a bit and find that Big Cars & Trucks has issued sixty million shares of ownership. To calculate the total value of the company, simply multiply $40 per share by the sixty million total shares.

You'll get $2.4 billion. That's the market cap of the company. That's the price tag on the entire business. What that means is that if another company wanted to acquire Big Cars & Trucks Inc., they'd have to pay at least the combined value of all the shares, or $2.4 billion.

Can you see, from running this calculation, why the stock price doesn't matter so much? Without knowing how many shares of ownership there are, it's impossible to value the overall company. If this isn't extremely evident to you, imagine that Big Cars & Trucks Inc. was trading at $40 per share but only had one million shares of ownership. The market capitalization would be . . . what? It would be $40 per share times one million shares, or $40 million. That's a long way from $2.4 billion!

In order to value a company, you must know both the stock price and the total shares of ownership. (This is a concept you can introduce to your parents and their friends. You may even be shocked at how few people understand it.) To find the listing of the total shares of a company, simply order its annual report from the company or, even easier, travel to www.freeedgar.com—where all public companies must file their financial information every three months.

Now, investors often categorize companies according to their market cap. Here's one way you can think about company sizes:

Large-capitalization: $5 billion or more

Mid-capitalization: $1 billion to $5 billion

Small-capitalization: $250 million to $1 billion

Micro-capitalization: Less than $250 million

Thus, Big Cars & Trucks Inc. is a mid-capitalization, or "mid-cap" company.

## Do It Yourself

Take a few minutes and calculate the market caps for the following companies by going on-line and finding their current stock price and then multiplying by their number of shares outstanding. We'll help you with the numbers on the first few. But complete the remainder yourself by cruising over to quote.Fool.com, entering the ticker symbol, then clicking on Snapshot. You'll find all data needed there.

| Company | Ticker | Stock Price | Shares Outstanding | Market Cap |
|---------|--------|-------------|--------------------|------------|
| Hershey | HSY | $65.50 | 105 million | $6.9 billion |
| Tootsie Roll | TR | $38.25 | 34 million | $1.3 billion |
| General Electric | GE | $38.25 | 9.9 billion | $ |
| Microsoft | MSFT | $64.00 | 5.4 billion | $ |
| Boeing | BA | $ | | $ |
| AOL Time Warner | AOL | $ | | $ |
| Amazon.com | AMZN | $ | | $ |
| Yahoo! | YHOO | $ | | $ |
| Starbucks | SBUX | $ | | $ |
| Wal-Mart | WMT | $ | | $ |
| Kmart | KM | $ | | $ |
| Ford | F | $ | | $ |
| Coca-Cola | KO | $ | | $ |
| PepsiCo | PEP | $ | | $ |
| McDonald's | MCD | $ | | $ |
| Johnson & Johnson | JNJ | $ | | $ |
| Gap | GPS | $ | | $ |
| Abercrombie & Fitch | ANF | $ | | $ |
| Nike | NKE | $ | | $ |
| Reebok | RBK | $ | | $ |

Once you're done, look closely at the market caps and see what you notice. Compare companies that are in the same or similar lines of business. You may be surprised, for example, to see how much bigger Wal-Mart is than Kmart.

Also, please note again that the stock price alone can't tell you the worth of a company. Both General Electric and Tootsie Roll are trading at $38.25 per share. Yet General Electric, one of the largest companies in the world, is valued in excess of $380 billion, while Tootsie Roll is worth not much more than $1 billion. Same *stock* price, but a very big difference in *company* price.

Market caps provide a useful gauge of how highly the stock market is valuing a company. It can provide excellent context for the size and scope of businesses in this world. And regardless of whether you ever invest in individual stocks or not, you should be able to calculate market capitalizations. They'll make you far more knowledgeable of the world around you.

# •STEP 12•

## Launching an Investment Club

· · · · ·

Never doubt that a small group of thoughtful, committed
people can change the world: indeed, it's the
only thing that ever has!
—*Margaret Mead*

You now have a watch list of companies that interest you. You also can calculate their market capitalizations, to get a relative sense of their size. Further, you've already learned not to carry credit card debt. You know to methodically save a little bit of money. You know to invest your long-term savings into the stock market. You know that a total market index fund is a wonderful first and last step for stock market investors. And now you want to build on all that knowledge and learn more about individual companies and their stocks.

Given all that, in our opinion, now's the perfect time to begin forming your own investment club. Investment clubs are popular with people of all ages. There are more than thirty thousand investment clubs in existence in America today. Some meet informally, others are incorporated like businesses. Some are limited to investors with more than thirty years of investment experience, others are formed to help people get started. Investment clubs are especially useful if you're in any way afraid of tackling investing on your own. Band together with some of your friends, relatives, or friends of friends. Bring food, stay up late, crack jokes, and gradually, cooperatively, learn how to manage your money better.

### How to Frame a Club for Teens

If you're a club of teens, you *could* operate pretty much like any other investment club. But teens have some special characteristics:

1. As minors, teens can't have brokerage accounts of their own.
2. In just a few short years, teens may be off in college or working in a separate town, distant from each other.

Because of these factors, we advise creating an informal investment club with your friends. In many clubs, members put in new money each meeting; the club incorporates as a business; and the earnings are split out over long periods of time.

Given the factors above, we recommend stopping short of pooling your money together. Rather, meet regularly (every week or two); assign responsibilities to each member; discuss what you've been reading and learning; study companies individually, in groups, or all together; debate the merits of each business; and above all, enjoy yourselves.

To start your investment club, you need not open a brokerage account together; you need not pay regular dues; you need not invest money together. Instead, you can each use the information from your meetings to make individual decisions and invest on your own. This saves you the hassles of accounting for everyone's share of the group investments, dealing with tax issues (such as getting a tax ID number and filing special forms with your taxes), and even having a club treasurer.

In fact, we recommend this sort of club structure for the vast majority of the thirty-thousand-plus investment clubs in America today.

---

**Famous Words**

---

*Please accept my resignation. I don't care to belong to any club that will have me as a member.*
—Groucho Marx

---

### How to Start and Run a Club

1. **Start by talking to friends.** See who's interested. In our opinion, your club shouldn't be exclusively about finding great stocks. Broaden the aims. Meet to talk about money—how to save it, how to spend it. What computer to buy. Whether to buy a car or not. Every financial topic should be fair game. Then mix in some

Ping-Pong, board games, or just general chatter along the way. And then, yes, study public businesses together. Will Krispy Kreme succeed or fail? Will Gap lose its leadership status in informal clothing? If biotechnology is the wave of the future in medicine, what companies will win?

2. **Pick a name for your club.** As silly as this might seem, hey, coming up with a great name is important. It brings spirit to the group. You might choose to be Bob Dylan's Wallflower Investors or America's Greatest Money Stars or The Early Retirement Club or the Own a Hawaiian Beach House Club. Eight years ago, we chose the name The Motley Fool and have turned it into a profitable company with many more than the two brothers we started with!

3. **Agree on how you want to learn.** This is an important step, too. You must figure out how you'll learn the *most* possible with

---

## Take It from Me

### Top Ten Reasons to Participate in an Investment Club

1. You'll learn what schools forget to teach—a subject that will have a huge impact on your life.
2. You'll improve your chances of making money.
3. You may form lifelong friendships with the friends you learn with.
4. It's another extracurricular activity that college admissions will look at.
5. It also looks good on a résumé.
6. You can make contacts in the business world that you would not have otherwise made.
7. Your parents might support the club by giving you money to get started.
8. You may even end up being covered on the news or in the newspaper.
9. You'll earn the respect of fellow classmates, parents, and teachers.
10. You'll have the opportunity to change your life for the better.

—Bryan Sims, 18

the *least* amount of effort. (This is a wonderful basic principle for learning in high school, college, and throughout life.) The faster you learn something thoroughly, the more you can learn. And the greater your learning, the greater your life.

Our recommendation is that you be sure *not* to underdelegate. Instead, expect each member to participate actively. To be a member of this club, everyone must do some work. For example, if you're learning together how best to negotiate for a new car, is it really fair that one of you does all the research work while the others eat chips? Do you really want to be in a club where two people do all the research and thinking while the rest of the members hack off?

Finally, you might consider inviting one or more adults (parents, teachers, or others in the community) to give a guest talk at your club. Maybe the local hot-shot money manager will come by. Maybe the CEO of your town's newspaper will give a half-hour explanation of how his business works. Maybe one of your moms has excellent advice for finding great technology stocks. Maybe one of your dads has a wonderful way to save money faster. Guest speakers can add a different, valuable, and fun perspective that educates, amuses, and enriches.

4. **Find the best resources out there.** Here are some educational resources you can use:

  - Go to Amazon.com and search for investing and personal finance books that get four-star ratings or higher. You can read about great companies like Southwest Airlines (*Nuts!* by Kevin Freiberg), gain insight into famous stock market collapses (*Famous Financial Fiascos* by John Train), and learn how to get started investing (*One Up on Wall Street* by Peter Lynch). You can read books on the world's greatest investors (*Buffett: The Making of an American Capitalist* by Roger Lowenstein). And you can read books by The Motley Fool, if you've enjoyed this one.

    There is no shortage of great financial books. Ask for suggestions from your parents and their friends. You could literally read a book on investing, business, or personal finance each month for the rest of your life and never run out of great reading material.

  - Surf the Internet for enlightening articles. You'll find articles with tips on how to keep your credit card bill to zero. You'll find articles with the CEOs of major video game companies.

You'll learn about the success of Neiman Marcus's retail stores throughout the last half century. You'll find articles explaining why Enron collapsed overnight. You'll find articles that can explain how the banking business works and why investors have made so much money with it over time. And, obviously, so much more.

5. **Have fun, darn it!** If you and the others don't enjoy yourselves, the club is doomed.

Take a few minutes to think of and jot down the names of ten to twelve people you'd enjoy forming an investment club with. Then approach them to see if they'd be interested. Again, investment clubs will pay handsome intellectual, social, and economic rewards throughout your life.

| | |
|---|---|
| _____ | _____ |
| _____ | _____ |
| _____ | _____ |
| _____ | _____ |
| _____ | _____ |
| _____ | _____ |

### Tips from a Club-Savvy Teen

Bryan Sims is an eighteen-year-old who has taken the initiative to set up several teen investment clubs in Oregon. He champions investment clubs for teens through his Web site, at www.StartSmartClubs.com. Here are some tips he shares:

- Start by talking to a few close friends about the investment club you want to form. Tell them to mention it to other people. Eventually, people will hear about the club by word of mouth.
- As you talk to people, explain why investment clubs are so great. Not many teenagers are yet involved in them. So you'll become one of the few. Most important, you'll learn together at a young age about investing. The power of compounding is something that cannot be duplicated. The average investor doesn't begin until his or her thirties—a big mistake. You will be ten steps ahead of other teenagers.
- Remember that just because you don't like some people isn't a rea-

son to keep them out. They could end up picking the next Microsoft.

- Having an informational meeting with both teenagers and parents is critical before the formation of the club. Half of the time it's the parents who push for teens to join. So how about getting them to reward you with investable cash if you join? In other words, mooch some money off your parents! They might be reluctant to just hand over money, but if you're looking for money to put into stocks, they might change their minds. Remind them that "it's an educational experience."

- Once you have enough people, visit a local brokerage and talk to a broker. See if the brokerage will give you a special discount on fees and trading commissions. Remember, it makes sense for them to do this because 1) they'll be expanding their client base, 2) they may meet parents (potential clients) of the teen investors, and 3) it's good public relations for them. (My clubs have been written about in newspapers, and the brokerage firm we use gets some good press that way.) Don't be afraid to remind them of these things if it will get you discount trading. My club pays only $5 per trade—and we get to hold our meetings at our brokerage's office!

- After you've formed a club, understand that people always remember first impressions. The first meeting is absolutely the most important one of all. If you know some things about investing, don't talk over the heads of members who don't know as much. Have fun at your meeting, but don't have so much fun that some members get frustrated because there isn't enough learning. There's a tricky balance between learning and having fun, but you can strike it.

- The first two months (at least) should be devoted just to education. Learning about stocks and investing strategies is a must. How can you expect to invest in good companies if you don't know how to research and evaluate them? While you spend a few months learning, you can still be chipping in your money and your account can be growing, in preparation for your eventual purchases. Encourage members not to invest until they've learned.

- When you invest for the first time (or after a few months),

> ## Famous Words
>
> *If the job has been correctly done when a common stock is purchased, the time to sell it is* almost never.
>
> —Philip Fisher

get the local media involved, if you think that would be fun. You might get written about in your local newspaper or even interviewed on TV.

- After you get into the full swing of things, and if you're investing as a club, remember to invest for the long term. Don't let yourselves be rushed to make a decision about a company just because someone gets anxious. Stocks will always go up and down. It's the smart, patient investors who do best in the long run.

## Resources

You can learn a lot more about investment clubs at www.Fool.com/investmentclub. There are also many helpful books on investment clubs, such as *Starting and Running a Profitable Investment Club* by Thomas O'Hara and Kenneth S. Janke and *Investment Clubs: How to Start and Run One the Motley Fool Way* by Selena Maranjian.

# ·STEP 13·

# Understanding the Business

**. . . . .**

> Every fortune ever made in finance has rested on a simple premise. Those with the most information make the most money. That edge, knowing what others don't, is priceless.
> —*Paul Gibson*

Our society today collectively comprises the most properly educated, well-read, sophisticated, and scientific thinkers in human history. Our brains, far and away the most powerful engines on the planet, have created an extraordinary quality of life for many.

Just think back to last century.

At the turn of the twentieth century, automobiles didn't exist. Neither did airplanes. We had no penicillin to fight infection. There were no steel-framed buildings. No computers. We didn't have television sets or radios. We had only the crudest of communications tools. It took months to travel from New York to California. There was no Internet. Neither was there any mapping of the human genome to understand the recipe of human life (no conception whatsoever of a double helix). More important, perhaps, there were no microwave ovens to accelerate cooking for overworked authors.

Information was, relative to today, in very short supply.

Today, the availability of information on every imaginable subject is extraordinarily high. Just in the first decade of its popularity, the Internet has exponentially increased our access to new ideas, to statistical data, to the rest of the world. It changes, every year, how we learn and how much we learn. This improved access to new information has extraordinary value, and it's specifically a boon for anyone with a dollar saved and a dollar invested. Your financial life has a very able assistant now: it's called the Internet.

To paraphrase Paul Gibson, above, information is the cake, the candles, and the icing of the investment world. Without it you cannot celebrate, because you can't win. On the stock market, publicly traded American businesses are required to feed a steady diet of valuable information to their investors. They must tell every shareholder—whether it's a banker with $10 million invested or a high-schooler with $100 invested—how their business is doing, in detail, every three months. These published reports are freely available. They show everything from how much sales and profit the company generated to how much cash and debt the business has amassed. Again, this key financial data is updated *every ninety days* for every interested investor.

If you're a shareholder, you should be eager to see these reports. You're a part owner, after all. You'll want to know whether Southwest Airlines is selling more tickets than it did last year. You'll want to know how many subscribers *The New York Times* picked up in the last three months. You'll want to understand the economics of the new release of Electronic Arts' NHL hockey game. You'll want to know if Donald Trump paid down any of the massive debt carried by his casino business.

If you own any stock in these businesses, you'll want to know. And, by law, you have a right to know. This right, though, begs your responsibility. Because if you're going to invest in individual stocks, you owe

---

### Famous Words

*I knew that the more I understood about the company, the better off I would be.*
—Benjamin Graham

---

it to yourself to learn about your companies. This chapter is dedicated to teaching you some of the basics of *corporate financial statements* (a nasty phrase that sounds worse than it is . . . we really just want to teach you how to know if your company is succeeding).

So let's get started.

### Business Basics

Whether you start your own private business (and own all its shares of stock) or invest in a public company, you obviously want it to succeed. What does help a company win? Why do some—like Microsoft—earn money each year for thirty straight years? And why do others—like Planet Hollywood—lose money, fade into obscurity, and file for bankruptcy? What is it, you should wonder, that distinguishes a great from a poor business?

The answers are relatively simple (far simpler than running a great business).

The foundation of a great business is sustainable profit. From month to month, and year to year, the most successful companies earn and save. It's just exactly what you'll want out of your own professional life—a regular salary, regular savings, regular investment, and the gradual accumulation of what will ultimately be an enormous savings stash.

Yes, great companies are like great professionals: they work hard, they earn their money, they save their earnings, they invest those savings, and they reap the long-term benefits. Sorting through a company's financial statements is really nothing more than a search for these qualities: a nose for earning profit (or wages) and the discipline of savings.

In this chapter, we're going to concentrate your attention on just a few critical factors of success. They're found on two of the financial statements. We'll be looking at the "balance sheet" and the "income statement."

## The Balance Sheet:
## The Owing and Owning of Business

If you were to make up a personal balance sheet about yourself, you'd list all that you *own* and all that you *owe*. Your stereo would be an asset. If you own a car, that's an asset. Your shoes and shirts and socks would be assets. And hopefully more significant in value than these, the money in your savings and investment accounts would be assets.

What debts might you carry? Well, some student loans for college. Maybe you borrowed money to buy a car. We hope you have no credit card debt, though that would be listed here as well. And maybe you borrowed $50 from your sister. That's listed as a debt, too.

Those are your assets (what you own) and your liabilities (what you owe).

Obviously, you'd prefer to look down and see significantly more assets than liabilities on your personal balance sheet. You'd love to own a car outright, have $1,700 in your savings account, and be holding $3,000 in your investment accounts. No credit card debt. No debts to siblings. And you'd prefer to have student loan debt *only* if you're really getting a lot out of your college education (and you should be, if you're paying to be there).

The simple truth is that businesses are just like you. They want more cash than debt. They want more assets than liabilities. They want the financial security to weather tough economic times and the means to invest in new markets and new opportunities when they present themselves. Company financial plans are just like your financial plans. They are designed *toward* earnings, savings, and investments and *away from* expenses, debts, and eventual bankruptcy.

For now, two items on the balance sheet can give us a basic view of corporate assets and liabilities: 1) "Cash and Marketable Securities," and 2) "Long-Term Debt." The first is simply a reflection of how much money the business has in savings and investment accounts. The second is simply a reflection of how much money a business has borrowed that won't be repaid within the year. Clearly, you'll want to focus on companies whose cash and investments exceed its debt.

Take a look at a few real-world examples and our performance grade:

| Company | Cash and Marketable Securities | Long-Term Debt | Our Grade |
|---------|-------------------------------|----------------|-----------|
| Trump Hotels & Casinos | $100 million | $1.8 billion | F |
| AT&T | $10.9 billion | $31.8 billion | D- |
| Nike | $360 million | $640 million | C |
| Abercrombie & Fitch | $100 million | $0 | A- |
| Microsoft | $36.1 billion | $0 | A++ |

Please jot down conclusions you draw from the numbers above.

_____

_____

_____

_____

_____

Our look at these two items on the balance sheet gives us a first impression of how well the business is saving and investing for its future. We'll have to look at other factors to fill out this picture. But for now, it's easier to understand why Microsoft is doing so well when companies like AT&T are struggling. Microsoft is the great saver among companies, looking to set aside enormous fortunes for its future. AT&T recently has been the great borrower in corporate America . . . taking out substantial loans to buy properties of questionable value.

## The Income Statement

We now know how much a company has borrowed and saved, but clearly that's not enough data upon which to base an investment decision. What if someone you know, your older cousin Alison, is thirty-three years old, has $1,000 in savings, and has college student loan debts of $9,000? Does this automatically mean she's in financial trouble?

No, actually, it doesn't. If Alison will be earning a salary of $72,000 this year writing software for an architectural firm in San Francisco, the debts might not be a problem. If she sets aside 15 percent of that salary this year, she'll have saved $10,800. That's enough to pay down the debt and put away $1,800 for her future. If she continues to be disciplined, she'll be saving $10,800 per year. Furthermore, if she invests that money each year in an index fund, at the age of sixty-five she'll have $2.5 million set aside. (And that assumes she never gets a pay raise!)

> ### Famous Words
>
> *Seek facts diligently; advice never.*
>
> —Philip Carret

Wow. That's precisely the sort of person you'd love to invest in. She borrowed for her education (not a home entertainment center) and now plans to earn and save her way to a very secure financial future for herself and her family. Now you understand that just looking at debt and cash doesn't tell you enough. If you'd just looked at Alison's debt ($9,000) and her savings ($1,000), you'd have missed the real story.

The same is true when you study a business. In addition to the cash and debt positions at a company, you must know how much profit, or wages, the organization generates from its work each year. A company's income statement summarizes these every three months. It tells you how much, for example, Krispy Kreme generated in doughnut sales and how much profit it made from those sales.

Those are the two items we'll now focus on in the income statement—sales and profits. Let's look into our stable of real-world examples:

| Company | Sales* | Profits* | Grade |
|---|---|---|---|
| AT&T | $16.8 billion | –$2.3 billion | F |
| Trump Hotels & Casinos | $310 million | –$17 million | F |
| Abercrombie & Fitch | $260 million | $20 million | B+ |
| Nike | $2.6 billion | $200 million | A- |
| Microsoft | $6.1 billion | $3.1 billion | A++ |

*For the first three months of 2001.

Please jot down conclusions you draw from the numbers above.

_____

_____

_____

_____

_____

_____

Studying the income statement helps us understand how well a company has operated its business over the past three months (or past year, depending on the time frame you study). In the case of AT&T and Trump Hotels & Casinos, the past year has not been a good one. Both have lost significant amounts of money relative to their sales. Conversely, Abercrombie (earning $20 million), Nike (earning $200 million), and Microsoft (earning $3.1 billion!) have had a pleasing go of it.

## Combining the Balance Sheet and Income Statement

Now let's combine the numbers for all five companies we've analyzed. Obviously, it isn't enough to just know how much a company earns each year. If it's in gravely dangerous debt, today's profits might be small comfort to the investing community. It also isn't enough to just look at the debt and cash totals on the balance sheet. That's because a company with loads of cash and no debt that happens to be losing $1 billion a year is a disaster in the making. Like most numbers, you have to look at these in the proper context.

Let's now look at all four of the highlighted factors to get a much better sense of how these companies are doing. And this time, *you* grade their performance.

| Company | Sales | Profits | Cash | Debt | Your Grade |
|---|---|---|---|---|---|
| AT&T | $16.8b | −$2.3b | $10.9b | $31.8b | _____ |
| Abercrombie & Fitch | $260m | $20m | $100m | $0 | _____ |
| Nike | $2.6b | $200m | $360m | $640m | _____ |
| Microsoft | $6.1b | $3.1b | $36.1b | $0 | _____ |
| Trump Hotels & Casinos | $310m | −$17m | $100m | $1.8b | _____ |

m = million,  b = billion

Please jot down conclusions you draw from the numbers above.

_____

_____

_____

_____

_____

From our perspective, the most compelling companies here, in order, are Microsoft, Abercrombie & Fitch, and Nike. The least compelling, in order, are Trump Hotels & Casinos and AT&T.

These numbers serve only to fill out your analysis of the quality of

---

## How to Get the Goods

In the old days (just a few years ago), to get a company's financial reports, you'd have to call or write to ask for them. What a chore! Stamps, envelopes, getting put on hold forever.

You can still call or write to a company for its investor information (simply direct your letter to the company's investor relations department). And companies are still more than happy to mail you their information free. But why wait for the mailman to bring you the information in a week or two when you can access it right this minute, on-line? Here are a few sites where you can get the goods:

1. **The company's own Web site.** If you want to review Ford's annual report, just click over to www.ford.com. Look for the link labeled _investor information_ in the "Our Company" section. Here, just as at other corporate sites, companies offer on-line access to their annual reports and quarterly reports. You can also read a company's history by poking around or clicking on links labeled _about us_ or _our company._ This is highly recommended.
2. **Web sites that specialize in delivering financial reports.** Click over to www.freeedgar.com and search by name through financial statements for all ten thousand public American companies.

the company. To our prior questions (Are its products great? Does it have a brand? Is it the leader in its industry? Does it have great management?), we now add: Does the company save more than it borrows, and does it earn a healthy profit from year to year?

You have an excellent investment checklist forming.

# ·STEP 14·

# Crunching the Numbers

· · · · ·

It was the steady investors who kept their heads when the
stock market tanked in October 1987 and then saw the
value of their holdings eventually recover and continue to
produce attractive returns.
—*Burton Malkiel*

Please note that the stock market is the greatest creator of long-
term wealth in America. As of this writing, the value of all U.S.
public companies combined is about $10 trillion. That wealth has been
distributed among the people and the families who have invested
throughout their lives.

It is these steady investors who, on average, win their financial freedom in this life. They invest through good times and bad. Yes, they suffer
for prolonged stretches. But ultimately they prosper, and significantly.
Most of the millionaires in America today got there through business
ownership (of private company stock, public company stock, or both).

Contrarily, there are also what we'll call shaky investors—investors
who go crazy investing (day trading, borrowing additional funds, checking their stocks twelve times a day) in good times, then panic and quit
altogether in bad times. Shaky investors never really have a good han-
dle on the historical returns of common stock. They often don't know
why they bought a particular stock (or a whole portfolio of them) in
the first place. They gamble on the stock market and, for the most
part, lose.

As we kick dirt together down the home stretch of this book, you're
already looking like a steady investor to us—you've got that new aura
around you, that happy shimmer. You've put together a plan of sorts,

budgeting where you're spending money. Consequently, you know that the value of a dollar is to be flaunted more than the dollar itself. Matched up with this experience, you've learned about the stock market and index funds. And now you're venturing out into the world of individual stocks. Congratulations on all this—you're well ahead of the pack.

And congratulations on entering this advanced section and learning the traits of great companies. They are competitive. They have a mission. They have true leaders at the helm. They love what they do. They're stalwarts in their industry. And, as you've just learned, they earn and save more money than they borrow.

Given that you've achieved all this in the course of reading our Foolish book, we believe that you're well on your way toward fitting the definition of an "all-star money manager."

It's now time to move forward one more step. You have a very good sense right now of what makes for a high-quality company. But truly, you have little to no sense of whether a company's stock is priced fairly on the open markets. Here's our analogy. Right now, you know that the oranges for sale in a market are the best in the nation . . . but you don't yet know if you should pay $0.25, $1, or $5 per orange.

It's time for answers.

Every day, the stock market opens and investors bid up and down the value of public companies. It's your job to wonder: Are they getting it right? Is pricing in this market perfectly accurate (efficient)? Are the stocks of my favorite companies overpriced or underpriced? To answer these questions, you'll need to get your hands a little dirty—with ink stains and pencil dust. It's time to learn how to crunch the numbers of valuation. Yes, we'll throw some mathematics at you, but stick with it. At the end of this, you can sit down and determine whether you really enjoy it. If you don't, simply stick to a total market index fund (an outstanding alternative), get the stock market's average return each year, and proceed with your wonderful life!

You should also know that the numbers we crunch here are just to get started doing valuation work. You'll get your feet wet now. But you'll learn to really swim by reading the ideas and strategies of other investors at Fool.com. And, of course, by doing your own investing for real.

### Growth Rates

First things first, we need to determine whether a company is growing. Yes, we know if it has more cash than debt. Yes, we know if it's made money off its sales. But is the company expanding? Is it earning more money this year than last?

Calculating how quickly revenues and net income are growing (or not growing) is elementary. After you've mastered this simple task, you can run the same numbers on all line items on the financial statements (debt, cash, and so forth).

Let's go back to one of our real-world companies, Abercrombie & Fitch. Business looks great. The company has $100 million in cash and no debt. Last quarter it did $260 million in sales and made $20 million in profit. College students—and slackers in their thirties who want to look like college students—have clearly taken to the Abercrombie brand and style. The business looks solid. But now, let's see if they're growing. Let's study their performance from February 2000 to February 2001.

**Abercrombie & Fitch**

|  | Year Ending February 2001 | Year Ending February 2000 |
| --- | --- | --- |
| Sales (revenues) | $1.27 billion | $1.03 billion |
| Net income (earnings) | $158.1 million | $149.6 million |

Obviously, the clothing company is growing. But by how much? Well, simply divide the 2001 number by the 2000 number. So, we'll start with sales. Tap in $1.27 billion divided by $1.03 billion. You'll come up with 1.233. That means sales have grown by 23.3 percent over the past year. What about earnings? Simply divide $158.1 million by $149.6 million. Tap, tap, tap. And? Yes, exactly. Nice job. Earnings have grown by 1.0568, or 5.7 percent (rounded up from 5.68 percent).

Let's put those numbers together:

|  | Year Ending February 2001 | Year Ending February 2000 | Growth Rate |
| --- | --- | --- | --- |
| Sales | $1.27 billion | $1.03 billion | 23.3% |
| Net income | $158.1 million | $149.6 million | 5.7% |

Our first conclusion is to celebrate that the company is growing.

Sales are up strongly, and earnings are up as well. Breezily, we'd give Abercrombie an A for this performance. However, we're going to dock it down to an A minus because of the disparity in the growth rates. While it isn't a danger sign that sales are growing much faster than earnings, we'd prefer that the growth rates were closer.

Why?

Because, over long periods of time, we don't want to see the company increase sales dramatically but increase their profits insignificantly. We want to see them earning as much or more for every dollar of sales as in the past.

### Profit Margin

Profits are the aim of every commercial organization (and every employee who wants a salary from them!). Our model company this chapter, Abercrombie & Fitch, has a good deal of profit. In fact, they earned

---

## Take It from Me

### The Tristan System

I initially thought that investing was something rich people did to get more money. Now I understand that the majority of people can invest. I began investing in order to buy a nice used car. My best stock has been Chico's, a small-cap women's clothing retailer. It's gone up about 25 percent since I bought it. Applied Innovation, a small-cap computer networking equipment maker, has been my biggest dog, dropping about 40 percent. I'm holding on to it, though, because I think it has great prospects.

I've sold only two stocks so far, Mellon Financial and DTE Energy, losing just 4 percent or so on each. Overall, I'm down about 10 percent over the last few months, which isn't that bad considering that the stock market has fallen much more in the same time period.

To find companies to consider for investment, I use stock screening tools on-line or I hear about a stock on TV or stumble onto an interesting company on on-line message boards. Then I look them up to see if their balance sheet looks good, how profitable they are, and so on. I make sure they're undervalued enough. I aim to buy a company when its earnings multiple [explained below] is below its five-year average and lower than its industry's average. I also read the company's last annual report (from its Web site) and see how fast it's growing. These are just some of the things I do.

—Tristan Crockett, 15

---

---

### Take It from Me

#### Value in *Value Line*

Around eighth grade, my dad started sitting us down with *Value Line*—the big green book you'll find in most libraries that's full of company reports. He would teach us some numbers—such as net profit margin or return on equity. *Value Line* is organized by industry, so Dad would have me go through, say, the defense industry and compare margins among the companies in it. He'd explain that higher is better, and when I pointed out which companies had the highest margins, he'd ask me why I thought that was. He pointed out how higher margins can lead to competition in an industry, but that companies that *maintain* high margins over time are strong, defensible businesses worth considering for investment. Dad taught me to look for companies with double-digit profit margins.
—David Gardner, 35, Motley Fool co-founder

---

$20 million in profits last quarter. Unlike a company like Amazon.com, which lost more than $1 billion in the year 2000, Abercrombie is actually making money and putting it in the bank for their future. And the company's growth rates are strong: 23.3 percent sales growth, 5.7 percent earnings growth.

Expanding sales, expanding profits, expanding cash.

Now it's time for an additional calculation—how much money Abercrombie makes on every dollar of sales. Let's look back at Abercrombie's sales and earnings numbers.

**Abercrombie & Fitch**

|  | Year Ending February 2001 | Year Ending February 2000 |
|---|---|---|
| Sales (revenues) | $1.27 billion | $1.03 billion |
| Net income (earnings) | $158.1 million | $149.6 million |

To calculate their profit margins, we simply divide the earnings by the sales in each year. So, let's begin. For the February 2000 column, divide

$149.6 million in profit by $1.03 billion in sales. You'll come up with 0.145, or 14.5 percent. Let's think about what this means.

For every $1 of sales (cargo pants, T-shirts, wool pants, and so on), Abercrombie makes 14.5 percent in profit. You'll see that a more effective way to say this is that for every $1 of sales, Abercrombie makes 14.5 cents in profit. After *all* expenses—rent payments, employee salaries, clothing materials, distribution, advertising, a big fat check to Uncle Sammy, and all the rest—Abercrombie makes 14.5 cents on $1 of sales.

That means that up to February 2000, Abercrombie had 14.5 percent margins.

Now what about the next year? Divide $158.1 million in earnings by $1.27 billion in sales. Presto. Your answer is 0.124, or 12.4 percent. In the subsequent year, Abercrombie made 12.4 cents on every $1 of sales, for a profit margin of 12.4 percent.

There is no question, dear Fool, that you'll want your companies to increase sales and profits *and* profit margins over time. You want to find companies whose expansion extends their total profit and their margin of profit. And while you'll never find a company that *perfectly,* from one quarter to the next and one year to the next, expands sales, profits, and profit margins, that is the ideal. That is the company's certain aim.

When they slip up, you'll want to figure out whether the problems are temporary (a tough year for the overall economy, as is the case with Abercrombie) or represent a longer-term trend of decreasing interest in the product (which has not been true for Abercrombie). Again, the former is temporary, while the latter might be terminal.

### Reviewing Where We Are

You've come a long way already in your stock analysis. You've focused on companies whose products and services you know well. You've applied a filter to locate those of the highest quality. And now you've run some numbers to assess their debt, cash, sales, and profitability. From there, you've calculated the growth rate in sales and earnings. And you've finished it off with a look at the company's margin of profit.

For Abercrombie & Fitch, let's put it all together for the years ending February 2000 and February 2001. (We've added in the year-end figures for cash and debt from the balance sheet.)

| | Year Ending February 2001 | Year Ending February 2000 | Growth Rate |
|---|---|---|---|
| Sales | $1.27 billion | $1.03 billion | 23.3% |
| Earnings | $158.1 million | $149.6 million | 5.7% |
| Profit margin | 12.4% | 14.5% | |
| Cash | $137 million | $149 million | |
| Debt | $0 | $0 | |

The view you now have of Abercrombie & Fitch reveals a well-managed business enjoying the fruits of its popularity. Sales are growing. Earnings are growing. The company has substantial amounts of cash in the bank and no long-term debt obligations. However, there are two yellow flags. The first is that the company's profit margins have declined—they are not bringing in as many pennies of profits on every dollar as they were the year before. Hmm. And the second is that the company has $12 million less in cash (owing to investments made by the company in store expansion).

You can and should be able to run an analysis like this on *any and every* company you consider for investment. At quote.Fool.com the analysis takes no more than thirty minutes. And that half hour of work might be the difference between making and losing money on the stock market. We hope you won't make a stock investment ever, henceforth, without taking that thirty minutes to create your own financial snapshot of a company.

## Finally, a Look at Valuation

You're now huddled over this book, wondering about pricing the company. Yes, everything looks great with Abercrombie & Fitch. But everything looked great with those beautiful oranges in the supermarket as well. The question is, were the oranges worth $0.25 each, or $1 each, or $5 each? Concomitantly, is Abercrombie & Fitch stock worth $10 a share, $25 a share, or $50 a share?

This is, frankly, the most difficult investing question of all. Were there an easy answer, we'd give it to you in the next paragraph, then root you on as you became a millionaire within ten years. You'd be able to make one investment after another, knowing throughout whether you'd found a great company at a low price (clearly the ideal) or not.

But it's not that simple.

We can provide you with a useful first tool, though, for evaluating a company's stock price. It's called, the "earnings multiple" (or "P/E ratio"). It's a simple measurement for comparing the earnings generated by a company to the price tag placed on that company. In the end, every business will be priced based on its ability to generate profits. The New York Yankees, for example, will be bought and sold by investors based on its present and future profits. The business of the lemonade stand you once ran also was valuable (to others, anyway, had you ever wanted to sell it to them) *only to the extent that it made you, its owner, money.*

So, the price of the company relies on what profits it makes.

The simple, effective calculation to carry out, then, is the relationship between the market capitalization (already covered earlier—what the overall company is worth) and the total earnings of the business. You are comparing total price to total earnings. Let's run the numbers for Abercrombie & Fitch.

First, we'll look at the market capitalization. We calculate this, again, simply by multiplying the price of one share of stock against the total number of shares of ownership. Okay. So in February 2001, Abercrombie's stock was trading at $30 per share. At that point, the company had a hundred million shares of ownership. Thus, the total value of the business was:

$$\$30 \text{ per share x } 100 \text{ million shares} = \$3 \text{ billion}$$

The Limited Inc., which bought Abercrombie & Fitch in 1988 and then later sold it (spun it off as a stand-alone business in the public markets), is pretty happy today. The company they helped re-create was worth $3 billion as of February 2001.

But our question as a potential investor is: Is $3 billion too much or too little to pay for this company? Now it's time to complete our earnings multiple calculation. We simply divide the market capitalization of $3 billion by the total earnings for the year (listed above) of $158.1 million. It looks something like this:

$$\$3 \text{ billion} \div \$158.1 \text{ million} = 19 \text{ (rounded from } 18.975)$$

And what does this tell us? It shows that Abercrombie & Fitch is being valued at 19 times its 2001 profits. Investors are saying that the entire company of Abercrombie & Fitch is worth $19 for every $1 of profit. You now know the relationship between the price and the profits of the company. This, also, is a calculation you'll want to run for any company you invest in.

But is $19 for $1 of profit too much to pay for Abercrombie or not?

Again, there's no easy answer to this question. But we can provide two pieces of context. The first is a comparison of a company like Abercrombie with the rest of the market and with its industry (retailing).

## Typical Earnings Multiples

| | |
|---|---|
| Less than 10 | Car, airline, auto part, and steel companies |
| From 10 to 25 | Chemical, bank, insurance, industrial machinery, hotel, oil, restaurant, **retail**, and traditional telecommunications companies |
| From 25 to 50 | Global consumer brand, pharmaceutical, and semiconductor companies |
| Above 50 | High-growth technology, biotechnology, and communications companies |

*Furthermore, the overall stock market's average earnings multiple, going back to 1926, is 16.* So, at 19 times its earnings, Abercrombie & Fitch is on the high end of valuation both for the general market and its industry (retail average being 10 to 25).

More specifically, we need to look at how quickly Abercrombie is growing. Our final simple valuation metric (which, again, is largely for general context) is to compare Abercrombie's annual growth rates of sales and earnings with its earnings multiple. When steady investors buy stock, they compare the price of that stock with all present and potential earnings. Thus, we want to take into consideration the present earnings multiple (19) with the rate of growth at the company (some indication of its future growth).

Our numbers above showed that Abercrombie grew its sales by 23.3 percent and its earnings by 5.7 percent. To us, this means a fair price tag for Abercrombie is somewhere between 23.3 and 5.7. The average of the two numbers is 14.5. In these terms, we'd like to see Abercrombie & Fitch trading at around 14.5 times its total earnings.

We now have three points of context:

1. **The stock market's historically average earnings multiple is 16.**
2. **The average earnings multiple range for retailers is between 10 and 25.**
3. **The earnings multiple for Abercrombie based on the average of its growth rates is 14.5.**

And we have the price tag placed on Abercrombie in February 2001 of 19 times its total earnings.

So what is our general conclusion? First, we believe that Abercrombie is a very fine company. It has lots of cash and no debt. It's a profitable company. Its sales and earnings are growing. And it makes more than ten cents on every dollar of sales. Further, it sells clothes that are very popular in the high school and college markets.

However, we also believe that as of February 2001, at a stock price of $30 and an earnings multiple of 19, Abercrombie & Fitch is too richly priced for us. Since our aim with stock investing is to do better than the average return of the general market (which we could duplicate simply by buying a total market index fund), we're going to hold off on purchasing Abercrombie. We love the company. We just want the right price. So we'll wait until its price compares more favorably to 1) the general market multiple, 2) the retail industry multiple, and 3) Abercrombie's own sales and earnings growth rates.

---

## Take It from Me

### Jumping In After the Crash

About the same time that I stopped collecting *Star Wars* trading cards, I started to follow the stock market. I began looking at the business section when our newspaper arrived each morning, and I began to track the stock prices of some companies that I found interesting. I was thirteen years old, so I started tracking companies such as Toys R Us and Coca-Cola. I had my mother get me graph paper so I could plot the daily prices of the stocks. After a long time, I had nice-looking charts showing the way stock prices moved. By watching and graphing stocks for a few years, I learned that they rose and fell over short periods of time or even over a few years.

Meanwhile, I had been saving money from a job as a caddie at a golf course. I was seventeen when I bought my first stocks. I bought them the day after the stock market fell 22 percent in one day (in 1987), the worst one-day performance in history. I had learned from years before that when stocks of good companies went down, they eventually rose again later, so buying on large dips could be a good idea. I bought shares of a Florida real estate company that went out of business a few years later, teaching me some good lessons. I also bought shares of Citibank because it was the nearby bank. Both were great learning experiences.

—Jeff Fischer, 31, Motley Fool writer

(Note: Abercrombie's price and earnings multiple became much more attractive between February 2001 and January 2002. Check the financials and the chart for the stock at quote.Fool.com.)

## More Numbers

We've covered just some of the many numbers that business-focused investors consider when studying a company. There are ever more ways to evaluate the quality and price of a business. Explaining them all is what you'd get in a second *Motley Fool Investment Guide for Teens* (if you'd like to see this, please e-mail us at Teen@Fool.com). For now, we just want to share the terms with you. Type them into the search box at www.Fool.com, and you can read extensively about them there. You can also pose questions to our staff at boards.Fool.com.

Enterprise value

Return on equity

Return on assets

Working capital

Inventory turnover

Foolish flow ratio

Cash flow margin

# ·STEP 15·

# Managing Your Portfolio

• • • • •

*Back in graduate school I learned that the market
goes up 9 percent a year, and since then it's never gone up
9 percent in a year.*
—*Peter Lynch*

As you prepare to begin investing on your own, remember Peter Lynch's words. Lynch became one of America's great investors when he managed the most successful mutual fund in history—Fidelity Magellan Fund. If you'd invested $10,000 in the fund in 1977, it would have grown to more than $250,000 by 1990. Lynch retired early, at the age of forty-six. Not a bad life. And he found many of his best investments by tagging along with his wife and kids at the mall.

Lynch's statement above reflects something that most investors either never learn or just keep forgetting: There are *very few* average years on the stock market. For these past hundred years, the market has advanced on average 11 percent per year. But it hardly ever returns exactly 11 percent in one year. One year it'll rise 18 percent. The next year it'll rise 4 percent. The next year it'll rise 14 percent. The next year it'll fall 6 percent. Rarely will you ever see a year where the market returns either 10, 11, or 12 percent.

What we're saying here is that you need to guard against becoming overenthusiastic when the market rises 20 percent or pessimistic when it falls 20 percent. It's easier said than done. Keep that perspective, though, and as time passes, you'll be pleased. Over the long haul, the annual average should be somewhere between 9 and 11 percent per year.

## The Home Stretch!

You've nearly made it to the end of this book. We hope you've enjoyed it. We hope you're feeling more confident about your finances with every passing chapter. There will always be more to learn, but you've got a great start. Let's turn on the metronome, plug in our amp, and get ready for a hot track from the rock band we're starting right now, just for this section, which we'll call Def Fool Jam.

One-two-three four, one-two-three four, one-two-three four, one-two-three four:

> *Pay down credit card debt! (pay it down, pay it down)*
> *Thumpity-thump, thumpity-thump.*
> *Save 10–20 percent of your salaryyyyyy.*
> *Thumpity-thump, thumpity-thump.*
> *Use index funds (yeah, baby, index funds!) for your*
>     *long-term savings.*
> *Thumpity-thump, thumpity-thump.*

(Okay, so Def Fool Jam doesn't generate great lyrics. Whatever. Our fans are happy enough with their "DFJ" body tattoos and black T-shirts—they don't need *words* and *music,* got it?)

Anyway, if you think you can outdo indexing by purchasing individual stocks, and if you want the intellectual rewards of learning about businesses, go for it. But always remember that you can plug in your amp, twang that electric guitar, and shout our little song above at the top of your lungs, anytime; follow its direction, and in the years ahead you will earn more than the financial resources you'll need to live well.

We'll use this last chapter to tie up a few loose ends and focus you on your entire portfolio of investments, before sending you on your way. So let's think aloud about your approach. Here are a few suggestions from us.

## Practice with a Mock Portfolio

Don't begin investing until you're ready—until you're relatively comfortable and confident about what you're doing. If you're unsure, consider starting out by investing just a small amount. As your confidence and knowledge increase, you can swim deeper. But start by putting on those water wings (yeah, we know they're a little embarrassing, but it's better to blush than drown). Wade in the shallow end until you feel certain you can conquer the darker water at the other end of the pool.

Until you're ready, or even while you begin to actually invest, consider practicing by using a *mock portfolio*. With it, simply go through all the motions of investing, stopping short of actually making investments with cash. We know it's tempting to get started with that $500 of birthday and holiday gift money. But won't you wish you hadn't rushed in if that $500 is reduced to $200 through poor investments?

Instead of racing to it, research some companies, decide which ones you'd buy, and then set up a pretend portfolio, either on paper or on-line. (Many Web sites, including Fool.com, let you create and follow portfolios on-line. That will save you a lot of paper and hassle. And you'll have the chance to check how your portfolio is doing from week to week.) Keep track of details such as when you "bought" the shares and at what price. Then track your performance over time, aiming to beat the market.

If one of your holdings suddenly tanks, see how you react. If that were your real money, would you be panicking and selling? Or would you hold while calmly studying the situation? With a mock portfolio, you can learn without paying for the education.

Below is how you might keep track of a mock portfolio in a notebook:

| Ticker | Company Name | Bought on (Date) | Bought at (Stock Price) | Number of Shares | Commission | Total Purchase (Less Commission) |
|--------|--------------|------------------|-------------------------|------------------|------------|----------------------------------|
| HDI | Harley-Davidson | 9/26/02 | $39.50 | 10 | $8 | $387 |
| SCHL | Scholastic | 10/30/02 | $40.25 | 8 | $8 | $314 |
| HAS | Hasbro | 12/17/02 | $13.00 | 25 | $8 | $317 |

You can check back on the stock prices as frequently as you like. You should, however, make it a practice to not simply check the stock prices but also to look into the businesses' performance at least once a year.

## Know What You Buy—And Why

After you research some companies and decide to buy stock in one or more of them, make sure you know why you're buying. Set down your rationale in a notebook. Spell out your expectations for the investment. Then test yourself. See if you can spend one minute (a full sixty seconds) telling a friend (or your parents, if you want to impress them into

giving you more money to invest!)
how the company makes its money
and why you like it as an investment. If you don't have much to
say, you probably don't know
enough about the company. If you
have *too* much to say, you probably don't know enough about the
company.

Yeah, we mean it. If you know
the business, you should be able
to explain it in sixty seconds.

---

### Famous Words

*The only investors who shouldn't diversify are those who are right 100 percent of the time.*

—John Templeton

---

### Diversification: The Problem of Too Few or Too Many

When you begin investing in companies, keep your head about you, dear Fool. Don't go overboard and continue adding more and more stocks to your collection. Too many investors today have too many different investments. Don't make the same mistake. If you end up invested in thirty companies—three shares here, ten shares there—you'll run into two problems:

1. You'll have trouble keeping track of all of them. One company could be falling apart, and you might not notice.
2. You'll essentially duplicate the market (having created your own broad index), but you'll pay more in fees to buy and sell all those stocks than you would with an index fund.

Conversely, there is also the problem of holding too *few* companies. When you save and invest in just two companies, if one of them tanks, your portfolio will take a big hit. That's why we recommend that stock investors buy five to ten different companies, alongside investments in an index fund. Obviously, if you're just starting out, with small amounts of money, it's inevitable that you'll begin with just a few investments. But you should build toward five to ten companies.

Furthermore, we think you should invest in companies of different size. Two or three might be old, established companies like Coca-Cola or General Electric. Neither is likely to double in short order. But neither is likely to perform dismally for you, either. Then consider matching them up with two or three emerging companies—companies whose products you're familiar with but whose products are also not *everywhere* yet. The balance of large and small companies, stabilized by significant investments in index funds, makes good sense to us.

## Portfolio Tracking:
## How to Follow Your Holdings

Once invested, you need to devise a strategy for following the businesses you own. Here again, you can run into trouble at the extremes. If you obsess daily over the movement of the stock and performance of the business, you'll lose all perspective. Each 10 percent rise or fall will overwhelm you. A company press release might throw your mind into chaos. Don't let that happen. We don't want you to go dizzy on us.

On the other hand, though, if you don't check back in on your businesses but once a decade, you might be horrified by what you find. A new executive team might be in place. Their misguided marketing strategy coupled with some ill-advised acquisitions might now seriously be threatening the company's future (compare the performance of Lucent at the turn of the century). As an investor, you'll want to minimize business surprises.

So what's the right balance? We suggest looking at your businesses (yes, they are *your* businesses—you're a part *owner* now!) at least once a year. Read through their annual report on-line or the copy you receive in the mail from the company. Further, check out your company's discussion group at boards.Fool.com. At The Motley Fool, we have discussion groups for over two thousand public companies. Thousands upon thousands of investors gather to talk about these companies. So join in, ask questions, and share your opinions. (Remember, we offer a free thirty-day trial to test-drive our discussion boards.)

Finally, when you review your holdings, you should be asking your-

---

## Famous Words

*The art of investing in public companies is . . . simply to acquire, at a sensible price, a business with excellent economics and able, honest management. Thereafter you need only monitor whether these qualities are being preserved.*

—Charles Munger

self: Is this company still on track? What progress is it making and what obstacles has it encountered? Is it becoming a higher-quality company? Is it doing better financially than it was last year? Is it going in any new directions? Is management clearly laying out a convincing strategy? Do I still believe in its future? Do I still want to hold on, or should I sell?

### When to Consider Selling

If you spot wildly waving red flags around a company you're invested in, do *not* automatically sell. Take at least a few days to mull it over. Many fine companies run into temporary troubles and emerge stronger than ever. When Johnson & Johnson's Tylenol was being poisoned by a lunatic, the media were having a field day and the company was in crisis. However, J&J rebounded and has proven a truly wonderful investment for the last decade, two decades, five decades, century.

That said, there *are* many valid reasons to sell a company's stock. Here are some:

- If the reasons you bought the company are no longer valid.
- If the company's performance is seriously flagging—especially over a full year.
- If you can't remember why you bought in the first place.
- If you've come to believe the company's leaders are either clueless or crooked.
- If you don't know what the company does or how it makes money.
- If you'll need the money in the next few years. Put that money in CDs.
- If, in your opinion, the stock has become significantly overvalued.
- If you find a much more attractive place to invest your money.
- If you're hanging on only for sentimental reasons.
- If you've lost confidence in the company and its management team.
- If you're just sitting there hoping the stock will get back to your purchase price.
- If the company has falsely accounted for its performance.

This is a good list to start with.

### Famous Words

*Falling in love with stocks in a portfolio is very easy to do and, I might add, very perilous.*

—John Neff

## Investing Strategies

As you learn more and begin to invest, you'll notice that there are myriad ways to invest. Some make sense, others are absurd (we have yet to be convinced by any astrological approach to the stock market, even if you think the stuff works for your relationships!).

Following are just a few of the many different approaches we've encountered. If you're intrigued by any, you might choose to use aspects of them in your own investing. Feel free to mix a little of one approach with a little of another. But remember, in the end, you'll be developing *your own* approach to investing, just as it should be.

### Dollar-Cost Averaging

When you dollar-cost average, you regularly invest the same amount of money into one or more stocks or mutual funds. You might invest, say, $25 each month or $100 each quarter. Doing so adds discipline to your financial plan. It also protects you against volatility in the stock market. You'll be buying whether the market is up or down. If the market's up, you end up buying fewer shares. If it's down, you end up with more shares. The downside of the approach is that you can pay a lot, in percentage terms, in commissions.

### Value Investing

Value investors pay very close attention to the price tag on a company (that is, its market capitalization). They then try to buy only companies they think are bargains. The rap on value investors is that they sometimes buy bad companies whose low price is no real bargain. But if they get it right, finding a strong company at a startlingly low price, value investors are wonders to behold.

### Growth Investing

Growth investors generally worry less about price and focus on finding rapidly growing companies. They're willing to pay high prices if they think they've found a truly great business. When they get it right—when they pay a high price for Microsoft in 1990—they can do extraordinarily well. But when they get it wrong—buying Amazon.com at $100 per share—they can suffer greatly. (There is no reason, by the way, that you can't work to combine value and growth investing. Makes sense to us to try.)

## Drip Investing

We wrote about Drip, or dividend reinvestment plan, investing earlier in the book. This method allows you to buy stock directly from companies. In doing so, you'll bypass the higher brokerage fees. This can be an excellent option for teens and adults with limited funds. You can dollar-cost average with Drips. The Drip Portfolio at The Motley Fool (www.Fool.com/dripport) has a lot of great information on this approach.

## Buy-and-Hold Investing

It's up to you how long you hang on to any stock. Some companies will turn out to be lousier than you expected, so there's no sense holding on forever. But remember that some of the greatest investing fortunes were made by investors who bought and held great companies throughout their lives. Companies like Pfizer, General Electric, Johnson & Johnson, Microsoft, and ExxonMobil have created extreme wealth for anyone who's bought and held—through good markets and bad. Again, few of your holdings will earn a permanent place in your portfolio. But remember that America's greatest investor, Warren Buffett, once proclaimed: "My favorite time frame for holding a stock is forever."

## Dividend Investing

Investing in stocks that pay high dividends can generate cash income for you from one year to the next. There are good and not-so-good things about this. On the plus side, if you find a solid dividend-paying company, your cash dividend payments from year to year can prove substantial. If you don't want to lock up all your investment money in the stock market, dividend-paying companies dole cash back to you along the way. On the minus side, dividends are an inefficient way for a company to manage its capital for shareholders. Why? Because they get double taxed. They are first taxed as earnings at the company. Then you are taxed on the dividend payments. Because of this, dividends have been increasingly out of favor. However, companies like tobacco maker Philip Morris (or, now, Altria) still pay very high dividends.

## Low-Earnings-Multiple Investing

A low price-earnings (P/E) ratio or earnings multiple means that a company's price is low relative to its earnings. This is taken by many investors as a sign that the stock is a bargain. A number of great investors refuse to buy any company with an earnings multiple above, say, 15. They prefer to find companies priced low against their earnings. The strategy does not *always* work, though. Sometimes, a low price tag or multiple correctly estimates poor earnings in the future. If you go hunting for companies with low multiples, be sure they are also companies with bright futures.

◆ ◆ ◆

There are lots of other ways to approach investing. Pop over to the Web site of the National Association of Investors Corporation (NAIC) at

## Take It from Me

### A Jump Start on the Future

From the very start, my parents encouraged me to save half of my earnings. At first, it felt like a chore to "give" my money to the bank. But I eventually realized that I was actually *paying myself.* I was paying my future.

When I was about twelve, my parents urged me to start investing small amounts—$150-$200—in the stocks of my choice. My eyes were wide with the prospect of riches, but I didn't really know how to go about finding promising companies and researching them.

In the summer of 1998, I attended CompuFest, an annual conference held by the National Association of Investors Corporation. In their youth program, I learned how to research a company, to evaluate the criteria that make a good investment, such as good management, a relatively low earnings multiple (also known as the P/E ratio), good growth rate, and solid prospects for future growth. I bought my first stock, in the Applebee's restaurant chain, when I was about thirteen. My approach to finding stocks has changed over the years, but each step is another part of the learning process. I expect to be learning throughout my life.

These days I often visit investing Web sites to get ideas—but I never buy a stock without first researching its history and management thoroughly. I expect to make money in the stock market if I invest for the long term. I'm currently saving for college—and eventually a house, once I'm out of college. I think it's essential to learn how to invest at a young age, to have a jump start on the future.—Tina Dressel, 18

www.better-investing.org, for example, and you can learn about their own approach, which is conservative and has done well over time for many of its adherents.

## How to Invest with Different Amounts of Money

If you can save and invest just a little each month ($10, $20, whatever), you have several options:

- You can save your money until you have several hundred dollars and then open a brokerage account. Start by buying shares of stock in one company. When you've saved a few hundred dollars more, you can invest in another company, and so on. (Be sure you're not paying too much in commission fees, though.)
- You can open Drip accounts with one or a few companies, sending in very small amounts to the accounts each month. (Some Drip plans accept as little as $10 at a time—others have minimums of $25 or $50.) Remember that some Drip plans require you to already own one share of the company's stock, usually through a brokerage, while other plans let you buy your first share through the Drip.
- You can save your money and invest it into an index fund. Some index funds require a relatively high minimum. If you can't meet that minimum, check out shares of S&P Depositary Receipts, also known as "Spyders." These trade on the American Stock Exchange under the ticker symbol SPY. They represent investments in the S&P 500 companies, just like an S&P index fund. However, they trade at one-tenth the value of the S&P. In other words, buying Spyders, you can get started with $100–$200 and buy a single share.
- You can look into extra-low-cost stock purchase organizations, such as www.sharebuilder.com and www.buyandhold.com.

If you can save or invest larger amounts per month, you can still use any of the approaches above. Even people who earn $100,000 per year use Drip plans to save on commissions. Having more money does not mean you should be wasteful. Investors with their eyes on the fees as well as the perfor-

### Famous Words

*I don't want a lot of good investments. I want a few outstanding ones.*
—Philip Fisher

mance, and who pursue the lowest-cost route to success, are often the stock market's biggest winners.

## Avoiding Investing Pitfalls

Throughout this book, we've tried to work through some of the many mistakes investors tend to make. Here are a few more common pitfalls.

### International Investing

Some investors think that to be fully diversified, they need to invest in international companies, too. The problem is, few countries are as demanding as the United States when it comes to making information about companies public. For instance, England requires that companies report on their performance just twice a year, rather than the four times we require in the United States. In addition, many countries are themselves risky—with governments or economies that could collapse.

If you're going to invest in a foreign company, you'd better understand it and its country very, very well. We recommend taking the easy way out. Invest in American companies (or the broad index funds that hold these companies) that do a ton of business overseas. By doing so, you'll get the international exposure some seek. Companies such as McDonald's, ExxonMobil, Citigroup, Coca-Cola, PepsiCo, Philip Morris, Ford, and General Electric rake in as much as 25 percent or 75 percent of their revenues from outside the United States.

### Penny Stock Investing

We designate any stock trading below $5 per share as a "penny stock." The first question most investors should be asking of these companies (and sadly, so few do), is How the heck did it get so low in the first place?! If more adults took the time to answer that question, they'd steer clear of what for so many people represents the poorest investments of their lives.

Anyway, you probably won't be surprised to learn that penny stocks are generally the stocks of companies that are in serious trouble. Many people love 'em because they mistakenly think that a stock trading for $0.15 or $1.80 per share is a screaming "bargain." They love the idea that instead of buying just ten shares of a $100 stock with their $1,000, they can buy a thousand shares of a $1 stock. And then if it goes up only a quarter, they muse, I'll be rich! Would "rich" count as "rich" if you could truly get "rich" this way? Nay, dear reader. Such thinkers—hopers—are terribly mistaken. The vast majority of companies whose stocks trade under $5 a share go bankrupt within ten years. Read our lips: This is a terrible universe to be searching for your next investment.

## Day Trading

Again, this is very risky. A *Washington Post* article once noted that 90 percent of day traders "are washed up within three months." Day trading, making very frequent trades in the market, is a great way to run up extremely high commission fees. If you do make a profit—and most day traders don't—you'll pay the very high short-term capital gains taxes on your earnings. In the end, if you're guessing at the momentary twists and turns of a stock price, you really are doing little more than gambling. It just doesn't make sense to us. Get a life! At least, at the racetrack you get to watch pretty horses kick up dirt. That seems a better way to lose money than by sitting in front of a computer monitor all day trading stocks.

---

### Famous Words

*This year I invested in pumpkins. They've been going up the whole month of October and I got a feeling they're going to peak right around January. Then bang! That's when I'll cash in.*

—Homer Simpson

---

## Hot-Tip Investing

Ah, the sizzling hot tip. Uncle Frederick knows of a diamond mine in Zaire that's a guaranteed winner. Your cousin's sister-in-law Wilma has a broker who likes a company with ticker symbol FEFE. Hot tips always sound great. The vast majority of them end up as losing investments, though. Why? Because when you "invest" on a hot tip, how will you really know if the company's succeeding or failing? If you don't understand the business, we think it's highly unlikely that you'll have any sense of whether to hold or sell the investment once you've gotten in. The best hot tip we can give you at The Motley Fool is to do your own homework, make your own decisions, and learn from your mistakes. The second best one is that hot-tip investing crossed with penny stock investing is a sad, sad way to go. Please, before investing in individual stocks, at least run the simple numbers we presented in this chapter. You'll likely spot a lot of losers to avoid.

## Story Stock Investing

A story stock is just what you think it is—a stock or company with a *great* story. Mayhaps its latest press release claimed a cure for cancer. Or maybe it's developed a new fat-free, good-cholesterol, lip-smacking bacon cheeseburger. There are any number of *great stories* out on the public markets. And, of course, stories are fine. But you need to pair them with facts before you invest. Is the story stock company actually earning any money? A lot of money? If so, how? If not, why not? Look at the company's financial statements and apply your standards. How much debt does it have? Are its sales growing? Many investors are taken in by story stocks. They then lose a lot of money when fraudulent activity is uncovered or those revolutionary developments never materialize. It happens every day. Try not to let it happen to you. Research even the best story. And need we add that story stock investing mixed with hot-tip and penny stock investing will most often result in embarrassment that may be hard to live down?

## Margin Investing

Buying stocks on margin means borrowing money to buy stocks. In the vast majority of situations, we simply cannot support the practice of margin investing. While it can accelerate your returns on the way up (by borrowing money, you can own more stock), it can do a real number on your financial life when the market falls. If you borrow to buy stock and your stock falls 50 percent, your lender might call for the money back at the worst time. Every year, thousands of investors go belly-up because they borrowed to buy stocks and couldn't repay the loans when the market fell. Please, Fool, don't let this happen to you. And as for buying hot-tipped, penny-ante story stocks on margin . . . ahem.

---

## Famous Words

*Investors operate with limited funds and limited intelligence: they do not need to know everything. As long as they understand something better than others, they have an edge.*

—George Soros

## Your Bright Future

You're one lucky Fool. In these pages, you've learned that

- many of your wildest dreams are within reach, if you plan and save and invest.
- as an investor, you can still enjoy a life of spending. Just live within your means.
- the power of compounded growth is awe-inspiring.
- you're probably the smartest young investor on your block right now.
- you have an amazing opportunity to retire early if you start now.
- you don't need to have much money to begin investing.
- even starting small with $10 can lead to enormous wealth in decades.

You also realize that

- you can buy index funds and spend no time on your portfolio from year to year.
- the only reason to buy stocks is if you think you can beat the index fund.
- all investors lose money on occasion.
- the stock market should rise an average of 9–11 percent per year in your lifetime.
- investing in the stock market is a marathon, not a sprint.
- if you invest in companies whose products you know well, you improve your odds.
- being a Fool has its benefits.
- life is about more than money!

# Our Grand Conclusion

Things won are done, joy's soul lies in the doing.
—*William Shakespeare*

We close with a call to action, prompted by the Bard. You cannot win if you do not *do*. There is little joy in merely *being* on this little globe of ours. The soul craves activity. Your soul does, we know it. So *act*. Our advice is this—close our Foolish book with a bit more conviction to

1. figure out what you want to do in this life.
2. plan financially to fulfill those dreams.

Like it or not, you will need money to make your grand (or even your pedestrian) plans a reality.

Had we brothers not grown up with parents that encouraged us to save and invest, we couldn't have started The Motley Fool. Yes, the world still would have been a fine place. But our lives in it would be only half as sweet. We were challenged by our parents at an early age to let our imaginations run free, to steadfastly pursue our interests, and to plan financially for our future. Not just any one of these, but all three—dream, pursue, plan. The upshot of all that is this, The Motley Fool.

Your dreams are as extraordinary and as beautiful as (perhaps far more so than) ours. Learn about them. Pursue them. Feed them. Plan for them. Without them, you might wake up one day, locked in a long line of traffic, bound for a job you do not love, caught in a world that feels devoid of charm, wit, joy, and comfort. Don't let that happen. Learn about your dreams. Pursue them. Feed them. Plan for them. They are yours. Without them, you might wake up one day locked in a long line of traffic.

You get the picture.

We hope that the result of your reading this book is a brighter financial future for you. Little would prove more gratifying for us in this life than to hear, years hence, that the pages of this book set you on a course toward financial independence, worldwide adventure, and a great life. Do your best to make it so, Fool.

If you have questions about anything you've come across, have suggestions for us, the authors, or want to share your story or a lesson, you can write to us at

David Gardner, DavidG@Fool.com

Tom Gardner, TomG@Fool.com

Selena Maranjian, SelenaM@Fool.com

Our e-mail address for help relating to The Motley Fool is Teen@Fool.com.

And we hope to meet you out in The Fool Community (teens.boards.Fool.com).

Farewell, good luck, godspeed.

# Glossary

**American Stock Exchange (AMEX)**—The AMEX is the United States' second-largest floor-based stock exchange. In 1998, the AMEX merged with the Nasdaq to form the Nasdaq-Amex Market Group.

**Annual Report**—A report issued each year by public companies that includes information about the company's business and its financial performance.

**Asset**—Anything that has monetary value and can be sold or converted into money. Typical personal assets include stocks, real estate, jewelry, art, cars, and bank accounts.

**Bear**—A person with a generally pessimistic outlook on the market, a market sector, or a specific stock.

**Bear Market**—A trend in the overall market to lose value over a period of time. There is no "official" definition of what makes a bear market, though many feel a drop of at least 10% is needed. A drop of something less than 10% is often called a "correction" (even though the term "correction" is never used when the market moves up 10%).

**Blue-Chip Stocks**—Stocks of established companies with strong records of rewarding shareholders. Examples include General Electric, Coca-Cola, Ford Motor Company, and Johnson & Johnson.

**Bond**—An interest-bearing or discounted debt security issued by corporations, governments, or others (such as David Bowie—really). A bond is essentially a loan made by an investor to an issuer.

**Broker**—One who sells financial products. (Whether in insurance, real estate, or stocks, most brokers work under compensation structures that often are at direct odds with the best interests of their clients. When using a broker, you should always find out how he or she is compensated.)

**Bull**—A person with a positive or optimistic outlook toward the general market, a market segment, or a particular stock.

**Bull Market**—A market that has been gaining value.

**Capital**—A business's cash or property, or an investor's pile of cash.

**Capital Gain/Loss**—The difference between the proceeds from the sale of an asset and its original purchase cost (or "basis").

**Capitalization**—See Market Capitalization.

**Cash Flow**—The cash that flows through (i.e., is generated or used by) a company during a specified period.

**Certificate of Deposit (CD)**—An insured, interest-bearing deposit at a bank, requiring the depositor to keep the money invested for a specific length of time.

**Churn**—Churning is overtrading in a customer's account by a broker. This generates lots of trading commissions and often leads to deteriorating returns.

**Commission**—A fee charged by a broker for executing a transaction.

**Commodities**—Goods such as grains, precious metals, and minerals traded in large amounts on a commodities exchange.

**Common Stock**—A security representing partial ownership in a corporation.

**Compounding**—The generating of earnings on reinvested earnings from an investment.

**Crash**—A market crash is a big drop in market value. It's what many shorter-term investors always worry about. The stock market never goes up in a straight line, so there will always be crashes. It can take a few days, months, or even years for a market to recover after a crash.

**Discount Broker**—A brokerage that executes orders to buy and sell securities at lower commission rates than a full-service brokerage.

**Dividend**—A distribution from a company to its shareholders from its earnings. Typically, dividends are paid on a quarterly basis.

**Dividend Reinvestment Plan (Drip)**—A plan permitting investors to invest small amounts of money in a company's stock, with the option of having dividends automatically reinvested in additional stock.

**Dow Jones Industrial Average (Dow or DJIA)**—The oldest and most widely known index of the stock market. The "Dow" represents the average of 30 actively traded major American companies.

**Earnings (or Losses)**—Earnings, also known as net income or net profit, are what's left over from revenues after a company covers all its costs and pays all its bills. (In the case of some companies, this will result in losses.)

**Equities (Stock)**—A name that comes from "equitable claims." Equities are just shares of stock. Because they represent a proportional share in a business, they are equitable claims on the business itself.

**Expense Ratio**—The percentage of a mutual fund's average net assets used to pay operating expenses—much of which goes to the salesmen and managers of the fund. If you're investing in mutual funds, look for those with an expense ratio of less than 1%.

**Federal Reserve**—The central bank of the United States. The Federal Reserve (or "Fed") oversees money supply, interest rates, and credit. The Federal Open Market Committee (FOMC) is the 12-member policy-making arm of the Fed that sets monetary policy, chiefly by setting interest rates. It also buys and sells government securities, which increases or decreases the nation's money supply.

**Fixed-Income Fund**—A mutual fund that invests in bonds.

**Front-End Load**—A sales commission charged by a mutual fund when the investment is purchased—typically around 3% to 5%. You can avoid this fee with no-load funds.

**Full-Service Broker**—Full-service brokers earn their name because they offer their customers not only executions of trades, but also investment guidance, research, and other services. For this, they've traditionally charged hefty commissions.

**Income Fund**—A mutual fund that invests in bonds and companies paying significant dividends.

**Index**—A selection of securities whose collective performance is used as a standard to measure the stock market. Some indexes reflect a specific sector, industry, or region. Examples include the Dow Jones Industrial Average, the Standard & Poor's 500, the Wilshire 5000, and the FOOL 50.

**Index Fund**—A passively managed mutual fund that seeks essentially to duplicate the performance of a particular market index. It typically charges very low fees, compared to actively managed mutual funds.

**Individual Retirement Account (IRA)**—A tax-deferred retirement account set up with a financial institution such as a bank or brokerage, in which contributions may be invested in many types of securities.

**Initial Public Offering (IPO)**—A company's first offering of common stock to the public.

**Institutions**—Institutional investors include pension funds, insurance funds, mutual funds, and hedge funds. These are the big players in the stock market.

**Inventory**—Inventory represents raw materials, near-finished products, and finished goods that a company has not yet sold. You'll find it listed as an asset on a company's balance sheet.

**Liabilities**—Outstanding debts.

**Limit Order**—An order to buy or to sell a security at a specific price or better. Example: "Buy 200 shares of Microsoft at $65." This would be placed when Microsoft is trading above $65 a share, and the purchaser is interested in waiting for a better price and accepting the possibility that his preferred price will not ever be available, in which case the order will not be filled. See Market Order.

**Load**—A sales fee or commission charged by some mutual funds when you buy or sell their shares. When a fund's (front-end) load is 5%, for every $100 you invest, you're only getting $95 invested into the market, as $5 goes to the salesperson and/or mutual fund company. You can avoid loads by choosing no-load funds.

**Market Capitalization (or "Market Cap")**—A company's total stock market value, calculated by multiplying the current price of a single share of stock by the total number of shares outstanding. This can be viewed as sort of a price tag for the company.

**Market Order**—An order to buy or sell immediately at the best price available at that moment.

**Money Market Fund**—A mutual fund that invests in very-short-term, high-liquidity investments. Essentially akin to a savings account, though usually offering better interest rates than a passbook savings account.

**Mutual Fund**—An investment company that takes the cash of many shareholders and invests it in a particular way, as defined by the fund's prospectus.

**Nasdaq Stock Market**—The Nasdaq began as the world's first electronic stock market, and today is the exchange where investors trade stock in more than 5,000 companies. It's often seen on television as a large wall of video screens showing individual stock price movements.

**Net Income**—Start with a company's revenues, subtract all expenses, and you'll end up with net income, aka earnings. Net income is listed on a company's income statement.

**Net Margin**—Net income divided by revenues. This measure of profitability indicates how much of the company's sales make it to the bottom line as profits. Expressed as a percentage, it tells you how many cents on each dollar of sales is pure profit.

**New York Stock Exchange (NYSE)**—The oldest stock exchange in the United States, this Wall Street haunt is the one frequently featured on television, with hundreds of traders on the floor staring up at screens and answering phones, ready to trade stocks on command from their firms.

**No-Load Fund**—A mutual fund that charges no sales commission, or "load."

**Odd Lot**—A number of shares that's fewer than 100. Trading in odd lots used to incur higher transaction fees. Today, with online computerized discount trading, buying and selling stock in odd lots no longer involve higher transaction costs.

**Penny Stock**—This term is generally applied to stocks trading for less than $5 per share. Penny stocks are notorious for their volatility and riskiness.

**Portfolio**—All the securities holdings of an individual, an institution, or a mutual fund.

**Price-to-Earnings (P/E) Ratio**—The share price of a stock divided by its earnings per share (EPS) over the past year.

**Principal**—The original cash placed into an investment.

**Prospectus**—A legal document usually written in extraordinarily tedious language that provides information about a potential investment, such as its investment objectives and policies, past performance, risks, and costs.

**Return on Equity (ROE)**—Return on equity is a measure of how much in earnings a company generates in four quarters compared to its shareholders' equity. It is measured as a percentage and serves as one measure of profitability.

**Revenues (Sales)**—Revenues are monies that a company collects from customers in exchange for products or services.

**Roth IRA**—Roth IRAs are retirement accounts in which contributions to the account are not tax-deductible but withdrawals are tax-free as long as certain conditions are met.

**Round Lot (Even Lot)**—A group of shares of stock traded in a multiple of 100, or $1,000 or $5,000 worth of bonds.

**S&P 500 Index (Standard & Poor's 500 Index)**—An index of 500 leading publicly traded companies in the United States. The S&P 500 is generally thought of as the best measurement of the overall U.S. stock market, though the Wilshire 5000 is a more complete index.

**SEC**—See Securities and Exchange Commission.

**Sector**—A group of companies with shared characteristics—usually operating in a common industry.

**Sector Fund**—A mutual fund that invests in a relatively narrow market sector (for example, technology, energy, the Internet, or banking).

**Securities**—A fancy name for shares of stock or bonds, "securities" is just a blanket term referring to any kind of financial asset that can be traded.

**Securities and Exchange Commission (SEC)**—The federal agency charged with ensuring that the U.S. stock market is a free and open market. All companies with stock registered in the United States must comply with SEC rules and regulations, which include filing quarterly reports on how the company is doing. The SEC, headed by five appointed members, was created under the Securities Exchange Act of 1934.

**Stock**—An ownership share in a corporation. Each share of stock is a proportional stake in the corporation's assets and profits. If you buy stock in a company, you own a share of the successes and failures of that business.

**Stock Split (or Split)**—A company-initiated increase in the number of shares of the company's stock. A stock split simply involves a company altering the number of its shares outstanding and proportionally adjusting the share price to compensate. This in no way affects the intrinsic value or past performance of your investment, if you happen to own shares that are splitting. In a typical example, a company announces a 2-for-1 split and, as of the effective date, if you own 100 shares at roughly $60 each, you suddenly have 200 shares, trading around $30 each. Before and after the split, the value of your holdings is $6,000.

**Ticker Symbol**—An abbreviation for a company's name that is used as shorthand by stock-quote reporting services and brokerages. For example, Kellogg's ticker is K, Coca-Cola's is KO, and the Dynamic Materials ticker is BOOM.

**Trade**—The purchase or sale of a stock, bond, or other security.

**Underwriter**—An investment bank or brokerage that helps a company execute an initial public offering or secondary offering of its stock.

**Valuation**—The determination of a fair value for a security.

**Volatility**—The degree of movement in the price of a stock or other security.

**Wall Street**—The main drag in New York City's financial district and the street on which the New York Stock Exchange is located, although the term is used mostly to refer to the professional investing establishment.

**Working Capital**—The lifeblood of a company, this is the money it has sloshing around, ready to reinvest in the business. Take the total current assets and subtract the total current liabilities. This measure compares money the company has at its disposal to money it needs to pay out in the near future.

# Additional Resources at Fool.com

We hope you have enjoyed reading this book and that it has provided you with valuable and helpful information. Throughout the book you have been pointed toward additional resources and services to help you make more money than your parents ever dreamed of. Fool.com offers many of these additional resources at your fingertips. Below is an abbreviated but helpful list of some of the key areas, most of which have appeared in this book:

**Teens and Investing**—http://www.teens.Fool.com

- Learn about all things money—how to make, save, spend, invest, and grow it.

**Fool's School**—http://www.Fool.com/school

- Get started with the basics. Learn the 13 Steps to Investing Foolishly, the skinny on mutual funds, and some beginner investing strategies like dividend reinvestment plans and index funds.

**Buying a Car**—http://www.Fool.com/car

- Follow a step-by-step plan for making a budget, finding the best fit, taking control of the test drive, striking the best possible deal and actually taking possession.

**Paying for College**—http://www.Fool.com/money/payingforcollege/
payingforcollege.htm

- Make the most of your education and your education dollars. Develop strategies for saving money for college and how to navigate the financial aid process.

**All About Banking**—http://www.Fool.com/money/banking/banking.
htm

- Learn the basics of banking; find the best services for you, and how to get the most for your bucks.

**IRA Center**—http://www.ira.Fool.com

- Get a head start to planning your retirement. Find out if you are eligible to invest in an IRA account and how to open one.

**The Fool Community**
Join other members online to interact, learn, question, and exchange ideas. The Community offers:

- An opportunity to post messages to get your questions answered
- Staff-monitored discussions

To check out what other Fools are saying, take a peek with a 30-day free trial. Visit the Teens and Their Money discussion board at http://teens.boards.Fool.com.

The Motley Fool's aim is to help you find solutions to the many and sometimes complex matters of money and investing. Whether you're looking for new investment ideas, how to get the best deal when buying a car, minute-by-minute stock quotes, or just a place to talk to other investors, Fool.com has all of that and more—available twenty-four hours a day.

# Index